World's Great
MYSTERIES

For India and Mathilde

The Five Mile Press Pty Ltd
1 Centre Road, Scoresby
Victoria 3179 Australia
www.fivemile.com.au

Concept and text copyright © John Pinkney, 2009
All rights reserved.

Cover design by Aimee Zumis
Cover image © JcJordanPhotography

The mysteries described in this volume were unsolved
at the time of going to press.

ISBN 978 1 74211 664 8

This US edition first published 2009

Printed in China

World's Great MYSTERIES

- Mystifying Murders • Unearthly Incidents
- Uncanny Deaths • Bizarre Crimes

JOHN PINKNEY

The Five Mile Press

Contents

Preface

I HAVE DEVOTED much of my career as a writer to collecting, chronicling and, wherever possible, investigating unexplained mysteries. This book contains some of the profoundest of the puzzles I have studied. The cases cover a broad spectrum, from pilots' fatal encounters with aerial "unknowns" to the question of how a novelist writing in 1914 managed to predict Japan's attack on Pearl Harbor – and its date: December 1941.

The mysteries presented here vary widely. But they do have one characteristic in common. All are unsolved.

JOHN PINKNEY, 2009

The Corpse, the Duke, and the Nazi Spy
Murder in the Bahamas

The death in 2005 of thrice-divorced heiress Nancy Oakes went largely unnoticed. Only a dwindling number of people recalled the scandalously sensational murder trial in which she had played a crucial role: a trial so explosive it occasionally elbowed World War II off the front page. At center-stage lay the corpse of Nancy's multi-millionaire father Sir Harry Oakes, whose burned, bludgeoned body had been found in his Bahamas mansion. The accused was Nancy's handsome young husband Count Alfred de Marigny, whom she ferociously defended. Lurking enigmatically in the background was the Duke of Windsor, who had abdicated his throne to wed Wallis Simpson – and whose intervention in the murder case was considered strange beyond belief. Also in the cast were a shadowy assortment of Mafia dons, and a suspected Nazi spy. The accused count was acquitted, and the true killer never found – prompting crime novelist Erle Stanley Gardner to describe the case as "the greatest murder mystery of all time…"

THE TINY PITEOUS CORPSE of Sir Harry Oakes had been subjected to indignities that one witness described as "demonic." Not content with savagely fracturing the diminutive baronet's skull, the frenzied killer had turned his bed into a funeral pyre by dousing the body in gasoline and setting it alight.

The murderer also started spotfires in corridors and adjoining rooms, obviously hoping the inferno would destroy Sir Harry's vast Nassau mansion and any forensic evidence that might remain. However, the plan failed when a thunderstorm exploded over the Bahamas islands. Rain, driving through open windows, doused the flames and saved the house.

A friend and business associate, Harold Christie, discovered the body – or so he claimed. He told investigating detectives that having slept relatively soundly and undisturbed in a guestroom at the mansion, he had risen to eat an early breakfast, then gone up to Sir Harry's bedroom. During the later court proceedings he said:

> *"Going up the stairs I noticed marks of charring. There was an odd pungent smell around. I suspected there had been a fire of some kind... when I reached the bedroom smoke was curling around the door. I went in and said good morning. Then I noticed that the mosquito net around the bed was burned. I rushed over to the bed and saw him lying at an angle. He was blackened. The fire had turned him black. I could see how the heat had raised big blisters on his skin – and his upper half was covered with feathers. His pillow was torn open and the feathers were stuck to blood from his head.*
>
> *"I had no idea he was dead. I lifted his head and tried to give him water from a bottle beside the bed... but he wasn't moving. I went to the porch and screamed for help. But the servants were off that day. Then I went down to the telephone."*

Sir Harry, an extraordinarily generous philanthropist, was loved by the Bahamian people, whose lives he had improved in numerous ways. Few believed he could have had any enemies at all – let alone the fiend who had intruded into his room. When the initially suppressed news of the murder leaked out the general expectation was that Nassau's police force, working with the Bahamas Criminal Investigation Department, would quickly track down the assassin.

But it didn't happen like that.

The Bahamas was a British colony, comprising more than 3000 islands and reefs scattered across the Atlantic Ocean, about 50 miles from Florida's eastern coast. It was an important strategic staging post in the struggle against Hitler – and enemy submarines often invaded its balmy waters at night to drop agents and saboteurs ashore.

The governor of the beleaguered islands was the Duke of Windsor, the former King Edward VIII, who had abdicated the British throne to marry an American divorcee, Wallis Simpson. Even before Sir Harry's corpse was cold, the duke began to behave puzzlingly. He placed himself in charge of the investigation, telling the local police and Bahamas CID that they would be acting as assistants only. His first order was that the murder be kept secret – an impossible demand in a community as tightly knit and talkative as Nassau. And his second decision was even odder. He entrusted the principal task of finding the killer to two detectives, Captains Ed Melchen and James Barker from the Miami police department. Public (and police) concern grew, as it became apparent that neither of these imported investigators knew much at all about Nassau or its people. The pair quickly proved to be bunglers whose flounderings would ultimately deprive the baronet and his family of justice. But the duke, an imperial satrap with unchecked powers, would not be talked into ditching his ill-chosen detectives. This bizarre behavior was a principal element in what crime novelist Erle Stanley would call "the greatest murder mystery of all time."

• • •

HARRY OAKES WAS BORN in Sangerville, Maine, to a lawyer and a teacher. He enjoyed a relatively privileged and affectionate childhood. But at the onset of puberty his world darkened. Short, slight and slow to develop, he was increasingly dwarfed by his friends. Convinced that no girl would want anything to do with him, he became depressive and introverted, devoting much of his time to daydreaming about the riches that (somehow) would be his one day.

At 16 he even predicted famously to classmates that he would become a millionaire and die violently: a forecast that was to prove accurate on both counts.

Parents William and Edith refused to take their son's flights of fancy seriously. They insisted that he qualify himself to make a "solid" income. Obediently, 22-year-old Harry enrolled as a medical student at Syracuse University. He drudged at his studies for two years – but then was distracted by what he perceived to be his destiny. Suddenly the newspapers crackled with reports of a gold strike in the Yukon. Harry had no trouble convincing himself that he would find his fortune there – and his doting parents astonished him by agreeing that he should try.

Sir Harry Oakes: the investigation into his murder was
muddied by the Duke of Windsor.

Everyone in the loving Oakes family contributed to the enterprise – little realizing that their loans would one day be returned to them a thousandfold. Harry's mother gave him most of her savings... his brother pledged to send him $75 a month from his lumber business... and even his sister said she would send what she could from her secretarial salary. As a biographer later remarked, it was easy to see where Harry's kindly nature and immense generosity came from.

The Yukon venture failed. The young prospector spent months chipping rock at temperatures which sometimes plunged to -76°F, but found nothing. He was equally unsuccessful in the Belgian Congo. Even Ontario, where many miners had struck fabled fortunes, was unyielding.

But then he drifted to the violent northern town of Swastika where he stayed at a miners' boarding house run by Roza Brown. As he acknowledged later, "With a few words, she transformed my life." Historians have described Mrs Brown as being a strikingly ugly and smelly female who was followed everywhere by snarling dogs. She was notorious for lashing tenants with her tongue – and sometimes even her fists – but the little American inspired a softer response. She shared with Harry Oakes – and nobody else – the gist of a circumstantial rumor she had heard about a remote stretch of water known as Kirkland Lake. Harry listened with growing excitement, the scholar in him recognizing the ring of truth in his landlady's story.

With only $2.65 left in his pocket, Harry knew he needed financial and working partners to help him stake and dig the claim. He offered the chance to four brothers, Tom, Hugh, Harold, and George Tough, whom he had met only hours earlier. The five men shook hands on the deal, then set out on foot for Kirkland Lake.

The temperature fell to -62°F as they trudged seven miles through lightly falling snow. On a shore of the icebound lake they drove in their stakes, then toasted what they christened the Tough Oakes Mine. This was only the first of several mines Harry Oakes would open in the area. One of them, Lake Shore, became the second-largest gold producer in the western hemisphere. Within eight years Oakes was the richest man in Canada, pocketing more than $60,000 daily – and he made sure that Roza Brown was lavishly rewarded for her help.

At 50, Harry invested a fraction of his daily earnings in a world cruise. During what had been intended as a brief stop-off in Australia he met Eunice MacIntyre, the quiet, reserved daughter of a government official. She was 26 years his junior and six inches taller, but he was so entranced by her that he canceled the remainder of his voyage. He proposed, and they were married in Sydney, a week later.

The multi-millionaire returned to live in New York with his bride. Between 1924 and 1932 she bore him five children: Nancy, Sydney, Shirley, William and Harry. But by the time his new baby arrived, Harry Oakes was angry and disillusioned – the principal reason being that the Canadian government was levying his companies $17,500 per day in taxes. In 1934 he decided to move with his family and his business interests to the Bahamas.

In Nassau's balmy climate, Harry Oakes thrived. Knighted by King George VI for his prodigious works of charity, he grew to love the islands with their sweeping beaches and vividly blue tropical waters. He often vowed that he would retire here. Instead, he would be beaten savagely to death.

• • •

The Duke of Windsor's imported detectives conducted the case casually from the start. After Sir Harry's body had been removed, the investigators allowed several of Nassau's most prominent citizens to inspect the room in which he had perished. Nobody was discouraged from handling the bloodied objects around the bed.

Unworried by this contamination of the crime scene, Captain Barker ostensibly lifted a fingerprint from a Chinese screen: a clue that would become central to the looming murder trial.

Captains Barker and Melchen established that no member of the Oakes family had been in the house when Sir Harry died. His wife Eunice was visiting her family in Sydney; eldest daughter Nancy was in Vermont – and the other offspring were with relatives or friends.

The policemen quickly became privy to one of the island's choicest items of gossip. On her 18th birthday Nancy had defied her father by eloping with a man he despised: Count Alfred (Freddie) de Marigny, a playboy and minor business entrepreneur who had been married twice before. Eavesdroppers described bitter, shouted arguments between the young aristocrat and his father-in-law, several witnesses suggesting that the count was a desperado, whose chief motivation in making Nancy his wife was his hope of benefiting from Sir Harry's will.

Captain Barker took fingerprints from Alfred de Marigny – and within hours had announced a match with the print he claimed to have collected from the bloodied Chinese screen in Sir Harry's bedroom. The count was bundled into Nassau's jail. The fire brigade formed a cordon outside, to protect him from angry islanders. Most Bahamians seemed convinced of his guilt, and a rope was quietly ordered for the hanging.

As soon as Nancy heard of her husband's arrest she hurried back to Nassau. Grieving for her father, she was nevertheless convinced that Freddie could not be the murderer. Strikingly beautiful and often compared to Katharine Hepburn, she quickly became a favorite of reporters and photographers. At one press conference she said: "I know my husband well. Not only would he never commit such a terrible act, he *could* never commit it. He is a gentle and good man and I will do all in my power to help establish his innocence."

The murder charge was postscripted by a series of dubious and suspicious events. Particularly disturbing was the telephone call that police "forgot" to make on Alfred de Marigny's behalf. Soon after arriving at the jail, he asked his captors to ring Nassau's most respected barrister, Sir Alfred Adderley, who had won many major cases. Sir Alfred did not call back. Subsequently, he told journalists that the police had never contacted him. "I would have accepted the case for the defense," he said.

The Crown (seemingly with a little help from Freddie's jailers) reached Sir Alfred first – and engaged him to lead the prosecution team. Freddie had to make do with a less-revered lawyer, Sir Godfrey Higgs.

Death-room Scrubbed

Also extraordinary was the Miami detectives' behavior in Sir Harry's room. Nancy, convinced that her husband was being railroaded to the gallows, hired an American private detective, Raymond Schindler, to monitor proceedings. Schindler subsequently described the case as one of the most alarming he had been involved in.

Accompanied by a fingerprint expert, he flew to Nassau to conduct an independent investigation. With his colleague he stepped unannounced into the murder bedroom to find detectives Melchen and Barker hard at work scrubbing down the walls. At the subsequent trial Schindler testified: "We both were astonished. The two were in the act of cleaning away a handprint formed from blood. When I enquired why they were destroying vital prints, Officer Barker said they were not Alfred de Marigny's prints and were therefore of no interest. He said further that he'd taken photographs anyway, so they would be sufficient evidence."

Later in the trial Captain Barker conceded that he had flown back to Miami to have plates of the handprint and other clues developed. However, all of these plates had been destroyed by exposure to light. The identity of the person who had left the bloody palmprint on the wall would never be known.

The Crown's principal piece of evidence against de Marigny was his fingerprint, which Barker said he had found on a Chinese screen near the bed on which Oakes died. The prosecution pointed out that as de Marigny had not paid a social visit to the house in many months – and as fingerprints swiftly deteriorated in Nassau's humidity – this clue would form conclusive evidence against him. But Sir Godfrey Higgs had already caught the Miami detectives out in a morass of evasions and mistakes – and he made short shrift of the fingerprint "evidence."

Under Higgs's polite cross-examination, Captain Barker said he had lifted the count's print cleanly off the Chinese screen. When Higgs enquired whether any trace of the powdered original remained on the screen, Barker mumbled a reluctant no. Higgs then asked where on the screen Barker had found the print. To the court's astonishment, Barker could not remember. It was the trial's turning point – lending further credence to the defense's suggestion that the detectives had framed de Marigny with a print from a drinking glass that also had been adduced as evidence.

Throughout the proceedings Nancy, the count's passionately loyal wife, played a role the world came to admire. Her outward demeanor was generally as low-keyed as the behavior of her ally Sir Godfrey. But she seemed expert, despite her mere 19 years, at attracting attention and sympathy to herself – and by indirection to Freddie. Appearing in the humid courtroom in a different dress every day, she demonstrated a powerful sense of the dramatic. Once, when giving evidence, she seemed close to fainting. Later, while the attorney-general was delivering his closing speech, she stormed from the courtroom, saying, "I won't listen to such filthy things being said against my husband."

The trial not only made headlines internationally, it brought the sailing and sporting activities of the island's rich citizenry to a halt. "Like playgoers," reported *Time* magazine (November 22 1943), "Nassau's lush sun set had paid early rising natives one pound a day for places in the tiny courtroom – unless, like the Baron of Trolle, they chose to have their servants bring their own chairs. Between sessions Count Freddy waltzed by himself in the police station, read books on sailing."

The all-white jury took two hours to reach its decision – acquitting de Marigny by a nine-to-three majority. The crowd outside the courthouse, no longer in lynch mood, chaired the count aloft and bore him, cheering, to his chauffeured limousine.

Freddie de Marigny had not waited to hear the jury's second recommendation: that he be deported immediately from the Bahamas. This stricture had little to do with the murder – of which he was patently innocent – but more closely reflected the dislike the colony's officials and mercantile classes felt for him. A free spirit, he had long enjoyed mocking Nassau's "ridiculous" conventions – and had inspired particular outrage when he described the Duke of Windsor as "a pimple on the arse of the empire."

With doubtful legitimacy, the duke's executive council approved the deportation. Nancy de Marigny followed her husband into exile: their first stop being the home of Freddie's close friend, novelist Ernest Hemingway in Cuba. The couple divorced in 1949. Nancy, always optimistic, married unsuccessfully twice more – never sure that her vast inherited wealth might not have been a fateful obstacle to her happiness. She died, frail and blind, on January 16 2005, aged 80. To her last days, she insisted that Freddie had been the victim of a conspiracy – and that her father's murder had actually been engineered by powerful enemies, motivated solely by the desire to increase their wealth and impose their political will on the idyllic island colony.

The person (or persons) who killed Sir Harry Oakes remained at large. The Bahamas, and the world, waited for a fresh murder investigation. But to public dismay, the authorities took little further action.

This monument to mysteriously murdered philanthropist
Sir Harry Oakes still stands in Nassau.

From this point the hunt for the killer was left largely to theorists.

Their consensus was that Sir Harry had probably died because his integrity and high moral standards were somehow blocking the ambitions of certain ruthless people. But who were those people? Analysts, in the years following the murder, speculatively suggested four principal candidates:

- The prime target of conjecture was Axel Wenner-Gren, the suspected head of a Nazi spy-ring in the islands. Oakes, a notoriously blunt man, had never concealed his dislike of this Swedish lightbulb millionaire who, having bought large land-holdings in the Bahamas, set about worming himself into a relationship with the Duke and Duchess of Windsor. Oakes was deeply suspicious of the Swede and his friendship with Hitler's Luftwaffe chief Hermann Goering – a link which British intelligence believed was enabling Sweden to remain neutral while her neighbors endured German occupation.

The British government, convinced Wenner-Gren was at the least a Nazi sympathiser, was deeply concerned about his closeness to the former king – and eventually managed, by means of diplomacy and force, to quarantine him in Mexico. But there were strong suspicions that a nest of Nazi agents remained intact in Nassau itself. According to some historians Sir Harry Oakes had information that might have helped identify these spies – but died before he could share it.

Under the heading "Strange Outing", *Time* (on November 22 1943) revealed, "One day in midtrial, banker John Anderson, friend and confidant of Sir Harry's, took the reporters on an excursion… to admire Shangri-La, the fabulous estate of Swedish tycoon Axel Wenner-Gren. US and British blacklistings keep (him) in Mexico for the duration, but the reporters found 17 gardeners pushing back the lush jungle growth, awaiting the end of the war and the master's return. One or two reporters wondered whether the excursion had a meaning."

- Next hypothetical candidate was Sir Harold Christie, who claimed he had found the body. In his capacity as a real estate broker, Christie had made large profits by selling Bahamian properties to Sir Harry Oakes. But he wanted more. With an associate, Frank Marshall, he had devised a scheme to introduce casinos to the islands – but when he proposed the idea, Sir Harry witheringly rebuked him. The philanthropist, who had spent years building free schools and hospitals for the disadvantaged native people, believed institutionalized gambling would cause great harm. Oakes assured Christie that he would use his popularity and moral authority to thwart the plan. Furious, Christie might have committed the murder himself, or through hirelings.

- The other cardinal suspects were Lucky Luciano and Meyer Lansky. Like Christie, these Mafia mobsters regarded the casino plan as a ticket to vast post-war wealth. They would have seen Harry Oakes as a simple obstacle to be removed. The possibility that the pair engaged assassins to dispose of the multi-millionaire gained some credence at the trial. A policeman told defense counsel that on the eve of the murder a nightwatchman had seen a speedboat, with two men aboard, berth in Nassau harbor. They were driven away in a dark car which, the defense hinted, might have been driven by one of Sir Harry's business associates.

The nightwatchman himself was unable to testify. Shortly after Count Alfred de Marigny was arrested, the man's drowned body was found floating in the harbor.

The behavior of the Duke of Windsor was one of the greatest mysteries of the ugly affair. As governor he had shown a remarkable lack of faith in the abilities of his own passably efficient local law-enforcers. Most historians agree that if Nassau police and Bahamas CID had been allowed to follow normal procedures, they would not have allowed visitors to contaminate the crime scene. Nor would Bahamian detectives have actively scrubbed clues from walls, or allowed photographs of evidence to be destroyed.

Possibly for reasons of protocol, the former king never publicly explained why he had so absurdly appointed those two incompetent detectives from Miami, or why the investigation into Sir Harry Oakes's death had descended so disastrously into farce.

The duke died in 1972, his motives unexplained.

Doomed Plane's Message
Mystified the World:
Airliner *Stardust*

When the British airliner Stardust vanished in 1947 on a routine flight from Buenos Aires to Santiago, rescue aircraft spent five days combing vast tracts of the Andes mountain range – and found nothing. But even after the search had been abandoned, a further puzzle remained. Just before contact with Santiago airport was lost, Stardust's radio operator had transmitted a single, strange word, three times in morse code: a word unknown in any language. For more than half a century, codebreakers, linguists and academic theorists have tried to make sense of what that word might signify – but without success. The meaning behind Stardust's final, haunting call remains a mystery...

Buenos Aires Airport.
August 2 1947

THE PASSENGERS occupying four of the window seats on the routine flight from Buenos Aires to Santiago, Chile, would not have been out of place in a Hollywood thriller.

Paul Simpson, 44, was a British Foreign Office diplomat. In his role as "king's messenger" he was carrying, in a secret panel of his briefcase, a message from His Majesty George VI to the Chilean foreign minister. Directly behind Simpson aboard the Lancastrian (a converted British bomber) sat a Swiss banker and a Pakistani businessman with a large diamond sewn into the lining of his jacket. In front was a black-clad German widow returning to Chile with the ashes of her dead husband.

The aircraft's captain, Reginald Cook, first officer Norman Coomb and second officer Donald Checklin had all served as Royal Air Force pilots in World War II. Experienced wireless operator Dennis Harmer was also ex-RAF – and the stewardess, Iris Evans, had been a petty officer in the WRENS. *Stardust* herself (registration G-AGWH) was one of 60 bombers which defense authorities had sold to the British Overseas Airways Corporation for conversion into passenger aircraft. She retained some of the outward appearance of a warplane – but her interior boasted every luxury available at the time. Even the nine passenger seats, placed in a line on the cabin's port side, could be converted into bunks.

At 1355 hours (1.55 p.m.) crew and passengers experienced a rush of raw power as their plane taxied for takeoff. *Stardust*, which could fly as high and as far as any commercial aircraft yet built, was ready to begin a run-of-the-mill trip of less than four hours across the Andes; past Aconcagua, the highest mountain in South America, then south to Santiago.

Throughout the journey wireless operator Harmer sent regular morse code messages confirming that the plane was on course. In the 1940s the dot-dash system, invented in 1832 by American painter Samuel Morse, was still the preferred method of long-range air-to-ground communication. Technology enabling pilots to make direct long-distance voice contact was far from being perfected.

At 1741 hours (5.41 p.m.) when the scheduled flight seemed almost complete, Harmer transmitted the words:

"ETA [Estimated Time of Arrival] Santiago 1745 hours. STENDEC."

• • •

The signal was logged by a Chilean Air Force officer at Santiago control tower. He subsequently testified that it was "loud and clear – and given out very fast." The officer had no trouble understanding the bulk of the message: aircraft G-AGWH would be landing in four minutes. But that final word – STENDEC – perplexed him. He asked the radio operator to repeat it. Dennis Harmer obliged, by transmitting STENDEC again – twice. He had now spelled the peculiar word, exactly the same way, three times. After Harmer's second confirmation there was radio silence. The British–South American Airways flight from Buenos Aires was off the air. It would never make its promised landing at Santiago airport.

A massive five-day search by planes of the Chilean and Argentinean air forces found nothing. Within hours of the disappearance the theories – and the wild conjectures – poured forth.

One popular supposition was that *Stardust* had somehow been sabotaged by enemies of Britain. During the war the continent of South America had remained neutral. Now, in this immediate postwar period, some of her nations had become welcoming havens for fleeing Nazis and other war criminals from ravaged Europe. Could it be that the presence on the plane of the king's representative, carrying secret papers, had inspired England's old adversaries to exact a murderous revenge?

- Another widely touted theory was that a group of armed Nazis (possibly among the passengers) had seized the Lancastrian and flown her to a concealed airstrip somewhere: her crew either captive or murdered. *Stardust*, suggested the promoters of this idea, might eventually become a small part of a Nazi plan to establish a resurgent Reich on the South American continent.

- Others preferred to believe that the silencing of *Stardust* might be the fruit of a plot hatched by the increasingly belligerent Soviet Union. But whoever had masterminded the disappearance, these theorists insisted, it had to be sabotage – and part of a sinister pattern. In the preceding four months, two other planes from the same airline had also disappeared.

One belief, however, gripped the imagination of a section of the public more powerfully than any other. It had its genesis in an event which reportedly had occurred over the United States just 38 days before *Stardust* ceased transmission.

On June 24 1947, while flying his private plane from Chehalis, Washington, to his home in Boise, Idaho, businessman Kenneth Arnold was startled by a "bright light". Looking to the north, he saw nine gleaming circular objects speeding above the Cascade mountain range. They seemed to be metallic. Arnold said he watched them for about two minutes before they streamed away over Oregon.

During a fueling stop, the clearly rattled executive described his experience to Nolan Skiff, editor of the *East Oregonian*. The objects, Arnold insisted, had shown unmistakable signs of being under intelligent control. And they had flown "like a saucer would if you skipped it across the water."

The Associated Press seized on the story. The "mystery disks" – which a journalist would soon re-christen "flying saucers" – made headline news around the globe.

Floodgates opened. On July 4 1947, Earl J. Smith, captain of a United Airlines DC3, said his plane had been "buzzed" by several disks while en route from Boise to Pendleton. On the same day, large crowds of people in Oregon, Vancouver and Washington saw formations of brightly lit disks hovering overhead. Numerous police were present at all three sightings.

Before long newspapers began to publish witnesses' purported photographs of the saucers. Many pictures were fuzzy and of arguable veracity – but in an era when the possibility of Russian attack seemed all too imminent, it was relatively easy to believe, also, that aliens might be preparing to strike.

Had *Stardust* been skynapped by beings from another world? And was that strange seven-letter word STENDEC the cryptic clue they had left behind? It has often been observed that the first three letters of STENDEC spell "ETs" backward – but this was not a term popularly used in 1947 (if used at all).

Through the ensuing decades, codebreakers, linguists, academics and ingenious members of the public tried desperately to deduce what STENDEC might mean.

• Many observers pointed out that the letters are an anagram of "DESCENT". But neat solution though this may seem, it makes little sense. The operator, in the early part of his message, had already advised that the

Lancastrian was preparing to land – so the addition of "descent", especially in anagrammatical form, would seem redundant, to say the least.

- Other theorists believed that paucity of oxygen at the plane's stated altitude of 24,000 feet might have caused the operator to scramble his message – but this too seems unlikely. While it is relatively easy to rearrange the letters of STENDEC into DESCENT, it's considerably harder to perform the trick in morse code. It stretches credibility to suggest that Dennis Harmer had performed precisely the same feat in code three times. And the "thin air" theorem was equally shaky. Every flight crew member was fully protected by oxygen equipment.

- There was a large body of belief – but not among pilots – that Harmer might have been trying to transmit his aircraft's name, *Stardust*, which, in morse, shares some characteristics with STENDEC. But aviation professionals quickly dismissed the idea. In air-to-ground communications, pilots and crew identified themselves with their registration numbers (in *Stardust*'s case, G-AGWH) rather than the fanciful names the airlines had given them. And why, in any case, would the operator have transmitted his plane's name at the end of a routine message?

- Another mind-stretching idea was that the enigmatic word was an acronym – standing, perhaps, for "*Stardust* Tank Empty. No Diesel. Expect Crash." But why a morse operator minutes from death would have troubled himself to invent a word puzzle, the theorists could not say.

- In the end, the most enduring belief among a considerable portion of the planet's population was that STENDEC might be a message from alien visitors.

The word, today, is virtually forgotten. But so widely recognized was it in the decades following *Stardust*'s disappearance that in the 1970s a Spanish publisher confidently made it the title of his new UFO magazine – corrupting the spelling to "STENDEK."

• • •

Mount Tupangato, near the Argentina-Chile border.
January 28 2000

A 23-YEAR-OLD member of an Andean climbing expedition saw it first. Far above him, on a rugged slope 3.2 miles up the side of the extinct Tupangato volcano was – something – glinting in the early-morning sunlight. For a painful hour he struggled closer, until he could clearly see that the object which had attracted his attention was part of an aircraft fuselage, lying in a field of debris.

Assuming that he had happened upon the site of a recent crash, the young climber signaled his companions. Before dusk fell, the group had studied and taken photographs of the wreckage, which they would later present, with a written report, to Argentinean authorities.

On February 21 an expedition comprising 17 soldiers led by Lieutenant Colonel Ricardo Bustos ascended the volcano. The climb was so difficult that one member of the team suffered a heart attack and was stretchered down the mountain.

After four grueling days, battling against high winds and vertiginous slopes, the party reached the glacier on which the wreckage had been found. Several feet from the scrap of fuselage lay a Rolls-Royce engine. An aircraft's main wheels – one still fully blown up – rested near a twisted propeller. There were human remains, also: clumps of hair, a hand, fragments of a torso.

The colonel led his men in prayer over this poignant evidence of lives lost.

Below, in the Andes foothills, the army established a base with 40 men and 100 mules. En route to what the officers were then erroneously referring to as the crash site, several mules plunged to their deaths from a slippery natural bridge. Others bolted.

But eventually, with the aid of military helicopters, the soldiers were able to convey all of the wreckage (tantalizingly estimated to be less than one-tenth of the plane) to crash experts for analysis.

Quite early in this perilous exercise, the officers had definitely identified the aircraft – or fragments thereof – as *Stardust*, vanished 53 years before. Now it was the analysts' task to ask perplexed questions: Where was the other nine-tenths of the plane? How was it possible that on a mountain often climbed and flown over, the wreckage had taken more than half a century to be found? And how had *Stardust*'s highly experienced captain and navigator managed to perpetrate such a gross navigational error – flying their aircraft 50 miles off course?

The first of these questions was tentatively answered by an Argentinean glacial specialist. *Stardust*, he surmised, must have crashed into the upper part of the glacier covering the slope of the volcano. There, over the long years, it had been gradually entombed by snowfalls, until it became part of the glacier itself. Slowly, the glacier – with scattered wreckage embedded – had moved down the slope until, in warmer weather, the leading edge melted, revealing a few tantalizing traces of what had been the Lancastrian and the people who flew in her.

As years elapsed, the expert accurately predicted, more and more of the aircraft would be thawed out of its hiding place in the ice.

• • •

But why had *Stardust* strayed so disastrously from her course? And how could the captain have imagined he was due to land at Santiago when in fact he was about to slam into an icy volcano?

To answer these questions, Argentinean and British aviation experts availed themselves of knowledge that would have had little meaning for the fliers of 1947. They theorized that *Stardust* had fallen victim to the jetstream: a high-speed, high-altitude wind that was barely known of – and even less understood – in the 1940s. *Stardust*'s captain, they agreed, must have decided, on that doom-laden August afternoon, to avoid the bad weather over the Andes by flying high above it.

It was a task for which the converted bomber was well-suited. But as he gained altitude, Reginald Cook little realized that he was climbing directly into the lethal teeth of the jetstream, howling 24,000 feet above the snowcapped Andean peaks.

The bad weather swirling below prevented Cook and his crew members from seeing landmarks. And the wind's colossal power slowed their aircraft to such an extent that it confused them about where they actually were. When Cook began to ease *Stardust* down for what he imagined would be a safe landing at Santiago airport, he was still on the wrong side of the Andes – with a towering volcano dead ahead.

Although some analysts disagreed with their findings the experts were generally judged to have given an accurate summary of what in all likelihood had thrown the Lancastrian off course in her final minutes. The 1947 crash of *Stardust* had not, after all, been a case of an aircraft encountering a UFO with deadly results.

However, such UFO-related cases *had* been chronicled earlier than 1947 and would recur subsequently.

Aircraft Disappearances of the Flying Saucer Kind – or events which at least bore the marks of "intervention by an unknown agency" – had occurred in Australia in 1934 and 1935. Two further cases – one involving the death of a pilot; the other of a pilot whose plane "merged" with a UFO before disappearing – occurred over the United States in 1948 and 1953. In 1978 a young pilot flying over Australia's Bass Strait vanished, along with his plane, after radioing that he was being "orbited" by an unidentifiable craft. I have documented these tragedies elsewhere in this book.

• • •

After 53 years the mystery of *Stardust*'s fate had been partially resolved. But what analysts of every shade failed to do was convincingly explain what the final tantalizing word in that doomed operator's morse message really meant:

STENDEC
STENDEC
STENDEC
STENDEC
STENDEC

QE2 – and the Spectral Radio Station

IN 1982 – 35 YEARS after the Lancastrian airliner *Stardust*'s final message perplexed the world – radio operators aboard the QE2 found themselves at the center of their own morse code mystery.

Over a period of 18 hours the ship received a series of morse signals in a format superseded long before. Purportedly the messages came from a ground station which had been shut down and its transmitters dismantled in 1977.

Broadcast engineers have devised numerous complex theories to explain the strange phenomenon away. But the phantom morse messages remain a mystery.

Puzzle of the Blood-Soaked Peer:
Lord Lucan

Did John Bingham, seventh Earl of Lucan, brutally bludgeon his children's nanny to death – stuffing her bleeding corpse into a canvas mailbag? Or did he fight courageously to save her; trying unsuccessfully to overwhelm a maniacal intruder?

The question of whether Lord Lucan was a monster or a hero divided England. Perhaps wisely, the seventh earl did not stay around to present his side of the story. Hours after the killing, he disappeared – and subsequently was declared dead. However, a British detective-superintendent challenges that finding. He claims that he helped police interrogate Lord Lucan in Perth, Western Australia, in 1987. A crucial question remains: did Scotland Yard ever act on the detective's report?

Belgravia, London.
November 8 1974

S EVEN-YEAR-OLD George Bingham and his sister Camilla, 4, were so deeply asleep in their upstairs nursery that they heard nothing of the crashing and screams from the basement.

In later life George would recall that he had been dreaming of lying on a beach, dazzlingly bright sunlight penetrating his eyelids.

He blinked into wakefulness. And a man said, "Sorry, sonny – you'll have to get up." It was a policeman, shining a flashlight into his face.

This was the dark, rainswept night of horror in which the lives of George, Camilla and their older sister Frances were changed forever.

The Earl of Lucan's three children lived with their mother Veronica (Lady Lucan) in a stately six-story townhouse a short walk from Buckingham Palace. Lord Lucan rented a comparatively modest flat nearby. The evening had begun in routine fashion in the fatherless Lucan household. Lady Lucan had given the nanny, Sandra Rivett, permission to go out with her boyfriend – but at the last moment Sandra changed her mind, deciding to avoid the bitter weather and remain in the warm comfort of the servants' quarters.

At 6.30 she dressed the two younger children in their pajamas and tucked them into bed in their nursery; George clutching his favorite teddybear, Big Ted. Lady Frances, aged 10, was allowed to sit up in her bedroom to watch television. Sandra read for several hours. Then, at about 9 o'clock, she rose and walked to Lady Lucan's sittingroom, to ask whether she would like a cup of tea. Lady Lucan thanked her and said, "Have it here with me." Sandra bustled downstairs to the kitchen.

Twenty minutes later, when the nanny still had not returned, Lady Lucan went down to the main level of the immense house to look for her. The kitchen and adjoining breakfast room were in the basement. Lady Lucan noticed, with mild surprise, that the light was off. She tried the switch, but it didn't work.

She called Sandra's name.

Silence.

The steps leading to the basement were bathed with light from the hall. Still calling for the nanny, Lady Lucan began to descend. But then, when she reached the breakfast room, recoiled. The walls and floor were splashed with blood. In a corner lay what looked like a misshapen sack. As if hypnotized, Lady Lucan stepped closer. It was a large mailbag. Crammed into it was a body, the head protruding. The face and skull were battered almost beyond recognition – but she knew it was Sandra's head.

Screaming, Lady Lucan turned to run for the steps. But someone – someone tall and powerful – grabbed her from behind and dragged her, struggling, into the dark kitchen. The assailant tried to force fingers down her throat. She bit them, hard. Enraged, he began to beat her about the head with what she would later describe as "some kind of club."

Lady Lucan was only five feet two inches tall. But the knowledge that her children were asleep upstairs and in mortal danger invested her with a strength she had never known she possessed. Blood clogging her eyes, reeling from the blows and punches, she groped desperately in the darkness, found the attacker's testicles – and squeezed them with an iron grip. Crying out in pain the man collapsed and fell to the floor. Lady Lucan fled.

* * *

Drinkers in the Plumber's Arms Hotel were enjoying their last orders when a young woman in a torn nightdress, her face a mask of blood, appeared in the doorway. She screamed, "She's been murdered – Sandra! And he tried to kill me, too. And my children are still in the house. Help me!"

While his wife Diana used hotel linen to staunch the woman's bleeding the landlord, Derrick Whitehouse, rang police. Within seven minutes an emergency team was at the Lucan house. Detectives quickly found the instrument that had caused Sandra Rivett's death: a nine-inch length of lead piping. Amid the smashed china scattered across the bloodied floor was a broken lightbulb. The killer had unscrewed it so that his victim would not recognize him.

But the children were safe: George and Camilla still fast asleep in the nursery; Frances crouched sobbing on the first-floor landing. Whoever had committed this appalling crime had no designs on them.

That night detectives interviewed Lady Lucan in her hospital bed. Facially bruised and with her skull severely lacerated she found it difficult to speak. But she managed to say she was sure that the man who had brutalized her in the darkness was her husband. He had shouted at her – and she would know his voice anywhere.

At this time Lord Lucan was 39 years old. He had married Veronica, daughter of an army officer, in 1963; separating from her 10 years later. The Eton-educated earl, who had served in the Coldstream Guards, was known in London as a playboy who regularly lost far more than he could afford at the gambling tables of Mayfair.

To the investigating detectives it seemed, on the surface, an open-and-shut case. Lucan, who had made no secret of his obsessive desire to gain custody of the children, had to be the killer. In all probability he had bludgeoned the nanny in the darkened breakfast room, mistaking her for his wife. When he discovered his error he went on to attack Veronica. It all seemed plain enough, but the police were properly cautious. Many of them expected that within a day or so the missing earl, lawyer in tow, would give himself up. That didn't happen – but it would, in any case, be five days before the detectives issued a warrant for Lucan's arrest.

However, police had wasted no time, on the night of the murder, in rushing to the earl's flat in a nearby street. Lucan's Mercedes was parked outside – but he had fled, driving a borrowed car (as his pursuers would later learn) to a friend's house 44 miles away. The friend subsequently recounted the story Lucan had told her – a story she believed – to the detectives:

Lucan claimed he had been walking past 46 Lower Belgrave Street, en route to the flat, to change for dinner at his club. He heard a scream – and through the basement's venetian blinds, saw what seemed to be Veronica being attacked by an intruder.

Using his own key, Lucan let himself into the house and rushed down to protect her. He found the killer cramming a body into a sack. He attacked the man, landing several blows – but then slipped in the slick of blood on the floor. The murderer ran off. Fearing that he would be blamed, Lucan fled also.

Police traced the borrowed car to Newhaven, Sussex, a port from which ferries ran to France. In the interior they found bloodstains and a portion of lead pipe matching the weapon that had killed Sandra Rivett. For Britain's tabloid newspapers this was proof enough. Ignoring the tenets of British law, which require a presumption of innocence, they showered opprobrium on the seventh Earl of Lucan – variously describing him as a "murderer", "dimwit", "snob", "racist", and "homicidal."

* * *

PRELUDE TO MURDER The Earl of Lucan and his bride Veronica on
their wedding day in 1963. Eleven years later, their children's nanny was
found bludgeoned to death – and Lord Lucan was a prime suspect.
Whether guilty or not, he became a fugitive and is either dead or still in
hiding – possibly in Australia.
Australian Picture Library

In June 1975 London's Coroner's Court found Lucan guilty of murder *in absentia* – a verdict that scandalized Britons with a regard for fairness under the law. So powerful was the protest that the government two years later was forced to pass legislation forbidding a coroner to deliver such a finding against an accused who was not present to defend himself.

Many people who had known Lucan (even those who considered him a wastrel) refused to believe he was capable of murder. His children, as adults, shared that view. In an interview son George said, "Our father loved us far too much to inflict this terrible pain. He did not try to kill our mother and he was not the person who murdered Sandra – of that I'm certain."

Before he disappeared Lucan did what he could to secure his children's welfare. In a letter to his brother-in-law, Bill Shand-Kydd, written several hours after the murder, he said: "The circumstantial evidence against me is strong, so I will lie doggo for a while. But I am only concerned about the children. If you can manage it I would like them to live with you."

Lucan's wish was not immediately granted. In the years following the slaying George and his sisters lived with their mother. But shortly after George turned 14 the arrangement was changed. He and sisters Camilla, now 11, and Frances, 17, went to live with their uncle and aunt, Bill and Christina Shand-Kydd.

* * *

Their happy life in the couple's house in Bedfordshire helped them overcome the trauma that had shadowed their childhood. Frances grew up and graduated in law from Bristol University. Camilla, with a double-First from Oxford, married a Queen's Counsel and had two children. George graduated from Cambridge and subsequently joined a London financial firm. After 10 years he resigned to research a book about what really had happened on that dark drizzling night in 1974.

"If I believe what the papers tell me, my father was a totally unpleasant person," he said. "And yet I can't find anyone who knew the man who was prepared to say anything but that he was the most wonderful company, incredibly generous and the nicest person to be with."

In 1999 Britain's High Court declared Lord Lucan dead. Thanks to his huge gambling debts his estate was worth only £14,000.

But not everyone is sure that the seventh earl *is* dead. Even the police who pursued him are divided. After retiring from Scotland Yard, Superintendent Roy Ransom, who led the search, said, "He killed the nanny by mistake, thinking he could dispose of his wife and get custody of the children he loved. When he realized the error he killed himself in some remote place, like a lord and a gentleman."

Superintendent Dave Gerring, who took part in the same pursuit, disagreed. "Lord Lucan is still in hiding somewhere," he said. "He's a lord and a gentleman, but he's still a gambler – and he's still gambling on the odds that no one will ever find him."

In the three decades since Lucan's disappearance, dozens of people – the sincere and the publicity-seeking – have come forward to claim they knew of his whereabouts. In September 2003 a photographer claimed he had taken pictures of the earl – and produced images of a long-bearded semi-naked hippie living in Goa. Skeptical reporters quickly established that, far from being an earl, the hirsute man (now dead) had been a tin whistle-playing elementary school teacher who moonlighted as a busker.

Further probing revealed that before leaving Britain he had lived with his mother in a red-brick semidetached terrace in Lancashire.

A "Lucan-sighting" which some observers have taken more seriously was reported by a senior Sussex policeman, Detective Superintendent Tim O'Connor, who was working in Newhaven when the earl's borrowed and bloodstained car was found.

Thirteen years after the murder, while visiting his brother in Perth, Western Australia, O'Connor became friendly with a senior policeman living next door. "He said he had information that Lord Lucan was living in a Perth suburb – and asked if I'd be interested in going along with the Australian detectives who'd be interviewing him," O'Connor recalled. Hoping he might be able to help in an unofficial capacity, O'Connor accepted the invitation.

He traveled, with two detective-constables, to a pleasant house in an affluent suburb.

"The man who answered the door was, to me, Lord Lucan," O'Connor recalled. "He was older and his height, looks and bearing were spot-on. So was the aristocratic English accent, which I feel he'd have found impossible to disguise. And his sitting room had photographs of army regiments on show.

"He went to a drawer and produced several British passports and driving licenses in another name – but they didn't convince me. He was too well-prepared. I believe the man I met was Lucan."

Tim O'Connor immediately submitted a report to Scotland Yard. That was in 1987. O'Connor, now retired, says he can only "assume" that his detailed brief was followed up – but no one has officially told him what the results were.

Is Lord Lucan still alive? And is he hiding, under an alias, somewhere on the vast Australian continent?

The question remains unanswered.

Mystery of the Many Mary Celestes: 1840-2003

On December 4 1872 the American brigantine Mary Celeste was discovered adrift in the Atlantic. The vessel was completely seaworthy; her cargo, provisions and water supply intact. On a table in the captain's cabin a meal lay uneaten. In the forecastle the crew's oilskins, boots, and tobacco pipes were neatly arranged. But the crew themselves, their captain and his wife and daughter, had vanished – never to be seen again. Historians habitually describe this bizarre episode as the greatest of maritime mysteries. But the facts suggest otherwise. Crews and passengers had puzzlingly disappeared from intact vessels before. And the extraordinary Mary Celeste phenomenon would repeat itself throughout the twentieth century and into the twenty-first, when a "ghost ship" was found floating and inexplicably abandoned off the Australian coast…

Dockside, New York,
November 7 1872. Morning

FOR THE DARK-HAIRED 17-year-old beauty Katherine Richardson, this was the saddest of days. Less than a month had passed since she married her beloved childhood sweetheart Albert – and here she was today, on a bleak wharf far from their native Maine, waving farewell to him; saying goodbye when their lives together had scarcely begun.

As the daughter of a seafaring family Katherine had always known that long separations and gnawing anxiety were the trials a sailor's wife must endure. But it was plain to her now that she had understood this only in theory. As she would later confess to her diary, the raw reality of parting was far more painful than she had ever imagined.

A cheer went up from the small knot of well-wishers around her. The 103-foot brig, sails spread, had begun to move away. Katherine's tears almost blinded her to the sight of her lanky, boyish-looking husband, Albert Richardson, first mate, craning over the rail, arms outstretched, as if intent on somehow diminishing the fast-growing gap between them.

Sarah Briggs, 30, wife of the captain, leaned by the rail with her 2-year-old daughter Sophia, waving, alongside Albert, to the forlorn girl on the dock. In her nine years of marriage Sarah had endured many such wrenching farewells.

On the bridge stood stern-faced, spade-bearded Benjamin Spooner Briggs, 37, captain, and part-owner of *Mary Celeste*. To those who would later recall in detail the events of that morning, he appeared quite untouched by the emotion on the dock. This was an important occasion in his life and he was according it the grave attention it deserved. Having extended himself financially to buy his interest in the brigantine he was determined to make this crucial voyage a success.

Mary Celeste steered a path through the clamor of the harbor, past cutters, customs boats, and noisy tugs and headed toward the open sea. To Katherine and her companions, the ship was a blur, now, their loved ones on the deck invisible. None of those left behind in New York guessed that they had seen the people aboard for the last time.

Less than an hour after weighing anchor, the 290-tonne brigantine was under full sail, en route to Genoa, Italy. Her principal cargo was grain alcohol in 1,700 red oak barrels: an investment from which Benjamin Briggs and his partners were confident of making a large profit. For weeks, the buoyant Briggs had been telling associates that this would be *Mary Celeste's* "maiden voyage." But the assertion applied, in reality, only to the name freshly painted on her prow.

• • •

Photograph of the *Mary Celeste* in port.

The vessel had been launched 12 years earlier from the Joshua Dewis shipyard on Spencer Island, Nova Scotia. Sailing under the name *Amazon* she had survived a long string of misfortunes, including a fire, two collisions, and a near-fatal wreck. In 1870 Captain Briggs's principal partner, the shipowner James Winchester, had bought the brigantine for the bargain price of £3,000. He refitted the ship and sheathed her bottom in copper. By September 1872 the sparkling, newly christened *Mary Celeste* had been re-registered as an American vessel and was sitting at Pier 44 in New York's East River, ready to go to work.

Captain Briggs chose seven known and trusted men to sail with him. Aside from first mate Richardson the crew comprised second mate Andrew Gillings, cook Edward Head and four seamen, Gottlieb Goodschaad, Ari Martens, and brothers Boz and Volkert Lorenzen. Mrs Sarah Briggs and 2-year-old Sophia were making the journey at the captain's request. Sophia's brother, 7-year-old Thomas, had hoped to come, too, but his father insisted that he stay home to continue his schoolwork.

Sarah Briggs had sailed with her husband before – and knew how tedious the long hours at sea could be. To relieve the monotony she had brought along a sewing machine, on which she would make clothes for her children, a box filled with toys for Sophia and a handsome musical instrument, the New Melodeon, which Benjamin had bought her for a past birthday and at whose keyboard she was now adept.

Travel in those distant times was infused with glamor. Everyone aboard was planning and imagining what they might do when the ship made landfall in Italy, a country which none had visited. But the travelers' dreams and hopes were to come to nothing. Not one soul aboard *Mary Celeste* would ever reach Genoa...

December 4 1872. Atlantic Ocean, near the Azores

David Morehouse, captain of the British cargo brig *Dei Gratia*, sensed immediately that something was wrong. The vessel, roughly two miles to the north-west, sails set and blossoming, seemed to be moving erratically in the light breeze.

Morehouse signaled. There was no reply. *Dei Gratia* steered closer. The keen-eyed deckboy was first to notice it. "There's no one at the wheel!" he shouted. "No one there!"

Before long the mysterious ship was looming above the little *Dei Gratia* – and everybody aboard could now read its name: *Mary Celeste*.

To Captain Morehouse, the revelation came as a shock. He knew this ship, and her captain, well. He and Benjamin Briggs had dined together only a few weeks earlier.

Morehouse ordered his first mate, Oliver Deveau, and two seamen to take a boat and board *Mary Celeste*. The three men searched the brigantine from end to end. It was completely, and eerily, deserted. But everywhere they found signs of seemingly recent occupation. Mrs Briggs's sewing machine had been used for hemming a small girl's dress, which lay folded on a chair. A phial of oil, standing beside the machine, bore witness to the ship's apparent stability at the time of its evacuation. There had been no natural disaster here – no storm or freakish wave.

The captain's clothes and fobwatch were hanging in his cabin. On a table nearby, a meal, cutlery arranged neatly beside it, lay untouched. In the forecastle hung what seemed to be most of the crew's boots and clothing. Fixed to a wall was a rack containing their pipes. For reasons that could only be guessed at, the men had quit their ship without tobacco or warm clothes. As Oliver Deveau and his subordinates would subsequently testify, everything aboard looked normal, as if the people who had sailed aboard *Mary Celeste* were about to return at any moment.

Deveau inspected the cargo. The 1,700 redwood barrels of grain alcohol were, with one exception, unbreached, and firmly secured. He checked the log. The last entry, made on November 24, recorded a position 800 miles from where the brigantine now drifted. A log-slate notation, dated November 25, revealed that captain and crew had sighted the island of St Mary, in the Azores.

And then, nothing.

Working night and day, Deveau and his two men sailed the ghost ship 600 miles to Gibraltar, where they dropped anchor on December 13. In the 40 years that followed, almost to the time of his death, aged 80, in 1912, Oliver Deveau courteously allowed himself to be subjected to hundreds of newspaper and magazine interviews. He answered all questions and constructively considered all theories, but insisted always that he could think of "no rational reason" for the mass exodus from *Mary Celeste*.

But the authorities were convinced that there must be an explanation for the strange affair. In late December 1872, F. Solly-Flood, queen's proctor in the Admiralty Court, ordered a "special survey" of the derelict vessel. The initial investigators were the master of the court, T.R. Vecchio, surveyor of shipping, Gerald Austin, and a diver, Ricardo Fortunato. The trio's findings, as reported in the *Gibraltar Chronicle's* January 30 1873 issue were that:

- The derelict known as the American brigantine *Mary Celeste* "appeared to be in a substantially serviceable condition." The hull exterior, below the waterline, "exhibited not the smallest trace of damage, and nor was there the appearance that the vessel had come into any kind of collision."

- The state of the ship's interior only intensified the investigators' puzzlement. "A very minute survey showed most clearly that not only had the vessel not sustained any accident, but that she could not have encountered seriously heavy weather... The deckhouse, made of thin planking, was perfect; there not being a crack, even in the paint. The seamen's chests and the clothing found were perfectly dry, some razors even being quite free from rust. Spare panes of glass were also found stowed, unbroken; and a small phial containing oil for use in a sewing machine was found in a perpendicular position which, together with a thimble and a reel of cotton nearby, had not been upset, as must have been the case if the ship had been subject to any stress of weather."

- And of the grain alcohol, valued at about $80,000, which might have motivated a pirate attack, the report said: "All of the barrels were well-stowed and in good order and condition, except one barrel which had been started. Nothing had been stolen."

Mr Austin concluded, "The captain, B.S. Briggs by name, is well-known in Gibraltar and bore the highest character... The effects found in his cabin were of considerable value... and proved that a lady and child had been aboard. Up to this date, not a word has been heard, or a trace discovered, of the captain and his crew, or the lady and her child."

The American Consul's Letter

ON JANUARY 18 1873 Horatio Sprague, the US Consul in Gibraltar, wrote an official memo, on the subject of *Mary Celeste*, to Worthington C. Ford of the State Department.
Sprague said, in part:

> *The case of the* Mary Celeste, *as you justly remark, is startling, since it appears to be one of those mysteries which no human ingenuity can recreate sufficiently to account for the abandonment of this vessel, and the disappearance of her master, family, and crew, about whom nothing has ever transpired. Believe me.*

Mary Celeste quickly became the most talked-about ship in the world. Theories about what might have befallen her doomed passengers and crew dominated the international press. A Board of Inquiry, established to throw a cool judicial light on the affair, only succeeded in fomenting further confusion.

A principal witness at the hearing was the brig's defacto captain, Oliver Deveau. He testified that during his search he had come upon "a ceremonial sword, stained with rust." Within days, rumor had transformed the weapon into a pirate's bloodied saber. The hysteria prompted a retired sea captain, F.W. Stainton, to write a letter to *The Times* of London, urging restraint. "Were a pirate band to bear blame," he wrote, "they would surely have been a group of men singularly lacking in greed, for nothing of value was taken."

• • •

On London's streets, earnest Temperance crusaders distributed a pamphlet, *The Matter of the "Mary Celeste" Resolved*. Responsibility for the tragedy, the publication averred, could be sheeted squarely to the "thousands of barrels of alcohol" carried as cargo. Fumes from these inadequately sealed containers had driven the sailors mad, prompting them to kill the captain along with his wife and child, then dumping them into the ocean before fleeing by boat. The fatal weakness in this argument was that the Gibraltar investigators had checked the cargo and found it securely stored.

Another theory, rejected by the inquiry, was that the crew had been eating bread made from rye, rather than wheat. When wet, rye breeds a fungus that can cause insanity if ingested. But again, the Gibraltar investigators and others that followed them had declared the brigantine's food and water stores to be in excellent condition and sufficient for six months at sea. No wet, or even previously wet, bread had been found.

In 1884 Arthur Conan Doyle, creator of Sherlock Holmes, muddied the issue further by writing a short story, Habakuk Jephson's Statement, for the *Cornhill Magazine*. The narrative, filled with sensation and surmise, described the fate of a brigantine, *Marie* (sic) *Celeste*. Forgivably, many readers confused this imaginary vessel with the *Mary Celeste* of 1872. More than one popular historian in the late nineteenth century ignorantly aped Doyle's spelling of the ship's name, presenting his fictions as fact.

False trails continued to appear up to the eve of World War I. In 1913 a schoolmaster, Howard Linford, published in London's *Strand* magazine a collection of letters and notes which, he claimed, had been given to him by a dying employee, Abel Fosdyk. In these journals, subsequently proved spurious, "Fosdyk" alleged that Captain Briggs had taken him aboard *Mary Celeste* as a "secret passenger" – after Fosdyk confided to the captain that he had to leave New York in a hurry.

One afternoon (the almost certainly fictitious Fosdyk wrote) the captain and first mate Richardson had had a bitter argument about a man's ability to swim fully clothed. To demonstrate that it was a simple matter, Captain Briggs jumped overboard – challenging Richardson to join him in the water. The entire crew, accompanied by Mrs Briggs and her child, crowded onto a small upper deck, which had been built exclusively for the little girl to play on. Abruptly the structure collapsed under the crowd's combined weight. All fell into the sea, where they either drowned or were devoured by sharks. Fosdyk, the only survivor, escaped by boat.

The report won exceptional sales for the *Strand* magazine. But it swiftly became apparent that the shadowy Fosdyk's tale couldn't possibly be true. Neither the scrupulous Gibraltar investigators, nor the exhaustive Board of Inquiry, had found the faintest evidence of a collapsed deck. Had they done so, the conundrum would have been resolved in an instant.

Despite all the purported revelations and proof presented over the years, the fate of the lost souls aboard *Mary Celeste* has remained a mystery.

But as this book will reveal, it is far from being a unique mystery.

The profound puzzle of *Mary Celeste* is part of a pattern which has repeated itself through the centuries. A pattern whose meaning, at this time, eludes understanding.

As any patient and painstaking researcher can ascertain, cases eerily similar to the enigma of *Mary Celeste* had been chronicled decades before 1872. And the roll-call of these inexplicable events continued through the nineteenth and twentieth centuries and into the twenty-first:

- Ships discovered drifting through open ocean, with no human life aboard.

- Systems intact, with no evidence of significantly disabling damage. Food and water supplies adequate. Meals sometimes found on tables. The crew's clothing and other personal effects left behind.

- No sign of violent impact, either from the weather or from intruders.

- Ships in whose cabins valuables (jewelry, cash, documents) remained undisturbed.

- Ships whose principal shared characteristic was, in short, *the uncanny absence of people*.

I will focus first on the most recent of these events: the disappearance, early in the present century, of the captain and crew of *High Aim 6*...

Indian Ocean, 155 miles off Broome, Western Australia. January 9 2003

It was the nauseating stench that alerted the captain and officers aboard Australian naval vessel HMAS *Stuart* that something was amiss. The afternoon was hot and cloudless, with the lightest of breezes – but the flow of air was strong enough, nevertheless, to be swamping the *Stuart's* decks with a foul odor.

Plainly the stomach-churning smell was emanating from the modern long-line fishing boat that bobbed on the swells ahead, drifting in circles. She was Indonesian-flagged. Her name, painted on the hull in both Taiwanese and English, was *High Aim 6*.

When he received no answer to his signals, the Australian ship's captain sent a party of men aboard the 150-tonne derelict. They found it silent, deserted. Seemingly it had been abandoned in a hurry. Clothes lay neatly folded in the lockers, along with international documents belonging to ship personnel. Seven toothbrushes hung neatly from a rack: a possible indication, an officer initially surmised, that there might have been a captain, a first mate, and five crew. On the dash in the wheelhouse lay a pair of reading glasses, subsequently identified as belonging to the captain; a jar of Nescafé, and an open carton of Marlboro cigarettes.

The boarding party followed their noses to the source of the fetid smell. In the hold they found a rotting mess of mackerel and tuna. Subsequent tests showed that the fish had been caught two weeks earlier and weighed a total of three tonnes. *High Aim*'s freezer had failed when its engine stopped.

Bemused, the Australians looked for further clues. There was no sign of violence or natural damage. If pirates had stormed the fishing boat, they had been exceedingly inefficient, leaving wallets containing considerable sums of Taiwanese and Indonesian cash behind – not to speak of the untouched documents, which would have fetched good prices in the wharfside underworld. The vessel was carrying sufficient drinking water, fruit, and canned food to last several months. Her fuel tanks were half-full. If the captain and crew had simply abandoned ship, it was hard to imagine what their motive might have been.

The men of HMAS *Stuart* nicknamed the ghost craft *Mary Celeste*. They towed her to a quarantine bay off Broome, where Australian Federal Police immediately began an intensive forensic investigation.

Meanwhile the Royal Australian Navy, aided by coastwatch aircraft and a PC-3 Orion conducted a 15,500 mile search around the area where the fishing vessel was intercepted. They found no trace of the missing seafarers.

Police established that the mystery ship had left Taiwan on October 31 2002, and had last made radio contact with the owners, Tsai Huang Shueheer on December 13, when she reported being near the Marshall Islands.

Her Taiwanese captain was Chen Tai-chen; her chief engineer, Lee Ah-Duey. There were 10 Indonesian crew. The search coordinator, Bill Graham, told media reporters that he could find "no plausible reason" for the men's disappearance.

Theories that pirates might have attacked the ship were widely dismissed in the press. A typical comment came from the *Taipei Times*, which described the notion as "unlikely." The newspaper added: "There was no sign of a struggle – and the hijackers almost certainly would have made off with the boat."

• • •

After eight months of fruitless investigation, the Federal Police transferred control of *High Aim 6* to the Australian Fisheries Management Authority. The Taiwanese owners wrote to say that they did not want the vessel back – explaining that it would cost too much to make her seaworthy again. (They omitted to add that superstitious seamen might baulk at sailing in her.) On January 13 2004, the fisheries authority announced that *High Aim 6* would be hauled from the Broome mudflats on which she had lain beached through the previous year – and sunk offshore as an artificial reef.

Next day Queensland's *Courier Mail* summated this decision in the terse headline: GHOST SHIP WILL TAKE HER SECRETS TO THE GRAVE.

As years passed, Taiwanese, Indonesian and Australian authorities continued to make it clear that they would welcome any information about the fate of the travelers aboard *High Aim 6*. However, as realists, they were unhopeful of hearing anything. Search coordinator Bill Graham had encapsulated the official feeling quite early when he said: "As time goes on, the prospects of locating the crew alive decrease."

In the annals of the sea, cases of sailors disappearing without trace from their abandoned *Mary Celeste*-like vessels can be traced back at least 17 decades. Probably the syndrome extends much further into the past, but contemporary chronicles, and official reports that distinguish fact from myth, are harder to find.

Among the maritime enigmas (both pre-and post-*Mary Celeste*) enumerated below, similarities abound. But the greatest similarity of all is that *not one* of the captains, crewmen or passengers who had traveled aboard these abandoned ships was ever seen again. Alive or dead.

Overture to the *Mary Celeste* Mystery: 1840-1857

Rosalie, 1840

THE RECORDS OF the British Maritime Museum reveal that the large French merchant ship *Rosalie* was built in 1838, from 222 tons of timber. The vessel came to the general public's attention in 1840, when *The Times* of London, in its November 6 edition, reported that she had been intercepted "in peculiar circumstances" in the Atlantic Ocean. *Rosalie*, laden with what the newspaper described as "valuable cargo", had been en route from Hamburg to Havana. She was discovered with sails fully set and on course, despite the fact that nobody was at the wheel.

In the forecastle, trapped in its cage, drooped a starving canary. Along the deck, domestic hens pecked desperately for any trace of nourishment.

Aside from the squawking of the fowls and the hushing of the calm sea, all was quiet aboard *Rosalie*. The ship's captain, officers, crew, and passengers were nowhere to be found. This, as *The Times* remarked, was a puzzle, because there seemed to have been no reason for the mass desertion.

Everything aboard the ship was in exemplary condition. There were no leaks. Food and water supplies were plentiful. The "obvious" explanation – that the voyagers aboard *Rosalie* had been murdered by pirates – was ruled out both in France and Britain. There was not a crumb of evidence pointing to criminal intrusion. There was no sign of a struggle. No trace of blood. No bodies. The cargo, along with money and valuables belonging to all aboard, was untouched.

For no discernible reason, every soul aboard *Rosalie* had vanished. No trace of them was ever found.

Hermania, 1849

In October 1849, 23 years before the fate of *Mary Celeste* would baffle the world, a fishing vessel happened upon a Dutch schooner, *Hermania*, adrift off the coast of Cornwall in southern England. Like the other craft in these cases she was in good condition, carrying adequate provisions. Her lifeboats had not been launched. But her captain and crew had vanished. Again, no remains were discovered.

Unidentified Bark, 1852

Another curious case, which preceded the *Mary Celeste* drama by two decades, was reported from the Gaspe Peninsula, Canada. The incident was recalled – under the heading MYSTERY SHIP – in the *Berwick Register* of December 15 1915. The newspaper republished a correspondent's detailed and circumstantial bulletin from Miramichi on February 23 1852:

> *The courier from Perce to Restigouche has informed me that when he left below there was a large barque in the ice off Gaspe. The barque had her fore-top sail and jib set.*
>
> *Two men by means of a skiff got on board and found her laden with red pine. There were 60 bags of bread and 20 barrels of flour, also the ship's papers. There appears nothing wrong with her apart from the loss of her rudder and part of the bow-sprit. A crew of men are going on board with the intention of working her out of the ice, and taking her to some port in Nova Scotia or Newfoundland.*
>
> *There was not a soul to be found on board, yet strange to say, none of the boats belonging to the ship were gone, all being in their proper place, so that what has become of the crew remains a mystery.*

James B. Chester, 1857

In October 1857 (December in some reports) the bark *James B. Chester* was reportedly found becalmed in the Sargasso Sea. Her chairs were upended, plates of food lay putrefying on a table – and nobody was aboard.

Mysteries in *Mary Celeste's* Wake

Resolven, 1884

THE 143-TONNE brigantine *Resolven* was built from softwood in Nova Scotia. During the 1880s she plied a profitable trade as a carrier. Her principal cargo was fish.

On August 27 1884, under the captaincy of Stephen James, with six crew and three passengers, *Resolven* left Harbor Grace, Newfoundland, for Snug Harbor, Labrador. Two days later a British naval vessel, HMS *Mallard*, encountered her, sails set and "steering strangely" in relatively calm waters, 63 miles from her intended destination.

When his signals were ignored, *Mallard*'s captain dispatched a boarding party. His officers and men could find no sign of life on the brigantine – but there was evidence that people had been present quite recently. The ashes of a fire that had been burning in the galley were still warm. There was no indication of damage, either natural or caused by man.

Neither the British officers, nor a subsequent inquiry, could find any reason why all aboard *Resolven* had suddenly abandoned ship.

Freya, 1902

In its April 1907 edition the British scientific journal *Nature* looked back on the eerie disappearance of yet another ship's captain and crew. The men, in this case, had been sailing on the German bark *Freya*.

On October 3 1902 the bark left Manzanilla for Punto Arenas on the west coast of Mexico. On October 20 fishermen found *Freya* at sea, partly dismasted and completely deserted. Her anchor was still hanging free at the bow, suggesting that a calamity of some kind had occurred relatively soon after she left port. This theory was strengthened by the date on a calendar in the captain's cabin: October 4 – one day after *Freya* had begun her journey.

Weather reports showed that on October 4 and 5 conditions in the area had been fine, with light winds. German maritime authorities could find no reason why the voyagers on *Freya* had abandoned ship. No bodies were found...

Carroll A. Deering, 1921

The fathomless enigma of the *Carroll A. Deering* sparked headlines and increasingly shrill argument around the globe.

The immense five-masted schooner, launched from Bathe, Maine, in 1919, had spent most of her brief working life carrying goods between US ports and South America.

On December 1 1920, she unloaded a cargo of coal at Rio de Janeiro, then set sail for her home harbor: Portland, Maine. Almost two months later (January 31 1921) the men of Ocracoke Island coastguard station, off North Carolina, spotted through their telescopes a five-masted ship, all sails set, hard aground four miles distant, on Diamond Shoals.

After three days in which surfboats, fighting mountainous waves, failed to reach the vessel, rescuers sent out a tugboat, whose crew managed to board the stricken ship. They identified her as *Carroll A. Deering*.

The men of the boarding party were greeted by an unsettling (but, in the context of this narrative) familiar scene. There was no sign of humanity aboard. The only living creatures were three famished ship's cats. On the galley table, plates of spare ribs, along with a large tureen of pea soup and a pot of coffee, stood untouched. The food seemed still to be fresh, but as the coastguards later testified, it could well have been preserved for days by the bitter weather.

The ship's boats were gone. The coastguards were at a loss to know why. The grounded schooner was stable – and the sailors aboard would have been sensible to use her as a shelter until they were rescued. Obviously, *something* had prompted this mass desertion. The coastguards searched the schooner from stem to stern. They found no blood, no bodies, no evidence of any form of violence.

* * *

The captain, on this tragic final voyage, had been a 66-year-old master mariner, Willis B. Wormwell. He had plied this and associated routes for 25 years. Witnesses at the subsequent inquiry found it inconceivable that a sailor of such experience would have led his crew to the lifeboats without firing distress rockets beforehand – signals that would easily have been seen by the 24-hour lookout four miles distant. By simply quitting the schooner,

Captain Wormwell and his men would surely have gone to certain death among the shoals.

What had driven them to such a suicidal act?

Over the following 10 days shipping and coastguard vessels scoured thousands of square miles of ocean, coves, and beaches, seeking any trace of the 11 missing men, or wreckage of the lifeboats in which presumably they had escaped. The search produced nothing.

The controversy surrounding the crew's fate inspired such enormous press coverage that the then US Secretary of Commerce, Herbert Hoover, placed himself in charge of the investigation. May 1921 brought an apparent breakthrough. A local seaman, Christopher Gray, went to coastguard headquarters with a letter which, he said, he had found in a bottle washed up on a beach near his Buxton home. The message, purportedly from *Carroll A. Deering*'s engineer, Herbert Bates, read:

> *Oil-burning boat captured us. Crew hiding all over ship. Some in handcuffs. Finder please notify authorities.*

Herbert Hoover promptly summoned Bates's mother, the schooner's owner, Gardner Deering, and three handwriting experts. All confirmed that the letter was indeed in the hand of the chief engineer.

But the bottle's finder, seaman Gray, seemed to be enjoying his new fame rather too much. Suspicious, Hoover dispatched two federal agents to question him at exhaustive length. Gray buckled under the tough questioning and admitted that he had written the note – basing its uprights and distinctive narrow loops on a specimen of the engineer's penmanship.

The federal investigation was back where it had begun. Despite attempts, decades later, to rationalize the mass disappearance with stories of "intrigue" aboard ship, the fate of Captain Willis B. Wormwell and the 10 who had journeyed with him would never be known.

Joyita, 1955

The 70-foot luxury yacht *Joyita* ("Little Jewel") was built in 1931 at the Wilmington Boat Works, Los Angeles. Her first owner was the film producer Roland West. He little imagined, when he took delivery of his expensive new toy, that it would one day become the focus of the Pacific Ocean's most uncanny mystery.

Joyita was a twin-screw, two-diesel-engine motor vessel, thickly insulated with cork: an addition, her designers boasted, that made her virtually unsinkable. But despite her palatial fittings and sybaritic comforts – and a sparkling cargo of French Champagnes and gourmet delicacies – the yacht brought little happiness to those who sailed in her. *Joyita* was the focus of trauma and ill-luck almost from the day she was launched.

At Roland West's invitation many motion picture performers enjoyed weekends and vacations aboard the spacious craft. One was West's lover, the then-celebrated actress Thelma Todd. When she was murdered, the more raucous American tabloids ascribed the tragedy to a curse. The accidents, illnesses and mishaps that had plagued *Joyita* during her first months at sea were evidence of a jinx, the journalists claimed.

Stung by the bad publicity Roland West sold the yacht for considerably less than he had paid. *Joyita* was passed among various owners until, in 1941, after the Japanese attack on Pearl Harbor, the US Navy requisitioned her as a patrol boat.

After World War II *Joyita* spent several years plying the Samoan and Fijian coasts as a fishing vessel and copra ship. During this period she ran aground three times. The writer Robin Maugham, who briefly owned the yacht in 1950, was so disturbed by her dark reputation that he asked an Anglican priest to conduct an exorcism ceremony on the deck. The request went all the way to the Archbishop of Canterbury, who is not believed to have given his assent.

In 1952 Dr Katharine Luomola of the University of Hawaii bought the yacht and chartered her to a Welsh friend, Captain T.H. ("Dusty") Miller. He would meet his fate aboard *Joyita*.

* * *

For much of the twentieth century the people of the Tokelau Islands had been fighting a bitter struggle for existence. Their Pacific neighbors were in the habit of helping out – and in September 1955 the Tokelauans urgently asked for aid again. Poor food crops and an ailing economy had reduced living standards to below subsistence level. The islands' flour, sugar, vegetables, and fruit were almost gone. Medical stocks were dangerously low. The farmers had more than 100 tonnes of cut copra awaiting export: a crop that would bring desperately needed cash, if only they could afford the transport.

The governments of New Zealand and Western Samoa commissioned Dusty Miller, captain of *Joyita*, to take a cargo of relief supplies to Tokelau, then to load the copra and deliver it to Australian buyers.

On October 3 1955 *Joyita* swept out of the harbor at Apia, Western Samoa, heading for Fakaofo in the Tokelau Islands, over 265 miles distant. Aboard were 25 people, comprising Captain Miller, 12 Samoan crewmen, three government officials, and nine paying passengers – among them, two children.

None of them would ever be seen again.

The voyage from Apia to Fakaofo should not have taken more than 48 hours. After three days, with no sign of *Joyita* on the horizon, the Tokelauans used their primitive radio equipment to raise the alarm. The Royal New Zealand Air Force mounted an extensive search which eventually covered more than 160,000 square miles of ocean – but found nothing.

The breakthrough came five weeks later, on November 10 1955. Captain Gerald Douglas, master of the *Tuvalu*, en route from Suva to Funafuti, spotted a vessel drifting off the Fijian coast. It was *Joyita* – waterlogged, but in no danger of sinking. She was completely deserted.

A Chinese tug towed the yacht into Fiji. Meanwhile, three RNZAF officers scoured the ship. They reported that the tanks contained fuel enough for 3000 miles and that there were ample supplies of water and food. The searchers opened hatches, forced a cabin door, and shouted continuously – encouraging anyone who might be lying injured somewhere to shout back. Silence greeted them.

One of the officers who went aboard that day was Gerry Ayre, a member of NZAF 5 Squadron. "It was scary looking for the people who should have been on *Joyita*," he later recalled. "We found nothing – not even a scrap of paper or a pencil. The ship was clean – no rags, nothing."

But there was one small trail of evidence. The searchers discovered clues that led them to believe the abandonment of the grand yacht had occurred in two stages. They deduced that someone must have stayed on board after the others left; using an awning, either to catch water or provide shelter from the furious Pacific sun.

* * *

In December 1955 a Commission of Inquiry sat in Western Samoa. After several weeks of intense investigation it delivered a 315-page finding. Its conclusion: the fate of *Joyita*'s passengers and crew was "inexplicable."

But the world beyond the sweltering courtroom, with its lazily thwacking ceiling fans, wanted more satisfactory answers:

- *Why* had every soul aboard abandoned ship? *Joyita* was partly waterlogged, certainly – but she remained safe for human occupation. Everyone, from Captain Miller down, knew that the ship's cork lining rendered her virtually unsinkable. Surely they would not have been so foolish as to take their chances in lifeboats, in shark-ridden waters when they could have stayed on board and awaited rescue.

This was the same question that had been asked about the vanished men of the *Carroll A. Deering*... and of the people aboard *Mary Celeste*... and of *Rosalie* and *Resolven* and *Zebrina* and...

- And *what* had happened aboard *Joyita*? The inquiry had offered no more than theories, assumptions, and exclusions. Could it be possible, some observers asked, that there might be a more bizarre explanation for the mystery than officialdom cared publicly to speculate upon?

* * *

The mysterious history of Mary Celeste and her vanished
captain, passengers and crew has been chronicled on the
postage stamps of several nations.

FOR MORE THAN 130 years writers and historians have habitually referred to the *case* of the brigantine *Mary Celeste*. This is a misnomer. The fate of Captain Benjamin Briggs, his wife, his daughter, and his crew was far less a *case* than part of a *syndrome* – a phenomenon so profoundly strange that it defies conventional analysis.

I have confined this survey to larger vessels from which there have been multiple arcane disappearances. But the *Mary Celeste* syndrome has also affected smaller craft with crews of two or three.

A common thread runs through all these ship-abandonments – namely that *every person* aboard *every vessel* has been missing.

It might seem reasonable to expect that the law of averages, or of fate, or even of sheer fumbling luck would dictate that at least *one* life on *one* of these ships had been preserved. That at least a single person had been spared to tell the world what actually happened.

But no. Nobody – from 1840 through to 2003 – has ever survived the *Mary Celeste* syndrome.

The vanishing rate is always 100 per cent.

The Glowing Cross
that Astonished Australia

In September 1907 a young Australian railway worker died while courageously trying to halt a runaway train carriage. Eleven years after he was buried in a country cemetery the stone cross above his grave began to glow with a bright white light. As decades passed, the graveyard fell into abandonment and neglect. But amidst the dockweeds and wild grasses the cross steadily continued to shine. Not until 1978, after the phenomenon had quietly persisted for 60 years, were the nation's major newspapers and TV networks alerted to the story. Scientific experts visited the site and offered conflicting explanations. But the mystery of the glowing cross remains unsolved...

THE NEW SOUTH WALES TOWN of Lismore at the dawn of the twentieth century was an idyllic place to live and rear children. Built along the banks of the broad Wilsons River and edged by dense subtropical rainforest, the district, with its rich volcanic soil, was home to farmers of all kinds, from dairymen and sugarcane planters to growers of tropical fruits.

William Steenson, aged 29, had spent most of his life in Lismore. On September 30 1907 he died in a town nearby. Everyone agreed that the accident need never have happened. During a shunting procedure at Mullumbimby railway station a carelessly secured carriage ran out of control. In an extraordinary display of bravery Steenson tried to slow the runaway with his bare hands. He was thrown to the ground and critically injured.

William Thomas Thurling Steenson was to leave behind him a legacy more enduring than anyone, in their wildest imaginings, could have foreseen.

His family buried him beneath a large stone cross in the North Lismore Pioneer Cemetery on the town's outskirts. For a long time his resting place appeared no different from the graves around it. Even the verse of an old hymn, which his wife had ordered engraved on the headstone, seemed unexceptional. It was not until decades later that a local journalist would describe that hymn's words as "prophetic."

According to witnesses who were alive at the time, the "strangeness" set in sometime around 1918 as World War I was drawing to a close.

Without warning, or an apparent trigger event of any kind, William Steenson's cross began to glow, with a light that was sometimes so intense it bathed graves in a wide arc around it.

Local inhabitants struggled to find a rationale. Could it be reflected moonlight? No, because the cross glowed on cloudy nights with no moon visible. Besides, nothing else in the cemetery had ever been known to glow. Might the cross be reflecting artificial light from somewhere? Repeated investigation failed to identify a source of such light. And again, why did it "reflect" from only one stone monument in a cemetery full of them?

For 60 years the Glowing Cross remained Lismore's "secret." Its very existence remained, to all intents, unknown to the world outside. Lismore's population contained few publicity seekers, but possibly there were two additional reasons behind the silence:

SHINING CROSS In 1907 a young railway worker died while trying to stop a runaway train carriage. Eleven years later the cross above his grave in Lismore Australia began to glow with a mysterious light. The phenomenon, pronounced unexplainable by experts of many disciplines, appeared internationally on TV. The light shone for 60 years.
The Northern Star

- Lismore was *accustomed* to the Glowing Cross. It had been a familiar part of the landscape for as long as most citizens could remember. It didn't seem at all "new" or worthy of outside attention. As one student of the cross phenomenon opined: "I guess nobody ever thought it important enough to report – not that a grave glowing inexplicably every night could be considered mundane."

- It was unlikely that any decent local would have dreamed of helping turn the cemetery light into a tourist circus while the descendants of William Steenson still lived in Lismore. (In 1984, long after the cross had become famous, Tom Steenson, William's grandson, told a newspaper that he and his father had paid quiet visits to the glowing graveside.)

But in February 1978 the six decades of silence were broken at last. A local woman, who had visited the cross with friends, happened to describe her experience to Alan Layton, a journalist with Lismore's *Northern Star* newspaper. Layton was the author of a human-interest column, Notebook. The woman wondered whether he would publish a brief piece discussing theories about why the stone emitted its peculiar light. Undoubtedly imagining that he was writing (as usual) for local consumption only, Layton obliged.

Anomalous Image in a North Dakota Church

A PHENOMENON described by witnesses as an "immense light" in the form of a cross has regularly appeared in the deserted Absaraka Methodist church in North Dakota, USA.

The church, built in 1888, was closed in 1983. The manifestation was first noticed 30 years earlier after new windows were installed.

Some analysts believe the representation of the cross is formed by refraction of light through the frosted windows. Visitors to the derelict church have said that the light profoundly moved them.

But his words caught the attention of a Sydney daily's chief-of-staff – and the media frenzy began.

Within 48 hours Lismore was aswarm with TV crews, reporters, photographers, and the merely curious. The cross, the fully occupied cemetery around it abandoned and neglected, posed patiently for its picture: glowing images that would travel, this time, around the planet.

Soon afterward the experts arrived: stonemasons, geologists, gemologists, physicists, refraction analysts and practitioners of many other disciplines. They offered a learned confusion of conflicting explanations, ranging from phosphorescence to radioactivity – but everyone's argument had a hole in it somewhere.

According to one theory the glow was caused by a combination of the stone that formed the cross (Balmoral granite) with its highly polished state. But that failed to explain why the base, made from the same material, did not glow also. At the end of all the measuring, analyzing, and opinionating there was no definitive answer.

For the first time the people of Lismore themselves began to speak out. Some admitted that the graveyard spectacle had frightened them over the years. Albert Dann, who had moved to the district with his family 60 years earlier, recalled one Glowing Cross trauma. While he was still a newcomer, local children had taken him to "the Ghost on the Hill", as they called the cross, and offered him a penny if he dared read the name on the "shiny grave."

In February 1978 Mr Dann told the *Northern Star*: "Forcing myself toward the main gate, suddenly, as I edged closer, a dazzling beam of white light flashed from the center of the cemetery and struck me in the eyes.

"I was rooted to the spot with a horrible fear, still indescribable to this day. Somehow I remember forcing my unwilling body about and with every ghost and devil after me I sprinted back along the metaled road to the comfort of a gas lamp, beneath which the boys were howling with laughter and yelling, 'You couldn't do it, you couldn't do it!'"

But most reactions to the cross were positive. Many locals entertained the idea that it might be sending some kind of supernatural signal, of a benign kind, from the long-dead railwayman.

In 1986, following a long string of vandal attacks, someone removed the cross from its pedestal. Despite a wide search by police and locals it was never recovered. One rumor suggested that the thief (or, because of the stone's muscle-wrenching weight) thieves, dumped it up-river.

The Steenson family erected a new cross in memory of their ancestor.

It was carved to exactly the same proportions and in the same Balmoral granite as the original.

The new cross has never glowed.

Visitors to the replacement cross can still read the curiously prescient epitaph on the original 1907 headstone. The verse is from a hymn by Bishop Heber, published in 1811:

Sacred to the memory of my
Dear Husband, WILLIAM THOMAS
THURLING STEENSON, who died
At Lismore 30th September 1907; from
injuries accidentally received in execution
of his duty at Mullumbimby; aged 29 years.

Though sorrow and darkness encompass the tomb,
Thy Saviour has pass'd through its darkness before thee...
And the Lamp of his Love
Is thy guide through the gloom.

Shadow of Cross Appeared in a Painting

BETWEEN MARCH and July 1896 the Canadian artist Henri Ault painted a large picture of Jesus standing on a rock lapped by water.

On an April night he returned to his studio to retrieve a book. In the darkness, he subsequently wrote, he was confronted by a sight that prompted him to run down the road to alert two friends.

The trio returned to the unlit room. The painting appeared to be "glowing with light" from an unidentifiable source. Against the bright background the figure of Christ was a dark shadow. Above his head was a white sharply defined halo; behind his shoulder the shadow of a cross. Ault insisted, throughout his life, that he had introduced none of these elements (invisible in artificial or natural light) into his artwork.

Through the early twentieth century Ault's painting was displayed under similar conditions to audiences and congregations.

The painting was bought by a series of private collectors. The last of these was Mrs Herbert Griffin of Wichita Falls, Texas. Regarding the picture as a religious work that belonged in a church, she presented it in 1952 to the Mission of St Francis of Assisi in Ranchos de Taos in the mountains of New Mexico.

The painting was hung in an alcove by the altar. The church instituted a series of displays, before each of which the priest told the congregation of locals and visitors that the changes which occurred in the picture had "never been explained."

He would then call for the lights to be switched off. In the darkness of the church the glow, the halo and the shadow of the cross would puzzlingly appear.

The mission (characteristically conservative about "miracles") regularly welcomed scientists interested in testing the painting for phosphorus, radioactivity or anything else that might be capable of creating such a grand and complex illusion. At the time of writing no mundane solution has been found.

Henri Ault was similarly baffled. In the years before his death he painted several duplicates of the picture in the expectation that it might evince the same characteristics as the original. But in darkness his copies, like all his other paintings, remained simply invisible.

The Mysterious Death that Almost Destroyed Hitler

The brutal career of mass murderer Adolf Hitler was nearly cut short in 1931, when the corpse of his niece and unwilling lover Angelika (Geli) Raubal was found in the Munich apartment they shared. If Hitler had gone to trial for the young woman's murder the truth about his sexual perversions and cruelties would inevitably have come to light – demolishing at a stroke his burgeoning Nazi party. Did Hitler really murder his niece? Could a deputy, the chicken farmer Heinrich Himmler, have been the culprit? Or did Geli commit suicide, seeing a bullet as the only escape from her uncle's enforced attentions? The mystery of Geli Raubal's death has divided historians for more than 70 years...

Munich, 1931.

A DOLF HITLER, at the age of 42, was enjoying greater worldly success that he had ever known. His National Socialists were now the second largest political party in Germany. His hymn of hatred, *Mein Kampf*, was moving so briskly out of the bookstores that his bank accounts were unaccustomedly awash with money.

The year was 1931. Hitler's Nazis had recently established an imposing headquarters in Munich – and the would-be Fuehrer, naturally anxious to be close to the action, acquired a luxurious nine-room apartment nearby.

When he moved to the city from his modest country house at Berchtesgarden Hitler took with him a young woman with whom he had become obsessed. Her name was Angelika (Geli) Raubal, daughter of his stepsister Angela, who had served as his cook and housekeeper for the previous three years. At 23 Hitler's niece was a pretty, lively brunette of great wit and charm. Although he was close to twice her age, the creator of Nazism behaved like a beau, buying her clothes and jewelry and showing her off at party rallies and in restaurants and theaters.

It was a dark, sinister relationship.

Many years later, when the National Socialist dream had died in the smoke and rubble of Berlin, Geli's confidantes dared at last to tell the truth about her life with Uncle Adolf. Yes, they had been sexual partners. But not in the manner that any "normal" European of that era would have understood. Night after night, Hitler had demanded that Angelika perform vile acts upon him – demeaning him in ways that psychiatric analysts would subsequently ascribe not only to an ugly and violent childhood but to an inherited psychosis. In the Nazi leader's family, incestuous marriages were regarded as acceptable. Little was known about the genetic penalties such bondings could exact.

Repelled by Hitler's physical demands, Geli often told friends that she longed to break away. But she was her uncle's prisoner. He forbade her to seek the company of men her own age. On the rare occasions she went out to shop or buy clothes he insisted she be accompanied by two chaperones: burly jackbooted Brownshirts prepared to assault any male who dared approach her.

Used and humiliated though she was, Geli retained some sense of identity. In Berchtesgarden she had fallen in love with an art teacher. After several months of incarceration in the Munich apartment she managed to escape and flee to him. When her uncle's men recaptured her she was pregnant.

Anti-Nazi newspapers of the time published accounts of "screaming rows" resonating through Hitler's lavish premises after Geli was brought home. Neighbors had no idea what the fights were about, but they told journalists that Hitler was incandescent with rage, shouting on several occasions that his niece had dealt him a mortal insult.

In early September 1931 Hitler traveled to Nuremberg to speak at a Nazi rally. The previous evening (according to eavesdropping staff) Geli had begged him for permission to visit relatives in Vienna. When another fight ensued she ran from his bedroom, weeping.

The following afternoon a cleaner found Angelika Raubal lying dead, her uncle's pistol beside her.

Hitler's deputy, Rudolph Hess, telephoned him at a Hamburg hotel to convey the news – if indeed it was news. Hitler hastened back to Munich, where police immediately subjected him to intense questioning. He and Angelika had fought frequently – the neighbors, the newspapers, and even one or two staff members had confirmed that. Had Herr Hitler flown into one of his already notorious rages and shot his niece through the heart? Hitler, seemingly grieved, denied it.

Editors who regarded the Nazis as dangerous reveled in the story. Some newspapers, in their coverage, even hinted in a veiled way at Hitler's obscene sexual practices. (After the Fuehrer's death it emerged that Geli had not been alone in her debasement. The film actress Renate Muller revealed that she too had endured "sickening" sexual encounters with Hitler.)

The boldest front page story appeared in the *Munich Post*. It stated, correctly, that Geli had been pregnant and that the baby was not Hitler's. Most embarrassingly of all, from the Nazi leader's viewpoint, the paper reported that Geli's nose was broken – suggesting that he had beaten her before pulling the trigger.

The article sent shockwaves through the Nazi party. Already its Brownshirts were running out of control on city streets. Their bashings and suspected killings were electoral poison enough – but a scandal in which the leader himself was charged with murder would almost certainly wipe out most of the party's 107 Reichstag seats at the next election.

The final straw came when another anti-Nazi editor, Fritz Gehrlich, told associates that he intended to publish an expose of Hitler, his sexual habits and his role in Geli's death. The story never appeared. Two days before its planned publication stormtroopers broke into the newspaper's editorial offices, viciously beat journalists and hauled Gehrlich away. In 1934, with the Nazis securely in power, he died in an SS cell.

Adolf Hitler, in the words of one reporter, was "shaken and palpably frightened" by the detectives' questioning. He insisted that Geli had been in good health and spirits when he left the apartment – and that the first he had heard of her death was when Hess rang him.

Some of the homicide investigators believed Hitler was telling the truth and that Geli had taken her own life. If her uncle had done the deed, they argued, he would hardly have left his own gun beside the body. Others felt that the angle of the bullet suggested someone other than Geli had pulled the trigger. The investigation leaked copiously – and the less politically inhibited newspapers were full of policemen's theories. One paper even suggested that the bespectacled chicken farmer Heinrich Himmler had murdered the young woman on Hitler's direct orders.

In those dying days of a free press in Germany it was all good for circulation – and potentially disastrous for the Nazi party.

But then, suddenly, the furor died away. Police announced that on the balance of probabilities, Angelika Raubal had committed suicide. They declined to offer an opinion on whether Hitler had driven her to it. One by one all but the most courageous of German journalists ceased to speculate about Geli's death. Why risk a home or office visit from the stormtroopers?

Adolf Hitler was never charged or required to explain himself in court. In the end he had too many friends (and frightened enemies) in high places to submit himself to that indignity. After the war journalists went in search of the policemen who had conducted the murder/suicide inquiry. None could be found.

Following Germany's defeat the accused war criminal Hermann Goering spoke frankly to British and American lawyers about Geli Raubal's fate. It was certainly true, he said, that the Fuehrer would have found it unacceptable for his lover to bear another man's child. But whether Geli had suicided or been shot by Hitler or someone else, Goering had no idea.

However, he added, Angelika Raubal had been the only woman Adolf Hitler ever really loved. Wherever he lived he kept photographs of her on his walls, ordering that they be garlanded with flowers on the anniversaries of her birth and death. The advent of Eva Braun made no difference to this tradition.

Goering further recalled that it was on the day Geli died that Hitler became a vegetarian, saying that he could no longer bring himself to "eat corpses." An ironic resolution for the monster who would be responsible for more than six million deaths in World War II.

Large numbers of Freudian and Jungian biographers have tried posthumously to psychoanalyze Hitler. A belief held by many is that he was permanently transformed by the death of Angelika Raubal, whether he brought it about or not. In his 1957 book, *Hitler*, the dictator's former foreign press secretary, Ernst Hanfstaengl, supports this view. He opines that Geli's death changed something in the tyrant's mind, clearing the way for him to "develop into a demon."

At Hitler's behest thousands of anti-Nazis had been secretly slaughtered long before September 1931. For someone who was already a master of murder Geli's death would have been easy to arrange. And as psychiatric analysts have observed there would have been no inconsistency in Hitler feeling sad after he had her shot. If he was indeed the killer it was possible, from his poisoned perspective, that he saw himself as having "cleansed" her of a rival's child – rendering her "pure" again and worthy of mourning.

Puzzle of Hitler's Underground Labyrinth

ARCHEOLOGISTS are unable to access the secrets of a vast subterranean city, built in Nazi-occupied Poland during World War II.

Constructed, possibly on multiple levels, by slave laborers, the immense complex dwarfs the infrastructure beneath Egypt's Great Pyramids.

It comprises more than 125 square miles of roads, bridges, tunnels, chambers, and laboratories whose purpose investigators can only guess at.

Thousands of starved and brutalized prisoners died during construction of the complex beneath the deeply forested Sowie mountain range in Lower Silesia. Captured Nazi records show that the workers poured more than 275,000 tonnes of steel-reinforced concrete into the labyrinth, erecting massive walls thought to have been designed to protect weapons and scientific projects.

But the prisoners' sufferings achieved nothing. In 1945, as the Red Army fought its way into Silesia, SS bomb squads blew up the secret site. Today less than 60,000 square miles of the underground city's highways and secured areas are accessible. The rest are hidden behind impenetrable boulders and rubble.

Occasionally excavators discover tantalizing relics at the site. One, Jerzy Cera found a mass of stoneware pipes, perhaps intended to convey liquid. "But where to?' he wrote. "We measured the pipes' depth, then inserted two lit flares into each opening. The smoke disappeared. It had obviously been sucked deep into the labyrinth, because we could hear the distant sound of an airlock working. We put in 28 more flares – and the air in the pipes was again quickly cleared. The complex must have an immense capacity to be able to suck away so much smoke.'

More than six decades have elapsed since the end of Hitler's war. But the secrets of his subterranean metropolis remain unknown – and unreachable.

Enigma of the
Empty Lighthouse

Historians have described it as the profoundest unsolved puzzle in British history. On the morning of December 26 1900 a supply ship, Hesperus, *visited Scotland's brooding Eilean Mor (Isle of the Dead) to check on the welfare of the three lighthouse keepers. Inexplicably the 150,000- candlepower light had not shone for 11 nights – and the crewmen sent ashore were fearful of what they might find. Their concerns were well-founded. When they shouted they were answered only by echoes. The high stone tower lay deserted. A search revealed that the keepers had vanished without trace – and seemingly without cause. Behind them they had left neatly folded clothes, a stopped clock and a slate bearing the chalked words "GOD IS OVER ALL..."*

THE FLANNAN ISLES, also known as the Seven Hunters, are Scotland's bleakest outposts. Comprising little more than jagged rocks, bearded with grasses whipped by North Atlantic winds, the islands have at times lain uninhabited for decades on end. During the seventeenth and eighteenth centuries shepherds from the Hebrides would sail out to the Flannans to collect seabird eggs and to graze their sheep on the steep mountain pastures.

But – believing that the islands were haunted by the spirits of dead sailors – the men stepped ashore with extreme caution.

According to antiquarians visitors so feared these resident phantoms that they would perform complex self-protective rituals from the moment they landed. Among the oddest of these behavior patterns was that newcomers felt obliged to speak in a dialect other than their own and were expected to give everyday items new names – as if memories of a long-vanished language were being perpetuated. There were many other rules. No bird must be killed with a stone. No sheep suet must be removed from the islands. No person should sleep on a Flannan island alone, lest the resident "faerie people" abduct them under cover of darkness.

The engineers in charge of the Northern Lighthouse Board gave little attention to such superstitions. Their task was to keep Scotland's coasts and outpost islands safe. As trade blossomed during the 1890s the number of cargo ships wrecked at night on the deadly rocks of the Flannans was becoming increasingly unacceptable to British and European governments. The board responded by announcing that it would erect a lighthouse whose 150,000-candlepower lantern would be visible for 40 miles in every direction.

Construction of the tower took four years. Engineers and workmen, operating from pitching supply boats, were obliged to haul steel girders and heavy masonry up sheer cliffs more than 200 feet high. In December 1899 the work was finally complete. The board appointed five keepers to work in groups of three around the clock. For 12 months the immense beacon, shining high above the ocean, made journeys safer for ships traveling to Scottish ports. But then the light went out.

Among the first to notice was an assistant keeper Joseph Moore, who was on leave at Loch Roag in the Outer Hebrides. On December 15 1900 he glanced from his cottage window, expecting to see the customary cheering glow of the Flannans Light, only to be confronted instead by the chilling primal darkness of the ocean.

As Moore would subsequently complain to an official inquiry, it took him many days to persuade his immediate superiors to investigate. Particularly obdurate was Captain Harvey, skipper of the lighthouse's supply steamer *Hesperus*, who repeatedly insisted that he must wait for calmer weather. Finally, on December 26 he seemed satisfied. The *Hesperus*, with an impatient Joseph Moore aboard, set out for Eilean Mor.

From a distance the island and its disabled light were almost invisible in low-lying fog. Sensing that "something was terribly wrong" Captain Harvey ordered sailors to take a boat to the island.

The men scrambled onto the jetty. Nothing was as it should have been. There were no welcoming flags, no empty provisions crates stacked for loading – not even a mooring rope. With Joseph Moore in the lead the sailors mounted the carved steps that led to the light station. The entry gate and the front door were closed but not locked. Moore and his companions ran up the path, burst into the tower and began to shout. Their voices echoed emptily around them.

Everyone feared now that the duty lighthouse keepers – Thomas Marshall, Donald McArthur and James Ducat – might be lying dead somewhere. While his companions searched the upper levels Moore looked for clues on the ground floor. In the hearth lay the cold ashes of a fire. The clock was stopped. The lamps were trimmed and ready for use. Plates had been washed and stacked away in the larder, where an abundance of flour, fruit and salted meat was stored. The three narrow beds in the sleeping quarters were neatly made. Folded clothes were stacked on cupboard shelves.

Curiously Moore could find only one set of oilskins and seaboots in the storage area. It was later established that these were McArthur's. The boots and skins belonging to Ducat and Marshall were gone.

The log revealed that rough seas had lashed the tower on December 12 and 13. There was no entry for the 14th – but chalked on a slate were the words: *"December 15th. Storm ended, sea calm. God is over all."*

Captain Harvey came ashore and led a search of the island itself. There was no sign either of the missing men or of any clue suggesting why they had disappeared.

But one of the sailors, climbing a high cliff, did make a startling discovery. In a rock crevice 112 feet above sea level crane operators had securely wedged a large wooden tool crate containing pieces of lashing gear and spare parts for the machinery. The crate was gone. Neither the members of the search party nor the subsequent inquiry could imagine any reason why the lighthousemen would have moved this unwieldy box – and if they did, what possible use they might have had for it.

A later theory suggested that the box was swept away by waves gigantic enough to lash at its 112-foot-high crevice. But although captains reported high seas for the 12th and 13th, none had experienced waves of such gigantic size as this – a magnitude which would surely have capsized ships.

The *Hesperus* returned to the mainland with news of the triple disappearance. Poignantly its cargo of food for the lighthouse keepers, along with Christmas presents from their families, had gone undelivered.

On December 30 an investigation team headed by a superintendent from the Northern Lighthouse Board searched the island and its tower again. The investigators concluded that rough seas must in some way have been responsible for the keepers' disappearance. They surmised that Marshall and Ducat, while working outside, might have been swept away by a wave. When McArthur rushed out to save them he too was drowned.

This theory did not survive the cool light of subsequent inquiry. Eilean Mor's light had continued to shine normally during the days of violent weather. It had gone out on the 15th when conditions were calm. Inspection of the beacon showed it was in perfect condition and ready to be ignited again. But no one had been present to do the job. Why?

Another popular theory was that one of the lighthouse keepers had gone mad, killed his companions and then, in a fit of remorse, drowned himself. But the Lighthouse Board had chosen Ducat, Marshall and McArthur because they were reliable and quietly responsible. Their families and friends, along with the board's managers, had difficulty believing that any one of the men could have been a killer. And there were, besides, the practical considerations. Nowhere, within the tower or around the island, could the investigators find any trace of a struggle. The lighthouse was full of implements – axes, hammers, knives and picks – which could have been used as weapons. But none had been disturbed.

One Scottish newspaper, desperate for an explanation, even darkly suggested that the three men might have been spirited away by the "little people" who secretly inhabited Eilean Mor. But no one could propose an answer that withstood scrutiny for long.

For more than a century the disappearance of the three lighthouse keepers has remained as mysterious as the ocean winds that moan across the bleak Flannan Isles.

Also Among the Missing ...

- On the night of August 3 1969 the light on the Great Isaac Lighthouse near Bimini in the Bahamas went out. Officials were unable to contact the two keepers. Searchers next day found the lighthouse building undisturbed but abandoned. The keepers' clothes and other personal belongings remained intact, but the men themselves had vanished. An inquiry was unable to reach a definitive conclusion about what might have befallen the lighthousemen.

  They were not seen again.

- In September 1924 two Royal Air Force pilots crash-landed their plane in a stretch of Iraqi desert. An RAF rescue party quickly found the aircraft. It was minimally damaged. There was no blood in the interior, or other evidence that the fliers had been injured. The rescuers followed a chain of footprints, still visible in the sand.

  They found no other prints, human or animal.

  After several hundred feet the trail abruptly petered out. Despite a prolonged air and ground search the pilots were not found.

- Malcolm Macmillan, a young London publisher and the forebear of a British Prime Minister, Harold Macmillan, created a sensation in the England of 1889, when he disappeared from the summit of Mount Hymmetus in Greece.

  Contemporary newspapers quoted friends who said they had clearly seen Macmillan waving to them from the summit. Moments later he was gone. This, they universally agreed, hardly seemed possible – as it was difficult to imagine any place to which he could have disappeared. Large parties of volunteers and government officials searched for days but found nothing. The Macmillan family offered a large reward to anyone with information that would reveal the fate of their son. The money remained unclaimed.

Were There *Three* Tunguskas?

On June 30 1908 a massive aerial explosion flattened vast stretches of forest across 2,400 square miles of the Siberian wilderness. The blast, whose cause has never been determined, sparked a thermal shockwave which set hundreds of thousands of trees alight, incinerated animals, smashed windows and flung reindeer herders to the ground. Astronomers theorized that a meteor had struck the area, but scientists could find no trace of a crater. One investigator asserted years later that he had discovered traces of radioactivity. For much of the twentieth century many analysts regarded the mysterious Tunguska phenomenon as having been one of a kind. But then, scientific journals began to publish eerily similar accounts of "Tunguska-like" explosions above the remote jungles of Brazil and British Guiana…

Tunguska River, Siberia.
June 30 1908. Early Morning.

S EVERAL OF THE OLDER reindeer herders were still asleep when the first titanic cracks of thunder rent the sky. Startled, the grizzled men rolled from their hide tents and joined their fellow Tungus tribesmen on the forest's edge – staring up, awed, at the immense object hurtling above them.

The thing, whatever it might be, was casting wildly changing shadows on the ground and emitting a whistling sound, so high-pitched it tortured the ears.

It wasn't a comet. There was no tail. Instead, in its wake, it was trailing band after band of rich rainbow colors. Colors like nothing they had seen before. The intruder hurtled toward the horizon and vanished. But the thunderclaps were still as loud as ever and the bands of hectic color remained, stretching across the heavens like a tropical snake's tail.

Then came the real shock. There was a violent detonation that shook the ground. Within a moment a colossal wind, so hot it seared the skin through layers of furs and underclothing, howled through the forest, hurling men into the air and onto the ground, flattening every tree, snatching up tents and throwing them, kite-like, to the sky. Animals, fur charred, panicked and bolted. Boys and men clawed at their faces, on which bubbling blisters would soon appear.

At Churgim Creek, 22 miles closer to the epicenter, Vasily Dzhenkoul's 630 reindeer were incinerated, along with his hunting dogs, stores and furs. All he found on his return was ashes.

The Irkutsk newspaper *Sibir* quoted one herdsman's recollection: "Everything around us was shrouded in smoke and fog from the burning and falling trees. The ground shook and we heard prolonged roaring. Eventually the noise died away and the wind dropped, but the forest went on burning."

Another witness, who lived 62 miles from ground zero, said: "I was sitting on the porch of the house at the trading station, looking north. Suddenly... the sky was split in two. High above the forest the whole northern part of the sky seemed covered with fire. I felt a great heat, as though my shirt was aflame. At that moment there was a bang and a mighty crash. I was thrown 20 feet from the porch and lost consciousness... The crash was followed by a noise like stones falling from the sky, or guns firing. The earth trembled... and a hot wind, as if from a cannon, blew past the huts from the north. It damaged the onion plants. Later we found that many panes in the windows had been blown out and the iron hasp on the barn door had been broken."

Over Europe and Britain that night there was no darkness. Houses, streets and fields glowed with a soft white light by which it was possible to garden or read a book. The effect lasted for days. A London correspondent for the *New York Times* (July 5 1908) wrote:

"Several nights through the week were marked by strange atmospheric effects which Dr Norman Lockyer of the South Kensington Solar Physics Laboratory believes to be a display of the Aurora Borealis, though personally I have not observed any colored streamers."

(Dr Lockyer was less a fool than he may seem. Neither he, nor anyone else outside Russia, had the slightest idea that there had been a freak explosion in Siberia. Russia would not, for many years, announce officially that the blast had occurred.)

The correspondent continued:

"Following sunsets of exceptional beauty and twilight effects remarkable even in England, the northern sky at midnight became light blue... The clouds were touched with pink, in so marked a fashion that police headquarters was rung up by several people, who believed a big fire was raging in the north of London."

Remarkably, strange phenomena had begun appearing in Europe's skies eight days before the June 30 explosion. Newspapers, from June 22 onward, reported "glowing and multicolored twilights" (similar to those following the Krakatoa eruption), solar haloes, bright nights and silvery clouds. In fanciful hindsight it might seem that the Tunguska object was somehow prefiguring its arrival.

* * *

Russia in 1908 was in such civil and political turmoil that no academic institution had the money, time or motivation to investigate the Tunguska disaster site. It was not until 1921, when the tyranny had settled in, that the Soviet Academy of Sciences was able to send a mineralogist, Leonid Kulik, to conduct a survey. Kulik and his student helpers spent months taking witness statements and scouring the scarred forest surrounding the Tunguska River basin. Like the scientists who would follow them they found plenty of flattened trees, but no evidence either of a crater or of meteorite fragments. Gradually Kulik formed the hypothesis that he was not dealing with a ground impact at all – but with an *airburst*.

Something had exploded above Tunguska, with such force that, seemingly, it had obliterated all evidence of itself.

The sheer mystery of the explosion dominated Kulik's mind for the rest of his academic life. In 1938 he arranged an aerial photographic survey of the blast area. The pictures revealed that the event had felled trees in an immense butterfly-shaped pattern. Kulik would not live to continue his research. In 1943, as a Red Army officer, he died fighting the Nazis.

In the decades following World War II numerous Russian and foreign expeditions visited Tunguska. They came home with more theories than evidence.

- Many scientists insisted that the explosion "must have" been caused by a **meteorite** – an explanation that can be questioned because of the absence of fragments or a crater. It was difficult also to explain how a meteorite could have exploded with the force of 40 megatons of TNT – 2,000 times the power of the atomic bomb that fell on Hiroshima in 1945.

- Other analysts blamed the blast on a **comet nucleus**, composed principally of ice and dust, which had evaporated on impact. In 1983 NASA astronomer Zdenek Sekanin attacked this theory, demonstrating that the "cometary body" could not have remained intact at the five mile altitude at which it had been estimated to be traveling through Siberia's skies.

- Some suggested that the object might have been a **black hole**, which penetrated to the Earth's core – an idea that attracted a particularly small following.

- The ante was raised by a Soviet physicist, Alexei Zolotov, who controversially asserted that he had discovered radiation at the impact site: unmistakable evidence, he said, of a **nuclear explosion**. This theory seemed to be supported to some extent by the fact that scientists had noted an increase in the rate of biological mutations among people, animals and insects – not only at the epicenter but along the object's entire trajectory over Tunguska.

- Predictably, Zolotov's announcement led to suggestions that a **nuclear-powered spaceship** had exploded over Siberia. Science fiction writers – and many of their readers – were unimpressed by this notion, arguing that superior beings traveling across galaxies would surely have developed more sophisticated ways of converting matter to energy.

- But perhaps the most bizarre theory of all laid blame for the blast at the distinguished feet of **Nikola Tesla**, inventor of the alternating current induction motor. In an article for *Wireless Telegraphy and Telephone*, published four months before Tunguska, Tesla had claimed that his magnifying transformer would be able "to direct electrical wave energy to any point on the globe." Whether Tesla actually conducted an experiment that targeted Tunguska – and whether (to use his words) he "projected wave energy" toward Siberia – will probably never be known.

The cause of the Tunguska explosion is as great a mystery today as when the Siberian reindeer herders first stared up at the dazzling anomaly that had invaded their skies.

But the puzzle deepened more than two decades later when news of another blast, uncannily similar to Tunguska's, began appearing in newspapers. This fresh explosion had flattened and scorched hundreds of square miles of Brazilian jungle. According to *New Scientist* (November 11 1995) it occurred near an upper Amazon tributary not far from the Peruvian border.

Despite graphic newspaper reports describing the devastation, Brazil's dense jungles appear at the time to have been too remote for American or British scientists to visit. The only first-hand study of the explosion's after-effects was conducted by a Brazilian Catholic missionary, Father Fidel d'Alvanio, who wrote an article for the papal newspaper *L'Osservatore Romano*. His long official report on the incident lay forgotten in the Vatican Library until Tunguska pioneer Leonid Kulik learned of its existence and published, in a scientific journal, an essay about Tunguska's "Brazilian twin." Kulik commented on the "pronounced similarities" between the two explosions.

Like his Russian predecessor, Father d'Alvanio had conducted scores of interviews with eyewitnesses, one of whom spoke of the blast's "immense and frightening power." The event, d'Alvanio wrote, occurred at 8 a.m. on August 13 1930. The sun suddenly became hectically red and the sky darkened. Next, there was "an ear-piercing whistle" (as at Tunguska). The display ended amid thunderclaps when three fireballs streaked across the sky and exploded, setting vast tracts of forest alight. Three months later, the priest observed, many of the flattened trees were still smoldering.

When tardy scientific observers finally checked the scene for themselves, they reached a general consensus that the explosion's force had been about one megaton: only one-fortieth the size of the Tunguska airburst.

However, on December 11 1935, an explosion reputedly "bigger than Tunguska" occurred over the Rupununi region of British Guiana. Serge Korff of the Franklin Institute visited Guiana shortly after the detonation. He traveled through an immense smoldering wilderness of tropical jungle, which he described as being "far greater than the area of damage in Siberia."

In 1937 the American Museum of Natural History sent an expedition to the devastated area. The party's members reported seeing from a mountaintop a vast region in which trees had been snapped off like matchsticks, almost 26 feet above their bases.

Perhaps the most chilling fact concerning the Tunguska object is that it was traveling *on the same latitude as Moscow*. Had it plunged to Earth three hours before it did, that city might have been devastated, with millions dead.

So far, the Tunguska-style spaceships, meteorites, black holes (or whatever other theory you prefer) have obligingly fallen on snowy wastes and jungles. We can only tremble at the thought of what might happen if one of these objects, one dark day, plunges into the ocean, creating unprecedented tidal waves. Or if a Tunguska-like anomaly annihilates a city – and is mistaken by that nation's defenders for the first missile in a nuclear attack.

Catastrophe Catalog: 1931

WHEN NEWS OF BRAZIL'S jungle explosion belatedly reached the outside world, London's *Daily Herald* (March 6 1931) led its front page with this alarming – and possibly prescient – article:

MENACE OF METEORS LIKE BOMBS FROM SPACE

Another colossal bombardment of the Earth from outer space has just been revealed. Three great meteors, falling in Brazil, fired and depopulated hundreds of miles of jungle.

News of this catastrophe has only now reached civilisation because the meteors fell in the remote South American wilderness. It was yet another lucky escape of mankind from an appalling and unrecognized peril.

The last great meteor fall in Siberia in 1908 fell in a district so remote that only last year were details of its destruction given to the world. Had either of these two meteor falls chanced to strike a city in a densely populated country, frightful loss of life and damage would have been caused.

"A meteor," Mr C.J.P. Cave, an ex-president of the Royal Meteorological Society stated recently, "carries in front of it a mass of compressed and incandescent air. When it strikes the Earth, this air 'splashes' in a hurricane of fire."

The Brazilian meteors are reported (says the Central News) by Father Fidelio of Aviano, writing from San Paolo de Alivencia in the State of Amazonas, to the papal newspaper, Osservatore Romano.

BLAZING FOREST

The meteors fell almost simultaneously during an amazing storm. Terrific heat was engendered. Immediately they struck the ground, the whole forest was ablaze. The fire continued uninterrupted for some months, depopulating a large area.

The fall of the meteors was preceded by remarkable atmospheric disturbances. At 8 o'clock in the morning the sun became blood-red and a penumbra spread all over the sky, producing the effect of a solar eclipse.

Then an immense cloud of reddish powder filled the air and it looked "as if the whole world was going to blaze up."

The powder was succeeded by fine cinders which covered trees and vegetation with a blanket of white.

There followed a whistling sound that pierced the air with ear-

breaking intensity, then another and another. Three great explosions were heard and the earth trembled.

President Bush – and the Doomsday Asteroid

THE HUMAN RACE narrowly escaped disaster early in 2004, when a chunk of rock about 1640 feet across hurtled toward Earth at colossal speed. NASA's Jet Propulsion Laboratory estimated that there was a one-in-four possibility of a collision.

First astronomer to notice the rogue rock was Timothy Spahr of the Harvard-Smithsonian Center for Astrophysics in Cambridge, Massachusetts. While processing data from an automated telescope in New Mexico he saw a pinpoint of light which seemed to fit an asteroid's profile. He named the object AS-1 and posted its description on the Internet. In the hours that followed more than a dozen astronomers around the globe contacted Spahr to say they too had observed the intruder.

NASA scientists predicted that the asteroid's brightness would increase by several thousand per cent over the next day: an indication that it was traveling at a speed seldom observed before. The scientists generally agreed that if the asteroid struck, it would come down somewhere over the Northern Hemisphere. Even if it disintegrated before hitting the planet's surface the detonation would equal the force of a one-megaton hydrogen bomb. Such an explosion above an ocean might create tidal waves; a blast above a city would kill thousands.

The general public knew nothing about the possible disaster – mainly because there were no protocols for dealing with so catastrophic an event. At the time President George W. Bush was preparing to announce America's return to the moon, in a speech at NASA headquarters. During what is now known as "the nine-hour crisis" American authorities weighed the odds – wondering whether the president should be asked to change his good-news message to a disaster warning. A preliminary analysis at NASA's Ames Research Center had shown that the asteroid could strike Earth within two days.

Happily the mega-rock narrowly missed Earth. It hurtled past the planet at a distance of only 27,000 miles – the closest approach on record.

Should someone have raised the alarm, to enable people to take whatever precautions they could? Scientists confronted by this question were divided. A strong proponent of disclosure in such emergencies was Chuck Chapman of the South-West Research Institute in Boulder Colorado.

"I do not feel we're entitled to keep such a threat secret," he said. "I think the public should be told when such a big event, with such a high level of probability, is involved."

The Chilling Case of the "Shark Arm" Slayings

For several fevered months it was the most argued-about mystery in the world. Before a horrified crowd of vacationers a gigantic tiger shark, swimming in a Sydney aquarium, suddenly disgorged a tattooed human arm. When photographs of the grisly relic appeared in newspapers a woman approached police to say she recognized the limb. It had belonged to her husband who disappeared several weeks earlier. Fingerprints and skin samples confirmed the wife's story. The ensuing arrests and court hearings opened an ugly Pandora's box that revealed a secret world of drug-trafficking, blackmail, revenge and murder. However, despite detectives' utmost efforts no convictions were ever recorded. Officially this strangest of dual-murder cases remains open. But no policeman today expects ever to discover the killers' names – or how a bookmaker's left arm found its way into the stomach of a shark…

Sydney, April 25 1935. 4.30 p.m.

IT WAS THE BIGGEST story of journalist Leo Young's career. The off-duty *Sydney Morning Herald* reporter was leaning across the rail at the Coogee Aquarium when a collective gasp rose from the vacation crowd.

The principal attraction, a recently caught 14-foot tiger shark began suddenly to convulse and thresh about, whipping the water into foam and splashing nearby spectators. When the turbulence subsided it became clear that the tiger had vomited. Floating on the surface were a partly digested seagull, the remains of a smaller shark – and something else.

Something that defied belief.

It was an arm: a human arm, its gray fingers clawing upward.

Albert and Charles Hobson, the aquarium's owners, hastily shepherded their customers outside. They called police, then, using a long-handled scoop, retrieved the limb.

Considering that it had spent an indeterminate time in a shark's stomach the arm (a left arm) seemed remarkably well-preserved. It had belonged to a man. Engraved into the flesh in faded red and blue inks was a tattooed picture of two boxers sparring. Trailing from the wrist was roughly three feet of rope. The man had been tied up – or had tied himself.

While Leo Young was telephoning the story's opening paragraphs to a copy-taker detectives arrived with a police photographer. Next day the official picture of the "Shark Arm" appeared in newspapers around the globe, together with a police plea for help in identifying its owner.

The investigators did not have to wait long. Just before noon a middle-aged woman in great distress appeared at police headquarters to say she had recognized the arm in that morning's paper, from the tattoo. It was her husband James Smith's tattoo. He had not been home for three weeks.

She was concerned but had not reported it because she was used to him being absent for extended periods. She still had hopes he might still be alive; that a shark had bitten off his arm but that he had managed to escape. Was that possible?

Anything was possible, a sergeant gently replied.

At this point detectives were not particularly inclined to regard the case as suspicious. As a Sydney newspaper reported:

"Police believe that the human arm belonged to a man who committed suicide by plunging into the sea with his arms tied. This theory is supported by the fact that a piece of rope was attached to his wrist."

But the investigators were paid to remain open-minded. They took skin samples and fingerprints and matched them with the prints a policeman had taken two years earlier from the then 43-year-old James Smith during a raid on a club he managed. Police at that time had charged Smith with allowing illegal betting on his premises.

Aided by Mrs Smith and the dead man's former associates the detectives began to piece together his background. Born in Lancashire he had been a moderately well-regarded boxer before he immigrated to Australia. From the time of arrival he had lived on the fringes of the law, but was never regarded as a serious criminal. He had worked for several years as a builder, but had filed for bankruptcy. After that he had worked at various jobs, operating on the side as an SP bookmaker.

Mrs Smith confided that her husband had sometimes been severely depressed. Increasingly, suicide seemed the likeliest explanation.

* * *

But then Dr Victor Coppleson, an eminent forensic pathologist and an expert on shark wounds, submitted his report. The arm, Coppleson said, had definitely not been snapped off by a shark. His investigation showed, beyond doubt, that it had been severed from the torso by "someone using a sharp instrument". The doctor added, "The operation was not well-handled, which might have led me to believe that it was performed by a surgeon of limited skills. However I have ruled out that conclusion because the two large slashes near the laceration indicate that extreme violence was used."

Police realized that they had a major murder case on their hands.

Albert and Charles Hobson had already told detectives how they acquired the tiger shark. On April 18, while checking their nets in the ocean off Coogee, they discovered the immense man-eater hopelessly entangled. They now surmised, in the light of later evidence, that the tiger shark had become trapped while trying to eat a smaller shark already caught in the net. Delighted that they had become the owners of a major money-making exhibit they had towed the big shark back to the aquarium and released it into the special enclosure.

This chronology posed a problem for police. If the tiger shark had been swimming in the enclosure since April 18, surely its gastric juices would have dissolved the arm long before April 25, the day it was disgorged. Zoologists estimated that James Smith's flesh and bone would have been totally absorbed into the shark's digestive system within 30 hours.

Might the murderer of James Smith have entered the aquarium itself, at a quiet time and fed the arm to the shark as it circled the enclosure? If so, the latest this could have happened was sometime on April 24.

But why would the killer have been walking around with an arm under his arm? And what had he done with the rest of Smith's body? Homicide investigators developed several conflicting theories:

- Someone had paid a hireling to murder Smith – insisting that the tattooed arm be shown to him as proof that the job had been done. Under this scenario the hitman might have disposed of the corpse first and the arm later.

- While dismembering and disposing of the body the murderer might have overlooked the arm. On finding it he took it to the aquarium.

- When the killer threw the sawn-up corpse into the sea the small shark (whose remains would subsequently be vomited up in the aquarium) might have swallowed the arm. Shortly afterward the large shark swallowed the small one, whose dead body preserved the human limb against the big predator's gastric juices.

Fundamental questions remained, however. Who had killed James Smith – and for what reason?

The detectives learned that Smith had occasionally worked for Reginald Holmes, a rich Sydney boat manufacturer. Holmes told the policemen that Smith had knocked at his door several days before he disappeared, asking for a £50 loan. Distraught, he had explained, "I've got to have the money tonight or they'll kill me."

Soon after this conversation a homicide sergeant interviewed a barman at the Cecil Hotel, Cronulla. The man said he had noticed someone fitting Smith's description drinking with a local, Patrick Brady. He later heard that for some reason the two men were renting a house together: a beach cottage on the sand.

Police knew Brady. He was a former shearer who had turned to petty crime. They rushed to the house he had rented. The managing agent said Mr Brady was no longer in residence – a pity as he had been an outstanding tenant, leaving the property spotless. The agent did have a few complaints, however. Brady, quite puzzlingly, had removed a large tin storage chest and substituted a smaller one. Also missing were a pair of weights from the sash windows and an anchor from the shed.

These clues were more than enough for the homicide investigators. They summoned reinforcements to conduct a massive local search for Smith's body.

The remains, they postulated, had either been crammed into the tin chest and buried in the area, or dumped into the sea attached to an anchor. The searchers' efforts yielded nothing. As the Sydney newspaper *Truth* reported, "The police dug up certain premises, dragged the bottom of the bay, scoured the sandhills, but to no avail. The mystery is still as deep and apparently unsolvable as ever."

Detectives remained sure, nonetheless, that Brady was their man. Their questioning of people who knew or had employed him led them back to the quietly elegant premises of the boat manufacturer Reginald Holmes. Detective Sergeant Frank Matthews, who was leading the case, would recall in later years that the businessman seemed nervous and uneasy from the moment they arrived again at his front door.

Matthews had done some homework. He closely questioned Holmes about a recent argument he had had with an insurance company. The firm had refused to pay compensation for a power yacht, *Pathfinder*, which had caught fire and sunk.

Wasn't it true that Holmes had employed James Smith as caretaker of that yacht? And hadn't he been aboard just before it went down? Holmes admitted that this was so.

And wasn't it also true, Matthews inquired, that Holmes owned a second yacht, identical in every way to *Pathfinder*? Again, Holmes nodded agreement. He seemed pale and shaken when his polite interrogators left the house.

Police evidence against Patrick Brady was flimsy. But they were confident by this stage that he was only a small player in a larger criminal picture. They charged him with the murder of James Smith.

Brady's wife immediately intervened, making a statement to the effect that

Brady was covering up for Reginald Holmes. Brady made a similar deposition. He claimed that he had last seen James Smith on April 9 when, accompanied by Holmes and another man, Smith had left the rented beach house.

Armed with Brady's revised story, the detectives made plans to question Reginald Holmes a third time. They could not have foreseen what happened next.

That evening Sydney Water Police were alerted that a speedboat was careering recklessly around Sydney Harbour, clipping buoys and other vessels and threatening a catastrophic accident.

The chase lasted two hours. At its climax the man in the boat tried to ram the police launch before he was outmaneuvered and overpowered. The crazed speedster was Reginald Holmes, dazed, his face glistening with blood. He babbled that a man had broken into his house and shot him in the head. He had managed to escape in the speed launch – and had assumed that the pursuing police were assassins, intent on finishing him off.

An ambulance took Holmes to a Sydney hospital, where doctors removed a bullet from his forehead. It had narrowly missed his brain. Holmes remained in the hospital under police guard for four days. After his discharge he told the homicide investigators that he wanted to cooperate to the greatest degree possible. He would give evidence to the forthcoming inquest on James Smith and reveal everything he knew.

"In court and only in court," he reputedly said, "I'll lift the lid off the biggest racket this country has ever known." Holmes sincerely believed that by naming prominent Sydney figures while he was under the court's protection he would buy safety for himself. He was wrong.

At 7.45 on the evening before the inquest Holmes received a phone call at home. He told his wife, "I'm going into town for a while. I have to see a fellow. It's important." He promised to be back before 10 p.m..

At midnight Mrs Holmes rang the homicide detectives – and a search began for the inquest's principal witness. Astonishingly the police had done nothing whatsoever to ensure the safety of Reginald Holmes.

At 1 a.m. Constables Bilton and Casey of the night patrol drove onto a dark wharfside road in the shadow of the Sydney Harbour Bridge. They pulled up beside a limousine, headlights burning and driver's door hanging open. Holmes was slumped dead over the steering wheel, in a pool of blood, three .32 bullets in his left side, just below the heart.

Nine hours later detectives told the coroner that they could not proceed with the Shark Arm murder inquiry. Their star witness had himself been murdered.

Mrs Holmes gave evidence in her husband's place. Weeping, she told the court he had revealed to her that Patrick Brady killed James Smith, cramming everything except the tattooed arm into a weighted trunk, which he pushed into the sea.

At the subsequent murder trial the judge disallowed this evidence on the basis that it was hearsay. He further ruled that a murder charge required a body. An arm was not enough. Patrick Brady walked free.

The homicide investigators later charged two men with the shooting murder of Reginald Holmes. They too were acquitted, on the grounds of insufficient evidence.

* * *

Many analysts have theorized about what Reginald Holmes knew and why he and James Smith were silenced. The general consensus is that the men had played subsidiary roles in a rich drug-smuggling operation based in Sydney. Smith, the theory goes, had been a small-scale smuggler himself when major Sydney figures moved in and forcibly took over his business. Incensed by the miserable wages his superiors were paying him, Smith tried to increase his take by blackmailing them. Death was the only possible outcome.

Holmes, the theorists surmised, had almost certainly made his power yacht available to transport drugs from visiting ships to a Sydney warehouse. Whenever one of his yachts set to sea to meet a passing freighter its identical twin would sail into Sydney Harbour, purportedly returning from a fishing expedition. It was the ideal alibi, until one of the craft caught fire and sank.

But none of this is more than supposition. To this day no one really knows who killed James Smith and his employer.

Or why Smith's arm was so gruesomely severed.

Or if indeed it did lie for seven days, perfectly preserved in the stomach of a shark inside a shark.

After seven decades one of the world's strangest murder mysteries remains unsolved.

Portrait of a Monster

FIVE DAYS AFTER it vomited up James Smith's arm, the tiger shark at the center of the Coogee Aquarium furor died of unknown causes.

The deadly predator belonged to a species common in seas lapping Australia's tropical coastlines.

Equipped for amputation: the deadly Tiger Shark. Illustration by Lee Krutop

In hot weather tiger sharks commonly migrate to the warm waters off subtropical cities like Sydney.

The name "tiger" was coined because the shark is born with dark stripes on its upper surface. These fade as the fish matures. A tiger shark can grow to 20 feet long, with weight exceeding 2,000 pounds. Its powerful gastric acids enable it to digest anything from sacking and rowing-boat paddles to cans of food.

This most feared of man-eaters would need no more than a second to snap up and swallow a human arm.

And it is well-equipped to perform the procedure. The tiger shark's distinctive teeth, shaped like a rooster's comb, are serrated, breadknife-like, on both sides. This dental configuration enables the shark to apply a death-grip to even the fastest-moving target. For this deadly carnivore, legs and arms make easy pickings. However, shark attacks are relatively rare, not only in Australian waters, but worldwide. In the 21st century the annual average number of people killed by sharks has been 10. Meanwhile, humans are killing countless millions of sharks annually, to supply the food, manufacturing and medical industries.

Fatal Contact:
The Dark History of Aircraft and UFOs

An old but still well-tended headstone, standing in the Sacred Heart Cemetery in Moreauville, Louisiana, reads: "In Loving Memory of Felix Eugene Moncla Jr, 1st Lt United States Air Force. Born October 21 1926. Disappeared November 23 1953 Intercepting a UFO over Canadian Border as Pilot of an F-89 Jet Plane."

Official USAF records reveal that despite a massive search, neither Moncla, his co-pilot Lt Robert Wilson, nor even a fragment of their fighter plane was ever found. On the far side of the world, on the coast of Australia, a plaque celebrating the life of another young pilot stands, whipped with spray from the ocean beyond. It is the memorial to Frederick Valentich who, on October 21 1978 (Moncla's birthday) also vanished without trace, along with his Cessna. These are three of the young fliers who, over the decades, have fallen victim to the inexplicable. There have been many more…

Pacific Ocean, east of Japan.
August 25 1998

THE NEWS, in the form of an unconfirmed report, first reached the Japanese public via a radio station. A jet pilot, the flash asserted, had vanished while participating in a training exercise off Honshu Island.

In the young flier's final moments a colleague had radioed that an unidentified object was on a collision course with him.

Newspaper and TV networks experienced difficulty in persuading Japan's ASDF (Air Self Defense Force) to confirm or deny this story. It was not until 11 days later that the press had enough to run with. One report, under the heading MISSING FIGHTERS, appeared in the September 5 edition of the *Japan Times*.

It revealed that not one, but two, jets had disappeared.

The prelude to the dark drama began at 6.25 p.m. on August 25, when three Mitsubishi F-1 fighters took off from Misawa Air Base for Honshu Island. At 6.57 p.m., as the training maneuvers were beginning, one of the pilots told air traffic controllers that he could see "a red ball about 10 foot diameter" moving toward the three aircraft. According to the Russian newspaper *Pravda* the pilot then maneuvered, narrowly avoiding a collision with the object.

His colleagues were not so lucky. Their F-1s simultaneously ceased radio contact and vanished from the radar screen.

Japanese newspapers identified the two missing men as First Lieutenants Hirokazu Nagai and Madoka Nakaya, both 29. The reports revealed that the national Maritime Safety Agency sent 11 planes and 13 patrol boats to search the area from which their jets had vanished. Only one of the boats found anything: a fragment from one of the F-1s, "measuring 20 by 12 inches – dark green on the top and white on the bottom." It was part of a jet's horizontal stabilizer.

Questioned about the unidentified object, Defense Force spokesmen announced that it had, in fact, been a "fireball." Far from being struck by it the missing jets had "collided with each other during a low-altitude drill."

So, in the end, despite all the speculation about a UFO-related double disappearance, it had all been a tragedy of human errors. No unidentified object. No collision with an unknown. Instead, a fireball observed by the third pilot – and a crash involving his colleagues.

Everything was explained.

Or was it?

* * *

According to *Pravda* another disappearance occurred near the same Misawa airbase less than two months later (October 9 1998). At 8.02 p.m. a pursuit aircraft with an experienced two-man crew encountered a "red spherical object" close to the base. Shortly after they announced their intention to fire on it, radio contact was lost. Searchers found documents and a wing fragment floating on the ocean. The pilots were posted as missing.

The Japanese authorities may well have had their facts right when they denied that anything describable as an unknown agency had played a role in the Honshu vanishings. But whatever the truth of the matter, the official response was in lockstep with that of every other government on Earth confronted with a purported UFO case:

Disseminate everyday explanations, whether or not they fit the observed facts. Silence government employees. Discredit witnesses. Cite Venus. Weather balloons. Marsh gas. Pilot vertigo. Pilot error. Never concede that anything sinisterly inexplicable might have been involved in a pilot's death or disappearance.

For more than 80 years pilots – and their crews and passengers – have been mysteriously vanishing and/or dying amid reports of UFO activity. In that period the number of harmless encounters and near-misses has of course vastly outweighed those that ended in tragedy.

But a roll-call of horrifying events – all denied or "fudged" by governments – has occurred nonetheless.

Fort Knox, Kentucky USA. January 7 1948

According to US Air Force Intelligence Report 100-203-79 (1952) the "flap" began at around 1.15 p.m. Several hundred witnesses watched a circular object, variously estimated to be 246–295 feet in diameter, moving south at a leisurely pace. It was clearly visible through light cirrus clouds. State Police, besieged by telephone calls, went outside to check on the arcane intruder. Not knowing what to make of it they called the Military Police at Fort Knox (repository of America's gold reserve) who, in turn, alerted officers at Godman Air Force Base.

At 1.45 p.m. the control tower reported that the machine (if it could be thus described) was hovering directly above Godman. Personnel described it as a huge metallic sphere with a circle of lights around its base. It was oscillating slowly and changing color from red to brilliant white.

Captain Thomas F. Mantell Jr, who would become the principal player in this calamitous drama, was a World War II veteran. He had participated in the invasion of Normandy, receiving the Distinguished Flying Cross. On this fateful afternoon Mantell was leading a flotilla of F-51 Mustang fighters on a training patrol. Colonel Guy Hix, operations commander at Godman, ordered the tower to contact Captain Mantell. The official transcript reads:

Tower: Godman Tower. Calling the flight of four ships north-bound over Godman Field. Do you read? Over.

Mantell: Roger, Godman Tower. This is National Guard 869, flight leader of the formation. Over.

Tower: National Guard 869 from Godman Tower. We have an object out south here that we are unable to identify – and we would like to know if you have gas enough, and if so could you take a look for us if you will.

Mantell: Roger, I have the gas and I'll take a look for you if you give me the correct heading.

Followed by two of his fellow pilots (the third was under-fueled) Mantell climbed to 15,000 feet, then radioed:

"The object is directly ahead of and above me now, moving at about half my speed... It appears to be a metallic object and of tremendous size. I'm still climbing... I'm trying to close in for a better look."

At 22,000 feet Mantell's companions turned back. Their planes had not been serviced with oxygen that day. But Mantell continued to climb, until at 30,000 feet his F-51 leveled off, then plunged to earth, crashing into woodlands on a farm owned by William J. Phillips of Franklin, Kentucky.

Lieutenant Richard Miller, who was stationed at Scott Air Force Base in Bellville, Illinois, listened to the entire dialog between Captain Mantell and the tower. He subsequently testified that Mantell's last words were, "My God! I see people in this thing!"

That evening Air Force Technical Intelligence Center officers from Wright Patterson Air Force Base arrived at Godman and ordered all personnel to hand over anything related to the crash. One of the officers said Mantell had died "pursuing an intelligently controlled unidentified flying object."

On January 8 1948 the *New York Times* published a report headed:

CHASING A FLYING SAUCER
Plane Explodes Over Kentucky as States Report Strange Object

Numerous newspapers quoted Base commander Colonel Hix, who said he had "observed the flying saucer for almost an hour."

But the US Air Force hierarchy was intent on finding a prosaic "explanation" for Captain Mantell's death. Over the years it announced several reasons for the crash – all conflicting with each other.

- In its Air Intelligence Report (1952) the USAF concluded that Captain Mantell had, in reality, been chasing the planet Venus. Objectors pointed out that on January 7 1948 Venus would have been the merest pinpoint of light. Astronomical records show that it was only 33 degrees above the horizon when the UFO appeared. The airbase witnesses, the hundreds of people in towns across Kentucky, the officers of two police forces and Captain Mantell himself could not possibly have mistaken the planet for a "metallic object of tremendous size."

- The air force must quietly have agreed, because it changed tack shortly afterward and announced that the object had been a weather balloon.

- One USAF spokesman also confusingly backed a Professor Donald Menzel, who insisted that Captain Mantell had been chasing a "sundog", in which sunlight is reflected off ice crystals. Analysts commented that this phenomenon is visible only from particular angles and could not have been viewed simultaneously from air bases and towns hundreds of miles apart.

Perhaps the most intriguing testimony relating to the tragedy would come many years later from a retired US Army Air Corps pilot, Captain James Duesler. After marrying an Englishwoman and moving to Britain, the elderly Duesler recalled (in 1997) that he had been on duty at Godman Base when the UFO appeared – and had watched its progress through binoculars.

"It was a gray-looking object that resembled an inverted ice cream cone," he said. "It seemed to be rotating, as evidenced by a black line moving around it. The bottom was red."

Twelve hours after Captain Mantell's aircraft had plummeted to earth, Captain Duesler, then a crash investigator at Godman, was belatedly ordered to inspect the wreckage. He recalled that the pilot's seatbelt was tattered in a strange way. "By the time I got there the body had been removed," Duesler said. "The other officers told me it had been in a puzzling condition. There were no breaks in his skin – but all his bones had been pulverized."

Oddest of all was the manner in which the plane had come down.

"Its condition seemed too good to be consistent with a high-speed crash to the ground," Duesler said. "It was lying in a clearing in the woods. The wings and tail had broken off but the propeller was intact. Because of the weight of the engine the F-51 should have descended nose-first and hit the ground at an angle.

"There were no scratches on the fuselage and no signs of blood in the cockpit. The trees around the crash site were intact. Even if the aircraft had managed to glide in it would have cut a swathe through the trees and a channel into the earth. But there was nothing. *It was if the plane had just belly-flopped into the clearing.*"

Captain Duesler wondered also why he had been ordered to the site so late. "Usually I'd be told to attend a crash immediately," he said. "I've asked myself since then whether something relating to Captain Mantell's death was being concealed."

Five years later, pilots would be posing a similar question about the disappearance of two more of their colleagues.

Kinross Air Force Base, Michigan. November 23 1953

The radar "blip" was unusually large. None of the operators at Kinross Base had the faintest conception of what type of plane might be producing it.

What they did know, however, was that it was flying over Soo Locks, in restricted airspace – meaning that it might be an enemy craft of some kind.

The commanding officer at Kinross alerted his opposite number at Truax Field, Madison, Wisconsin. The "unknown" had to be identified immediately.

Within 100 seconds two young pilots were aloft in a Northrup F-89C Scorpion jet interceptor.

At the controls was Lieutenant Gene Moncla, 26, holder of a Bachelor of Science degree from Southwestern Louisiana Institute. Moncla had interrupted his studies toward a medical qualification to serve as a pilot in the Korean War and was now on temporary assignment to Truax airbase. He was married with two small children.

Sitting behind Moncla was the jet's radar operator, Second Lieutenant Robert Wilson, 22.

Guided by a GCI (Ground Control Intercept) controller the jet streaked upward at 500 miles per hour into wintry darkness. When it had reached 30,000 feet the twin blips on the glowing ground radar screen indicated that the Scorpion was in the vicinity of the unknown intruder. But then the gigantic "blip" changed course and moved away at colossal speed. The controller notified Moncla of the object's new bearing – and he pursued it out over Lake Superior.

The chase lasted 30 minutes – and the jet seemed to be gaining – when the object suddenly changed course again, dropping an estimated 23,000 feet. GCI ordered Moncla to descend also, asking if he and Wilson could lock onto the target visually.

There was no reply.

Then, as the GCI crew watched, appalled, *the radar blips representing the jet and the unknown object abruptly merged into one.*

The object subsequently headed north, quickly disappearing from the radar screen.

Assuming that the Scorpion and the UFO had collided the base commander sent search and rescue crews equipped with flares to the scene. Perhaps Moncla and Wilson had managed to bail out and were floating, even now, in their lifejackets or on a self-inflating raft. In the bitter cold they were unlikely to survive more than a few hours. Rescue planes and boats scoured a 160-square-mile area throughout the night and all the following day. But they found no bodies and no wreckage. Pilots Gene Moncla and Robert Wilson had vanished without trace.

Ground crew at Truax base were convinced that the pilots had been swallowed by a UFO. News of the incident leaked to a local newspaper and then became international news. The US Air Force tried to scotch the media's claims. After an investigation it announced that the radar blip had not been as large as originally reported. It had in fact been created by a Royal Canadian Air Force C-47, flying from Winnipeg to Sudbury, Ontario.

This explanation held firm for several hours – until the RCAF released a press statement denying that the "unknown" had been one of their aircraft.

The United States Air Force cast around for another way of hosing the crisis down. The ever-reliable Professor Donald Menzel, Harvard astronomer and dedicated UFO debunker, came to the rescue. Probably, he surmised, the pilot had suffered a vertigo attack and crashed. And the merging radar blips? Plainly the radar equipment had registered an atmospherically created "echo", which had blended with the Scorpion's radar returns.

As would occur in later cases, journalists requested a transcript of the final conversation between Eugene Moncla and his ground controllers. The air force refused the request on security grounds.

The young pilots' families were hurt and dissatisfied. They had talked privately with the fliers' friends – some of whom had followed the drama at first-hand – and were convinced the air force was not telling the truth. The widow and parents of Gene Moncla responded in the only way they could – by placing a remarkable headstone above the pilot's grave.

Its simple text confirms their conviction that Gene Moncla and his co-pilot died while chasing an unidentified flying object.

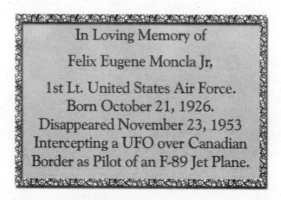

In Loving Memory of

Felix Eugene Moncla Jr,

1st Lt. United States Air Force.
Born October 21, 1926.
Disappeared November 23, 1953
Intercepting a UFO over Canadian
Border as Pilot of an F-89 Jet Plane.

When Lt Gene Moncla and his co-pilot disappeared while pursuing a UFO the US Air Force did everything in its power to discredit the hundreds of military and civilian ground-witnesses. Moncla's distressed family responded by erecting a memorial in a Louisiana cemetery, telling "the true story."

Bass Strait, Australia. 1920-1978

Bass Strait is the 80–130 mile stretch of ocean separating the Australian mainland from Tasmania. It was named to commemorate the explorer George Bass who, with Matthew Flinders, sailed through the strait to prove that Tasmania (then known as Van Diemen's Land) was an island.

Inexplicable light displays, associated with unsolved vanishings of ships, planes and people were chronicled in Bass Strait throughout the twentieth century. The most famous disappearance was that of the young pilot Frederick Valentich in 1978.

But there were many before him.

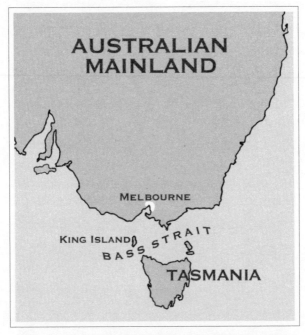

Many ships, planes and people have vanished without trace
in Bass Strait, the stretch of ocean separating Australia's
mainland from Tasmania.

From January 1982 to June 1984 Bill Chalker, the UFO analyst and author of *The Oz Files*, was given unprecedented access to the Royal Australian Air Force's UFO investigation records and photographs. The material, held at the Defence Department's premises in Canberra, gave Chalker, an industrial chemist, detailed information on UFO activity as it had impinged on Australian Defence Force pilots. He made some surprising discoveries.

Researchers are well-acquainted with the story that an "unknown" trailed a Beaufort bomber over Bass Strait during World War II. But the RAAF files offer considerably more detail. The Beaufort was flying at 4,500 feet over the strait in February 1944 when, at about 2.30 a.m., a "dark shadow" appeared alongside. It had a flickering light and flame belched from its rear. The object stayed with the bomber for 15–20 minutes. During its visit all radio and direction-finding instruments ceased to function. Eventually the UFO accelerated away at roughly three times the bomber's speed. When he landed the pilot reported the incident to his superiors – but claims he was only laughed at.

In retrospect, Bill Chalker writes, this reaction seems extraordinary. "It turns out that Beauforts figured heavily in the official RAAF list of planes that went 'missing without trace' during World War II in the Bass Strait area – an area that was not linked to any significant enemy activity." (Chalker adds a proviso. The Beauforts, he was told, had mechanical problems which could have accounted for some of the losses.)

The "Cigar" and the Missing Plane

IN OCTOBER 1981 four German tourists disappeared, with their Piper Lance aircraft, near Lake Eildon in Victoria, Australia. The vanishing triggered a massive search involving military planes and helicopters and seven volunteer pilots. No trace of the Piper Lance or the tourists was found.

Bill Buying, a professional photographer who worked in nearby Monbulk, approached me (this book's author) with information he felt "might have some connection with the mystery." He said:

"On October 24, two days after the plane disappeared, my whole family spent two hours watching a silvery cigar-shaped object hovering in the sky. The thing was so far away we had to use binoculars to see it properly – but I had a go at taking shots anyway, using a tripod and a 350 mm tele-lens on my Pentax camera.

"We all knew the thing we were watching was not a star, because it stayed in the same spot for hours and was never obscured by clouds. We were thunderstruck at one stage when we saw a second

object – dark with a long tail – seemingly emerge from the UFO and plunge behind trees several miles away."

I also spoke to Bill Buying's wife Dina. "It was the most frightening experience of our lives," she told me. "For the entire couple of hours that we watched the UFO the bush was absolutely silent. There were no bird or insect sounds and no dogs barking.

"When the thing finally disappeared, the noises returned as if a radio had been switched back on."

I studied Bill's negatives. Disappointingly the distant object appeared only as a dark dot when enlarged by conventional photographic means. Gerard Lie of the University of Melbourne's photographic department, with whom I had worked before, kindly offered to conduct an experiment that might reveal more about the pictures. The department's micro-unit made closeup negatives of the distant dot itself. Aside from confirming that a solid object had indeed been hovering in the sky, the tests were inconclusive.

However, other witnesses also described the UFO.

- A summer visitor, Perry Schneider, said he had seen "a strange metallic shape" hovering above the hills.
- A local pilot, Alan Weeks, told me he and several neighbors had watched for about an hour as "a metallic object" hovered over the district.
- The aerial anomaly was seen, too, by summer campers at the Thorton caravan park. The consensus was that it was "shining, with patches of red and white."

Like many other large bodies of water on the vast Australian continent, Lake Eildon is no stranger to inexplicable events.

7 Pilots, 14 Passengers Disappear

In July 1920 the schooner *Amelia J.* was lost in Bass Strait. Among the aerial searchers were Captain W. Stutt, a government aviation instructor, and his mechanic, Sergeant Dalziel.

They failed to find the schooner – and vanished themselves, instead.

A witness in an accompanying plane, Major Anderson, reported that

Stutt's plane *flew into a cloud* from which it did not emerge. Neither the schooner, the search plane, nor Stutt and Dalziel were ever found.

In terms of lives lost, the most significant disappearances over the strait occurred in 1934 and 1935. Newspapers of the time chronicle these baffling cases in exhaustive detail.

On October 19 1934, 12 people aboard the mailplane *Miss Hobart* were lost. Two pilots and the 10 passengers they were transporting from Launceston to Melbourne disappeared without trace minutes after the pilot had radioed a routine message that all was well.

No one pretended to have the remotest understanding of what had happened. The weather was fine with a slight breeze.

The aircraft was a DH-86, a model renowned for its reliability. The owners, Holyman's Airways, later said that even if two of its four powerful Gipsy VI engines had failed, the plane could have maintained its height with full load. It would have been impossible for all four engines to cut out.

The last words heard from *Miss Hobart* were transmitted at 10.20 a.m., when she was 8 miles from Wilson's Promontory. Co-pilot Gilbert Jenkins radioed, "Everything OK. Captain Holyman requests that Captain Haig of the Vacuum Oil Company meet him at Laverton at 11.30 a.m."

Unusual phenomena surrounded the disappearance:

- On October 20 1934 the Melbourne *Age* published a statement by two Works Department surveyors (A. Campbell and R. Henry) that while working near the lighthouse they had "heard the drone of a plane suddenly stop." This happened at 10.20 a.m., the time pilot Gilbert Jenkins made his final radio contact.

The witnesses said they had expected the plane, as usual, to come around a point of Mt Oberon and cross the sea – but nothing appeared. "If it had been a plane going on its journey the drone would have gradually died away," surveyor Campbell said. "But that didn't occur. The sound suddenly stopped as the unseen plane was coming towards us."

- On October 21 the *Age* reported that the crew of the collier *Kooliga* had seen an "unusual white flare" at 7.30 p.m. on the day of *Miss Hobart*'s disappearance. "The helmsman, Mr J. Millington, said it could not have been lights carried by search parties ashore as it was too large and did not move."

- On the same day the Melbourne *Herald* described another puzzling phenomenon: "A report has been received in Foster that a woman at Mt Best has stated that about the time the plane is thought to have disappeared, she saw a peculiar cloud, low down over the water, some distance out at sea."

Late in November a chair, thought possibly to have come from *Miss Hobart*, was found on a beach. An official inquiry failed to find a cause for the aircraft's disappearance or what had become of the pilots and passengers.

On October 2 1935, less than a year after the disappearance of *Miss Hobart*, the airliner *Loina* vanished in similar fashion. The plane left Essendon Airport, Melbourne, for Western Junction, Tasmania, at 8.15 a.m. At 9.51 the captain, A.N. Evans, radioed, "Approaching Emita [a small township]. Height 1,000 feet. On course 136 degrees closing down."

Loina was never heard from again.

That afternoon a search party retrieved, from a beach, three chairs and a petrol tank so telescoped that it suggested the plane had crashed at colossal speed. No trace of the rest of the aircraft, its two pilots or their three passengers was ever found. The subsequent official inquiry could discover no explanation for the disaster.

The Ides of October

A brief recapitulation is appropriate here. *Miss Hobart* vanished over the strait on October 19 1934. Loina followed her on October 2 1935. And it was on October 21 1978 that the young pilot Frederick Valentich vanished after reporting that an unidentified craft was "orbiting" him.

The Valentich case is probably the most famous UFO-related disappearance in history. Frederick, 20, was a qualified pilot who planned to make a career in aviation. He had hired a $43,000 single-engine Cessna to fly from Moorabbin airport across Bass Strait to King Island.

It is probable that he had never heard of Gene Moncla, the USAF pilot who disappeared 25 years earlier while pursuing a UFO. But the two young fliers were linked by a dark strand of coincidence.

At 6.19 p.m. on October 21 (a date which happened to be Gene Moncla's birthday) Frederick Valentich waved farewell to colleagues at Melbourne's Moorabbin Airport, taxied and took off. At 7 p.m. he radioed Melbourne

Flight Service to say he was over Cape Otway. All OK.

At 7.06 he radioed again with a question that was to intrigue the world for decades to come.

Melbourne, this is Delta Sierra Juliet. Is there any known traffic below 5,000?
No, the operator said. There was no known traffic.

Valentich responded: *Delta Sierra Juliet, I am... seems to be... large aircraft below 5,000 feet.*

After describing the object as having four bright lights, similar to landing lights, he went on to say that it had "just passed over" him – "at least one thousand feet above" and had begun to orbit his Cessna. And then: "It's not an aircraft, it's... as it's flying past it's a long shape... it's got a green light and sort of metallic (like) it's all shiny on the outside."

At 7.11 the young pilot reported that his engine was rough-idling. Thirty seconds later he transmitted his callsign, Delta Sierra Juliet, for the last time. The microphone stayed open for 17 seconds after that – accompanied by unidentifiable noises, subsequently described by some analysts as "metal on metal."

In October 1978, while flying a Cessna over Bass Strait, young Australian pilot Frederick Valentich radioed that he was being "orbited' by an unidentified aircraft. Neither Valentich nor any fragment of his plane was ever found.

Within minutes of Valentich's final transmission the Rescue Coordination Centre had a light plane in the air to conduct a night search. Next day, in perfect weather, an RAAF Orion and seven other aircraft, backed by ships and fishing vessels, conducted a massive sweep covering over 10,000 square miles. The Cessna was constructed from modular units, designed to float in the event of a crash into water. Aboard were polystyrene lifejackets, colored orange so they would easily be seen from the air.

The searchers found no floating wreckage. They found no body. The onboard VHF emergency beacon which automatically transmits a distress signal remained silent.

The RAAF was busy that day. Within 12 hours of Valentich's disappearance, it helped in an intensive search for an airliner with nine passengers aboard which had vanished over the Solomon Islands. Neither wreckage nor bodies were ever found.

Government agencies went into their usual debunking mode, suggesting among other things that Valentich might inadvertently have been flying upside-down – and that the strange craft he had seen was no more than reflections in the water.

Pilots and aviation experts dismissed this theory, pointing out that not only would the carpets have come off the floor, but that the Cessna, with its gravity-fed fuel system, would have ditched after 60 seconds. Further, according to the Department of Transport, Valentich had spoken to the Flight Service operator for six minutes. He would have found it hard to conduct such a conversation flying upside-down.

In 1998, 20 years after pilot Frederick Valentich's disappearance his family placed a memorial plaque in the grounds of Cape Otway Light Station.

The Valentich case revived memories of a previous incident involving an aircraft which had attempted to travel an opposite route above Bass Strait. On Christmas Eve 1969 a Fuji light plane vanished while flying from King Island to Moorabbin Airport. No trace of wreckage or of the pilot was found.

On October 11 2000 – 22 years after Valentich's disappearance – an Apollo Bay man came forward to say he had seen the incident. He explained to Melbourne's *Herald Sun* newspaper that he had feared ridicule if he spoke – but that his conscience had troubled him ever since. The man said that on the evening of October 21 he had been hunting rabbits with his son and two nieces at Cape Otway. Visibility was still good after 7 p.m. – and all four witnesses had seen "a green light" hovering above a light aircraft flying over the strait. The light and the plane were lost from sight when they flew behind the hills.

The mystery of Frederick Valentich remains unsolved.

In 1998 in the grounds of Cape Otway Light Station Frederick's family dedicated a plaque to his memory. It reads:

THE UNKNOWN

This plaque commemorates the landmark of the mysterious disappearance of FREDERICK VALENTICH on 21 October 1978.

Frederick was flying a Cessna 182L, and at this point he changed direction to south from the lighthouse towards the sea.

Twelve minutes flying south from here at precisely 19.12.28 his radio transmission was cut off and in his last radio contact he explained "that strange aircraft is hovering on top of me again, and it is not an aircraft..."

After an extensive land and sea search, no trace was ever found of the Cessna VH-DSJ or of FREDERICK VALENTICH.

And so to this day, his disappearance remains a mystery.

* * *

Language barriers and the secretive nature of governments make it impossible for any historian to chronicle all the known cases in which the deaths of pilots, passengers and crews have apparently been UFO-related.

But accessible reports are numerous nonetheless.

The Cuban UFO Tragedy, 1967

According to *Pravda* an "unidentified spherical object" invaded Cuban airspace in March 1967. Two MIG-21 jets were ordered to shoot the intruder down. As the pilots drew close to the UFO they radioed that their navigation equipment, including targeting and missile-firing systems, had failed.

One of the MIGs disintegrated. Shortly afterward the second disappeared from radar. No trace of the pilots or the wreckage of the second plane was found.

The old Soviet Union was not immune from inexplicable aerial disappearances. *Pravda* reports that aircraft mysteriously lost over Russia have included a TU-154 passenger jet and an MIG-31 pursuit plane in the Archangel region. "The pilots had reported no malfunction or state of emergency," the article adds. "The St Petersburg engineer Yevgeny Voronin [theorizes] that a plane can find itself inside an electromagnetic field in which all its equipment stops working. The aircraft starts spinning and blows up. The fragments can be scattered over a wide area."

Christiansfeld, Denmark, 1970

On September 16 1970 the Danish newspaper *Sonderjyden* published a report headed YOUNG SECOND LIEUTENANT KILLED IN PLANE CRASH. The article revealed that the previous morning four Hawker-Hunter fighters had taken off from Vandel Air Force Base to fly to Holland.

After the planes had been aloft for 20 minutes one lost radio contact with base and crashed vertically into a field. The explosion gouged a crater 50 feet wide and 20 feet deep, killing the 23-year-old pilot. The newspaper's conservatively worded report saved the most controversial paragraph until last:

A witness has told police that a few seconds after the plane hit the ground he observed a glowing ball in the sky, moving away with great speed in a northerly direction.

Air force spokesmen had a simple explanation for the tragedy. The weather that morning had been foggy – and the pilot must inadvertently have been flying upside-down. When he was ordered to climb above the clouds he took his aircraft in the opposite direction – crashing straight into the ground. A subsequent theory was that the Hawker-Hunter had been struck by a fireball.

Lviv, Ukraine. July 27 2002

SELDOM IN PEACETIME had there been a more horrifying aviation accident.

A military jet flying low over the air show at Lviv blew up and crashed into the crowd, killing the pilot and 85 spectators.

After interviewing witnesses and studying TV news footage a Commission of Inquiry found that the plane had gone into a spin, then burst into flames, exploding and collapsing onto the crowd. The investigators were at a loss to explain the cause of the disaster, other than to table a list of speculations.

But there was other evidence. Two spectators who had occupied widely separated vantage points at the show independently approached organizers with amateur video of the aircraft's final moments. Clearly visible on frozen frames of both tapes were images of an unidentified object, streaming near the plane seconds before it crashed.

The anomaly was neither a bird nor missile. It was cylindrically shaped. There was no smoke exhaust. Initial attempts to interpret the images as an insect or flaw on the lens came to nothing. The two video cameras had from different perspectives captured what was clearly the same object.

What was it? Was it simply a misidentification of some kind? Or could it possibly have been suggestive of an incident in which an unknown agency had caused a pilot's death – and the deaths of scores of others besides?

Ukrainian authorities declined, at least publicly, even to discuss the taped images, or to seek to dismiss them with reasoned arguments. Their attitude toward the purported "cylinder" was no different from that of any other government suddenly confronted with a possible UFO event.

The reasons underlying this code of official secrecy have never been satisfactorily explained. The universal silence of governments is almost as great a mystery as the UFO phenomenon itself.

Stalin's Secret UFO Probe

DICTATOR JOSEPH STALIN was convinced that UFOs posed a danger to the Soviet Union.

In 1948 he ordered mathematician Mstislav Keldysh, chemist Alexander Topchiyev and physician Sergei Korolev to conduct a "deep analysis" of reported sightings and incidents across Russia. He also kept the investigative trio supplied with data from his spies in USA – including stolen classified material from the alleged 1947 flying saucer crash in Roswell.

Stalin never believed the US authorities' announcement that the Roswell saucer had been a misidentified weather balloon. He noted that the specialists entrusted with inspecting and removing the wreckage comprised members of the USAF's elite nuclear weapons team – men whose time would never have been wasted on balloon retrieval.

In the years to his death in 1953 Stalin established UFO research departments in seven of the USSR's leading scientific institutes. Ten secret arms of the Defense Ministry were also dedicated to the study and hoped-for retrieval of UFOs. All researchers reported to the KGB.

Soviet pilots were often ordered to shoot at unidentified intruders. But it is unclear whether any flier managed to down a flying saucer.

Declassified documents detailing Stalin's UFO projects were published in newspapers after Russia was democratized. A particularly tantalizing scrap of information suggests that he might have succeeded in obtaining at least one anomalous artifact for scientific study.

It was a "silver rocket", assessed as being several thousand years old, found during an archeological dig in Kiev. The object, says the report, was cut up and transported to a testing area in Moscow, where it was found to be marked with inscriptions in the ancient language, Sanskrit.

The silver rocket's status as fact or myth still inspires argument in Russia.

Church Walls Were "Haunted"
– by Faces of the Dead:
Dean Liddell and His Wife

Twenty-five years after he died, the face of Dean Henry Liddell inexplicably appeared in mold on a wall of Christ Church, Oxford. This bizarre event created such intense public interest that after three years embarrassed church authorities finally summoned resolution enough to have the image scrubbed off. Within days, however, the dean's likeness re-emerged. When it was removed again, an image of his deceased wife appeared in its place. These occurrences were not unique. For centuries, portraits of people long buried have spontaneously appeared –seemingly without an artist's intervention – on the walls, windows and floors of churches and private dwellings. In 1971 an inquiry into one "face-crowded" cottage in Spain revealed that it had been built over an ancient graveyard. What causes such pictures slowly to well up from stone, cement and plaster? Investigators can find no answer…

O N JULY 17 1923 London's *Daily Express* published an unusual report under the headline FACE OF DEAD DEAN.

The article's posthumous subject was the famed cleric Dr Henry Liddell (1811-1898), Dean of Christ Church, Oxford, and father of Alice Liddell, the inspiration for Lewis Carroll's *Alice in Wonderland*.

In mold on the wall of the church's south aisle a perfect representation of Dr Liddell's face had gradually appeared over a period of several months. *(See photographs opposite.)*

The church and the university conducted parallel investigations. Both concluded that the remarkably lifelike portrait was a freak of nature: a "natural formation" in the mold, which had burgeoned too slowly for any artist or prankster to have been involved. Public interest in this purportedly spontaneous portrait grew so strong that visitors over the ensuing three years sometimes lined up to see it, creating disruption in the church's hallowed and normally quiet precincts.

In its September 11 1926 edition the London magazine *TP's and Cassell's Weekly* described the picture thus:

"It is a faithful and unmistakable likeness of the late Dean Liddell, who died in the year 1898. One does not need to call in play any imaginative faculty to reconstruct the head. It is set perfectly straight upon the wall, as it might have been drawn by the hand of a master artist. Yet it is not etched; neither is it sketched nor sculpted, but it is there plain for all eyes to see."

After a tense series of meetings, ecclesiastical authorities agreed that the portrait, on balance, was doing Christ Church more harm than good. The mold image was scrubbed away.

Several days later the dean's picture resurfaced. Workmen removed it again. Ten days passed. Then, in the precise spot which Dr Liddell's image had occupied, a mold portrait of his wife Lorina Liddell emerged.

These events caused a furor in the press – especially when journalists discovered that Henry Liddell was not the first dean posthumously to have appeared in a mold picture. The February 8 1902 edition of the journal *Notes and Queries* had reported:

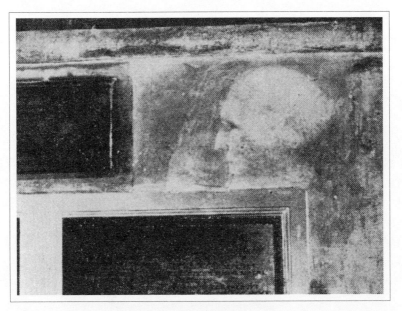

IMAGE IN MOLD In 1923 a perfect profile of Dean Liddell bloomed in mold on a wall of Christ Church Cathedral, between two plaques. When authorities had it scrubbed away, the face of the Dean's wife Lorina (also deceased) gradually appeared in its place. Neither University nor Cathedral investigators could find any explanation.
Fortean Picture Library

HENRY LIDDELL Former Dean of Christ Church Cathedral, Oxford, he is principally remembered today for being the father of his famous daughter Alice – and for an extraordinary occurrence after his death (see above).
Fortean Picture Library

Alice melts into the Looking Glass in a Tenniel illustration
from Lewis Carroll's book. The heroine's character was
based on Alice Pleasance Liddell, daughter of Dean Liddell,
who would eventually have his own rendezvous with
the bizarre. Twenty-five years after he died, the Dean's
image mysteriously appeared on a wall of Christ Church
Cathedral, Oxford.

"After the death of the late Dean Vaughan of Llandaff, there suddenly appeared on the wall of Llandaff Cathedral a large blotch of dampness or minute fungi, formed into a lifelike outline of the Dean's face."

And in Christ Church itself the phenomenon began to proliferate. In October 1931 Mrs Hewat McKenzie wrote that the "beautifully clear" image of the dean had returned – and that new mold pictures elsewhere in the church were also attracting attention. The most notable was on a gray pedestal base. "About a foot from the floor," she wrote, "a white patch appears on the marble, containing a very clear likeness of an elderly man with bushy hair, full whiskers and a beard... An even clearer face is to be seen on a wall behind the organ and within 20 yards of the choir stall. It is thought to be a chorister who sang in the church for many years."

Earlier cases had been chronicled in the United States. On August 20 1870 the *New York Herald* described the experience of a man in Lawrence, Massachusetts, on one of whose windowpanes "a perfectly executed portrait of a young woman" appeared overnight. Hoping to rid himself of sightseers the householder tried to erase the picture with a scrubbing brush. The portrait remained resolutely in place. On January 18 1871 the *New York Times* reported that "likenesses of human faces" also defiant of scrubbing-bristles had mysteriously invaded windowpanes in Cincinnati.

A century later the still-unexplained phenomenon was showing no sign of petering out.

No. 5 Rodriguez Acosta, Belmez, Spain. August 23 1971. Morning

Maria Gomez Pereira took great pride in the whitewashed cottage she shared with her husband and son. Owned by the Pereira family since it was built in 1835, the house was set high in the Andalusian mountains – its tiny windows offering exquisite glimpses of olive groves and densely treed slopes.

Mrs Pereira kept her house spotless. She was distressed therefore when an ugly stain of unknown provenance appeared on her kitchen's cement floor. Nothing, from hot soapy water to salt, seemed powerful enough to remove the mark. And day by day it grew, spread.

On the hot still morning of August 23 Mrs Pereira bustled into her kitchen and saw to her alarm that the stain had transformed itself into what seemed to be the portrait of a face. A distorted male face, staring up at her. She was terrified. This morning and this moment would stay with her for the rest of her life. She ran to fetch her husband Juan and son Miguel. They would know what to do.

But they were as frightened as her. They called in neighbors to see whether anyone could suggest an explanation. No one could. But two or three agreed that the picture did resemble Santa Faz, an icon displayed in the church whose tower dominated the village.

No one in the family would consider allowing so dreadful an image to remain in the house. Miguel Pereira smashed the cement with a pickax. His father hired a man to lay a new floor. Maria's kitchen was pristine again. Perhaps in time she could forget about the twisted face.

But it was not to be. On September 8 the face reappeared in the newly laid concrete – just as the features of Dean Liddell, 48 years earlier, had grown again in the wall mold on Christ Church's south aisle.

Two priests visited the Pereiras' cottage. They prayed for the family, but could offer no explanation for what was happening. Neighbors asked the mayor to help. He conferred with his fellow councilors, then sent in workmen, instructed by an archeologist to excavate the kitchen floor. Everyone hoped that the expert would somehow discover a cause for the past month's grotesque occurrences. And – arguably – he did. At a depth of 9 feet lay a jumble of skeletons: all headless. Also in the pit were thigh bones, ribcages, legs and arms – but there were no skulls anywhere. The archeologist surmised that victims of ritual execution had been buried here – or that there had been a battle whose decapitated dead had been flung into a mass grave.

GRAVEYARD FACE In 1971, images of human faces began to appear on the kitchen floor of a cottage in Belmez, Spain. Police sealed the building against possible hoaxers, but the faces – many of them seemingly troubled – continued to surface by the thousand. Scientists could discover no cause for the phenomenon. Archeologists established that the cottage was built over an ancient cemetery.
Fortean Picture Library

A laboratory tested the bones and declared them to have belonged to teenagers, male and female. They were about seven centuries old.

Meanwhile an ecclesiastical historian produced records which showed that the Pereiras' house, in common with its neighbors, had been built over an ancient graveyard. Most recently (in an historical sense) this cemetery had accommodated Christian dead: before that, Muslims and Romans.

Church authorities reburied the teenagers' remains in a nearby Catholic cemetery. The local council filled the excavation and covered the kitchen floor with its second fresh layer of cement.

The mayor dared express the opinion that this might be the end of it. But his hopes were quickly dashed. Within the week a veritable mass of new faces – many with expressions of anguish – began to appear in the cement. The images were accompanied by something new: representations of human hands, Greek and Latin crosses and the claws of unidentifiable animals.

The Pereiras were so distressed that local authorities closed their kitchen and built a new one at the rear of the house. This, to everyone's relief, remained image-free. But on the floor of the old kitchen the pictures became more numerous by the day. As word spread crowds of visitors arrived at the cottage, demanding to see the sinister display.

The house eventually became one of the most celebrated addresses on Earth, attracting TV news crews, photographers and scientists of numerous disciplines. Kodak, in conjunction with Freiburg University, analyzed photographs taken at the site and found them to be a genuine, unaltered record of the shifting twisting images that were appearing constantly on the kitchen floor. Particularly disturbing to television audiences were those faces whose expressions drastically changed as the film rolled.

The tourist frenzy gave no pleasure to the Spanish government. Authorities felt that the Belmez incident had got out of hand – and was reflecting badly on modern Spain by presenting her as a superstitious and primitive society. Officials quietly invited scientific debunkers to visit the house and to provide "rational" explanations for the phenomena. The skeptics produced theories aplenty. The most popular was that the faces were an elaborate hoax, created by a local artist who (with the family's collusion) slipped into the kitchen at night to paint images on the floor.

The villagers reacted angrily to this suggestion. A local councilor, Jose Garcia, retorted, "I know the family well. They would not be capable of such deception." A photographic researcher, Dr Antonio Arjona, concluded, "Trickery appears unlikely. The impressions are deep, unlike those surface representations which would be produced by a paintbrush. In addition the images are expressive and closely related to each other. To produce such a fraud it would be essential to have a team of good actors and even better artists. Also those artists would require access to the kitchen not only at night, but during the day, to produce the constantly changing pictures."

Convinced that the images were a hoax nonetheless, the government placed a 24-hour guard on the cottage, to prevent any rogue artist getting in. This measure's effect was opposite to what had been intended. Every morning new faces were found on the floor.

At the local governor's request two prominent parapsychologists, Professor German de Argumosa and Professor Hans Bender, traveled to Belmez.

The two men conducted a rigorous scientific experiment. Watched by journalists and fellow scientists and filmed by television crews they divided the kitchen floor into numbered sections, photographed each section, then covered it with a canvas sheet. Finally, in the presence of a notary, they sealed the kitchen's windows with wax. The 24-hour guard resumed.

Three months later the professors recalled witnesses, the notary and the TV crews, unsealed the kitchen and removed the canvas sheets.

The result: the faces on the floor had moved and changed expression. Many new faces and symbols had appeared.

Meticulously the researchers now tested the muralled concrete itself. They found:

- No trace of dye or paint.

- No evidence of X-rays.

- No chemical or organic traces.

- No radioactivity.

Nowhere could they find any indication of how, or through what process, the teeming facescapes had been created. Professor Bender said, "This is without doubt the most important paranormal phenomenon of this century."

Colleagues of Bender subsequently spent several weeks assessing Maria Pereira's relationship to the images. They noted that the faces seemed often to respond to her moods, mirroring the emotions that played across her features. During her absence for a month in hospital the floor mural – although continuing to change its outlines – became muddy, the colors leaching away. The investigators concluded that Maria Pereira was unconsciously psychic, "both influencing and being influenced by" whatever was creating the pictures in her kitchen.

When Juan Pereira died the cement floor darkened, almost obscuring the images swarming there. Several months after Juan was buried, his face, to his widow's distress, appeared on the cement floor.

For more than three decades scores of scientific investigators have traveled to the Pereiras' cottage hoping to find an explanation for the enigma in its kitchen. All have failed. The Belmez faces are as deep a mystery today as they were in 1971.

Monks Stare into Welsh Farmhouse

IN JANUARY 1999 religious words and pictures began to appear on the sittingroom walls of 400-year-old Pennyffordd farmhouse in northern Wales.

At first the new owners, the Gower family, were confident there was a logical explanation. The walls are carved from old Welsh stone and covered with white plaster. The family assumed that workmen had written and drawn on the stone years before – and that the brown pigment was now slowly seeping through.

This theory was scotched when additional words, crosses and monk-like shapes began to appear in stains on the stone fireplace. As had happened at Belmez 28 years earlier, TV news crews descended on the cottage – whereupon events took an increasingly strange turn.

The first word in the plaster had been TANGNEFEDD: a Welsh peace blessing. It was followed by Welsh expressions for love, joy and hope.

But the next word, MYNACH (monk), noticed in April 1999, appeared in more permanent form. It had been neatly carved into the hard stone at the top of the staircase – and was chiseled close to a monk-shaped stain on the same wall.

Was Stalin Poisoned – to Prevent Nuclear War?

When Soviet dictator Joseph Stalin died of a brain hemorrhage in March 1953 Russia's newspapers mourned the passing of a great leader. Eulogists described Stalin as a genius, the savior of the Russian people – and even as "a god." His hallowed remains were laid in Lenin's Red Square tomb – and shuffling thousands lined up to pay tearful respects. Not until 1956 did Nikita Khrushchev dare to announce that Stalin had in fact been a monster, responsible for the murder of 43 million Russians and the banishment to slavery of millions more. Understandably Khrushchev failed to mention the rest of the story. Today evidence is emerging that he and three frightened colleagues probably killed Stalin with rat poison, to save their own lives and to prevent him from starting a nuclear war with the West...

Stalin's dacha, near Moscow.
February 28 1953. 11 p.m.

THE USSR'S LEADER-FOR-LIFE was in an expansive mood. He had been greatly amused by the comedy screened for him in the Kremlin's private cinema – and now, over a lavish banquet, he was enjoying the company of the Central Committee's four most senior members: Lavrenty Beria, Georgi Malenkov, Nikita Khrushchev and Nikolai Bulganin.

As usual, Stalin dominated the conversation. The four stalwarts of his political inner circle responded occasionally, but for the most part sat smiling, nodding and sipping their drinks.

They were, however, listening with full attention. Stalin was feared among the political elite for his habit of asking sudden searching questions.

There were no brandies, liqueurs or vodka on the table. The leader had decreed that this would be an evening for Majari (a young grape wine) and quiet discourse.

Behind the diners, on either side of the long table, stood the bodyguards, black holsters unclipped for instant response. One of them, Alexei Rybin, would in later years write a memoir, *An Iron Soldier*, that included a detailed description of events on this epochal evening. Unpublished and largely unnoticed, his revelations about one of the greatest turning points in world history would molder for decades in Russia's Museum of the Revolution.

An observer without the benefit of inside knowledge might have imagined that Stalin's beaming cronies were happy and carefree on this occasion. But in cold fact they were filled with dread. Each one of these ruthless and powerful men knew that he was in mortal danger, either of summary execution or of a more protracted death in a labor camp. The four colleagues had received reliable intimations that the Leader was planning a purge of the Communist Party's Central Committee.

So deep was Khrushchev's disquiet that he had dared to risk denunciation by consulting with his colleagues. To his relief Beria, Malenkov and Bulganin all admitted that they shared his misgivings. Stalin's mind, the four agreed, had snapped. He was now a danger not only to the politicians around him, but to the entire Russian population and the world beyond. Lately he had been privately making it clear that he wanted to provoke a nuclear conflict with the United States. Russia, impoverished and weak, could never hope to win such a war – if, indeed, anyone could win it.

Stalin must not be allowed to take the first insane step toward Armageddon.

He must die. And the fatal blow must be struck tonight.

Rybin in his memoir recalls that the distinguished visitors remained at the table until 4 a.m. After they left, Stalin went to bed.

Ivan Khrustalev, a recently appointed guard, accompanied the dictator to his rooms and closed the door behind them. Later he summoned his colleagues. "Well, fellows," he said, "this is the first time ever – but the master [Stalin] has told me he won't need us tonight. He says we should all go to bed."

To the weary security men this was astonishing news. Stalin, ever paranoid about shadowy enemies who might strike at any moment, had always insisted on 24-hour surveillance. His guards were under strict orders not only to watch him, but to spy on each other. However, knowing how dangerous it could be to disobey any order the mercurial master might give, the guards repaired dutifully and gratefully to their lodge.

At 10 the following morning they gathered in the kitchen to plan the day's activities. Surprisingly the new man, Khrustalev, had gone home. The chef was standing by as usual to serve breakfast the moment the master appeared. But by 11 a.m. there was still no sign of him. As midday passed – and then 1, 2 and 3 p.m. – the guards grew worried. But none dared disturb Stalin. The penalty for waking him unnecessarily from sleep could be severe.

At 6.30 that evening one of the grounds security staff rang to say a light had gone on in the leader's small private diningroom. The deputy commandant Pavel Lozgachev said, "Thank God! Everything's all right." For long hours more, the light continued to burn – but Stalin still did not appear. The timorous guards took no action.

At 10 p.m. a messenger delivered a parcel from the Central Committee. Knowing they could be punished if they failed to pass on mail promptly the men argued among themselves over who should take it in. Pavel Lozgachev lost the debate.

Forty-four years later, in the June 1997 edition of the Russian magazine *Sputnik*, he described what happened next:

"I said, 'All right, then – wish me luck, boys,' and headed off to the Master's quarters. Normally we would go in there making some noise.

He didn't like it if you came in quietly. You had to walk in with confidence,
sure of yourself, but not stand too much to attention. Or else he'd tell
you off for imitating the Good Soldier Schweik.

"I opened the door and tramped loudly down the corridor. Then I
looked into the small diningroom and saw the Master lying on the floor,
his right hand outstretched. I froze. My arms and legs refused to obey me.
I asked, 'Comrade Stalin, what's wrong?' I saw that he'd wet himself. I
said to him, 'Should I call a doctor?' And in reply he just mumbled, 'Dz…
Dz…' incoherently."

Lozgachev noticed lying on the floor a copy of *Pravda* and a pocket watch
which had stopped at 6.30. On the table stood an unopened bottle of mineral
water. He assumed that Stalin must have walked from the bedroom to get
it, switching on the light before he collapsed.

In his book *Stalin* the Russian historian Edvard Radzinsky reproduces
witnesses' accounts of the confusion that followed. Lozgachev, terrified that
he might make a wrong move, telephoned his immediate superior, dacha
commandant Sharostin, who was on two days leave. Sharostin rushed to
the dacha, inspected the snoring dictator and recommended that he be lifted
onto the sofa, where he might be more comfortable. Then he rang KGB
headquarters. The senior official who took the call panicked and refused
to accept any responsibility. He passed the buck by ordering Sharostin to
ring Malenkov and Beria, two of Stalin's guests of the previous night. They
would know what to do.

Sharostin called Beria, whose sole contribution to the emergency was to
say, "Don't tell anyone Comrade Stalin is ill."

Hours passed. No one came to see the dying leader. Still snoring, his
urine dripping from the sofa onto the carpet, Stalin lay surrounded by his
nervous guards.

In his *Memoirs* Nikita Khrushchev tells a very different – and patently
self-serving – tale:

"Suddenly Malenkov phoned. 'Look, the security boys have rung from
Stalin's place. They are very worried. Something has happened to Stalin.
I've already called Beria and Bulganin. You go straight there. I'm coming
and they'll be along shortly."

"I immediately ordered my car. When I got there I first dropped in at the guardhouse and asked, 'What's happening?' They explained, 'Usually by this time (11 in the evening) Stalin has phoned us, ordered tea – but not this time.'"

Khruschev claims that he and his colleagues then hurried straight to the dacha. Remarkably he continues:

"When the guards told us something untoward had happened and that he was now asleep, we decided it would be a mistake to go in while he was in such an unseemly state. So we all went back home."

For 13 hours Joseph Stalin, supreme leader of the Union of Soviet Socialist Republics, lay in his own waste without medical help. Finally – and only after the desperate guards had telephoned him again – Khrushchev ordered 10 doctors to the dacha. But, as the guard Rybin recalls, they were too frightened to take decisive action. The practitioners simply milled uselessly around the snoring dictator, taking blood pressure, asking each other for prognoses and hoping that someone else might have the courage to act. Jumpiest of all was the dentist attached to the group. Hands trembling, he removed the patient's plates then accidentally dropped them to the floor.

One doctor asked, "Shouldn't Vinogradov [Stalin's personal physician] be here?" Deputy commandant Lozgachev took the man aside and whispered, "That would be impossible. He was arrested last week." This was a time at which numerous medical specialists were being imprisoned for imagined plots against the regime.

When it became officially apparent that the doctors were achieving nothing of value the Soviet Academy of Sciences convened an emergency meeting. It voted to rush several of the nation's most distinguished specialists to Stalin's side.

They arrived accompanied by an iron lung machine. But it was never used. As Stalin's daughter Svetlana subsequently revealed, "That huge contraption just stood there idle while the specialists stared about wildly."

In 1972 an academy member, Professor D. Myasnikov, looked back at the scene:

"Malenkov hurried in. He was sweating. He told us we must do all we could to prolong the patient's life. We all understood that time was needed

to get the new government together and prepare public opinion.

"Stalin sometimes groaned. At one point, briefly, his conscious gaze seemed to go around the faces by the bed. Then Voroshilov (a member of the Central Committee Presidium) said, 'Comrade Stalin, we, all your true friends and colleagues, are here. How are you feeling, dear friend?' But already Stalin's eyes were devoid of expression. We spent all the day injecting him and writing press releases. Politburo members walked up to the dying man. The lower ranks just looked through the door. I remember that Khrushchev was also by the door…"

At 9.50 p.m. the mass-murderer whose barbarism had rivaled Hitler's sighed gutturally and died. In Russia and beyond, millions mourned. Legions of comfortable Western academics wrote essays, articles and books lauding Stalin and the great good he had done for humankind. In bleak Siberian gulags and in the torture cells of the Lubiyanka even greater legions of victims allowed themselves to hope that their nightmare might soon end.

What really happened to Stalin? Did he (as officially promulgated) die as the result of a stroke – or was he killed?

Unless an autopsy is performed on his embalmed corpse the truth will never be known. But an increasing number of Russian and Western historians lean to the view that Stalin was poisoned. The consensus among these scholars is that the new guard Khrustalev (who sent his colleagues to bed after the banquet) was the likely assassin. Acting on orders from his master, KGB chief Lavrenty Beria, the guard is thought to have injected the sleeping dictator with the blood-thinning rat poison warfarin, a compound which can cause strokes and hemorrhages in humans.

According to Professor Jonathan Brent of Yale's Russian History department "the circumstantial evidence is overwhelmingly in favor of non-fortuitous death. And to support this further we now have solid evidence… of a coverup at the highest level."

In his book *Stalin's Last Crime* Professor Brent says Malenkov, Beria, Khrushchev and Bulganin would have been powerfully motivated to plot the death of their leader. Stalin had provided ample evidence that he was planning a second Great Terror in which he would kill hundreds of his colleagues, along with tens of millions of other Russians. But worst of all Stalin had become dangerous enough to destroy the entire world.

"It wasn't simply that (the four plotters) were afraid for their own lives, and they were," says Brent, "but it was the fear of a nuclear holocaust that drove them."

A motivating force behind Stalin's ambition to destroy the West was his violent anti-Semitism. In 1947, only two years after the closure of Hitler's death camps, the Soviet leader had launched a vicious campaign against Russia's Jews, having them dismissed from university positions, humiliated, arrested and executed. By 1953 the policy was careering out of control. Documents released after the USSR's collapse show that Stalin was spending hundreds of millions of roubles on equipment for new Siberian punishment camps in the Arctic north, Kazakhstan and Siberia. Into these sub-zero prisons the entire Jewish population, in company with other purported dissidents, would be herded. Relics of these mass jails, whose construction was abandoned after Stalin died, survive today. In Siberia and Kazakhstan, locals still point out the remains of the flimsy wooden huts in which hundreds of thousands of Jews were meant to live, and prematurely die.

Day by day the USSR's captive press promoted policies of hatred. Under the headline SIMPLETONS AND SCOUNDRELS *Pravda* (February 8 1953) listed the names of "scoundrels" (Jews) to whom wrong-headed Russians ("simpletons") were giving employment. The article unleashed anti-Semitic hysteria. As on Nazi Germany's *Kristallnacht*, Jews were attacked on the streets and their shops smashed.

But Stalin was pursuing an even more sinister agenda. He launched a new propaganda campaign designed to convince the Soviet people and world opinion that *Jewish doctors, secretly backed by America, were conspiring to destroy the USSR by killing its leaders.*

An early victim of the so-called "Jewish doctors' plot" was alleged to have been the senior Politburo member Andrei Zhdanov, who had died in 1948. The death had not been natural, Stalin insisted. Zhdanov's deliberately negligent Jewish specialists had killed him. To emphasize the magnitude of the danger facing the Soviet State Stalin then announced that even his own personal physician – the long-serving and seemingly trustworthy Vinogradov – was involved in the conspiracy. The hapless doctor was arrested, sentenced and sent to a labor camp.

The Soviet public was scandalized. Rumors, deliberately spread, described how Jewish doctors were killing newborn Russian infants and injecting toddlers with diphtheria.

The purported doctors' plot caused outrage in the West. Patently it was no more than an excuse for a second Holocaust. Diplomats tried desperately to persuade Stalin to reconsider his headlong policy – but he was adamant that the first in a series of physicians' trials, scheduled to begin on March 15 1953, would go ahead.

Stalin died 10 days before the proceedings were scheduled. The Soviet government immediately dismissed all charges against the doctors. In the years that followed, people who had known Stalin came forward to say that he had hoped, by murdering hordes of Jewish physicians, to begin a nationwide pogrom that would provoke America to declare war on Russia. "Using atomic weapons this is a war we can win," he told confidantes. "Europe will fall to us – but only if we act now."

In his book *Stalin* Edvard Radzinsky records a conversation with the dacha guard Pavel Lozkachev.

"About a week before his death, Stalin mentioned the Jewish doctors' trial, which was due to start in a few weeks, then asked, 'Will America attack us?' I replied that they wouldn't dare. This made him angry. Later on he walked up to me and said, 'They will attack us.'

"I could see very clearly that he wanted that to happen."

Such testimonies suggest that when Joseph Stalin died, either from natural causes or from the ravages of poison, he had been on the brink of fomenting the greatest disaster in the history of the world.

Australian Magazine Foretold Reagan Shooting 3 Months Ahead:
The Puzzle of Precognition

The near-fatal gunning down of President Ronald Reagan in March 1981 was predicted in an Australian magazine – 12 weeks before it happened. In a detailed article a young astrologer correctly foresaw the bodily organ in which the bullet would lodge (the lung) and accurately stated that the president "would survive the assassination attempt". This uncannily accurate foray into unvisited time made international headlines. But it was by no means the only prediction, committed to print, that has come true months and sometimes years after publication. Forecasts of this kind, preserved in books, newspapers and on film, offer puzzling but arguably powerful proof that some people (sometimes) seem able to catch glimpses of the future...

ON JANUARY 7 1981 the *Sydney Morning Herald*'s magazine *People* published an article headed PRESIDENT REAGAN WILL BE GUNNED DOWN, SAYS ASTROLOGER. The story began:

"During a strife-torn term in office, President Reagan may be struck down by a sniper's bullet. But it's likely that he will survive the assassination attempt – and, despite serious lung trouble, go on to complete his allotted span in the White House.

"These predictions were made by Melbourne astrologer Gary Wiseman...

"Wiseman believes that the Reagan chart contains mixed omens for America and the world. The good news is that Reagan will create a strong stable image for his nation overseas..."

The article was quickly forgotten. But three months later it became a news story, transmitted around the world.

On March 30 1981 President Reagan gave a speech to the Building and Construction Trades Conference at the Washington Hilton Hotel. As he was returning to his motorcade a crazed loner, John Hinckley, shot at him and his aides with a .22 caliber handgun. Hinckley hoped by this action to impress a woman he was currently stalking – the movie actress Jodie Foster.

Secret Service agent Jerry Parr shoved the president into the limousine and told its driver to head for the White House. When he realized the president had been shot he ordered the driver to divert to George Washington Hospital.

President Reagan underwent surgery to have a bullet removed from his left lung. He was full of praise for the three men wounded while trying to protect him: Secret Service agent Tim McCarthy, policeman Tom Delahanty and press secretary James Brady.

Probably the president knew nothing about the efforts of someone else, on a distant continent, who also had tried hard to help. Gary Wiseman, a 31-year-old former schoolteacher, was so continuingly disturbed by what he "saw and felt" in the astrological charts he was studying that one week before the shooting he repeated his warning in a circular letter to major Australian newspapers. None took it seriously. The letter read, in part:

Ronald Reagan has several ominous signs in his birth chart and some extremely dicey planetary influences. Vulnerable areas are the lung and head. There will be at least one assassination attempt on him...

In a subsequent interview with the magazine (April 15 1981 edition) Gary Wiseman made a further forecast which also would be proved stunningly accurate. *"I get a strong impression of war brewing up in Lebanon," he said. "There will be a conflict lasting 16 days that will be described in the press as 'The Siege of Beirut.'"*

Israel's Beirut siege (lasting 80 days, not 16) began in June 1982 – 14 months after Wiseman's published prediction.

Skeptics who flatly assert that precognition is impossible have difficulty explaining away cases of this kind. Detailed premonitions trapped in the amber of newsprint are hard to argue with when their forecasts come true.

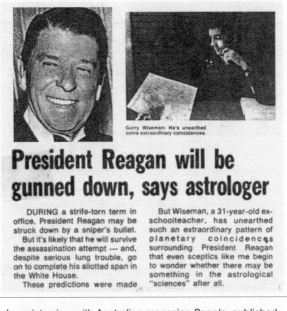

Garry Wiseman: He's unearthed some extraordinary coincidences.

President Reagan will be gunned down, says astrologer

DURING a strife-torn term in office, President Reagan may be struck down by a sniper's bullet. But it's likely that he will survive the assassination attempt — and, despite serious lung trouble, go on to complete his allotted span in the White House.

These predictions were made

But Wiseman, a 31-year-old ex-schoolteacher, has unearthed such an extraordinary pattern of planetary coincidences surrounding President Reagan that even sceptics like me begin to wonder whether there may be something in the astrological "sciences" after all.

In an interview with Australian magazine *People*, published January 7 1981, astrologer Gary Wiseman predicted that President Reagan would be struck by a sniper's bullet and would suffer "serious lung trouble" thereafter. Three months later, on March 30 1981, the President was shot. The bullet entered a lung.

Gary Wiseman later noted that he had based his Reagan and Beirut statements on "more than simple astrology". He said, "While I was reading the charts I became aware of an *overlay* – a kind of picture that floated just above the page, showing me what would happen." He insisted that he had never regarded himself as being clairvoyant. But he had come to believe that in some inexplicable fashion his concentration on the charts had triggered perceptions of future events.

An American, Joseph de Louise, experienced a similar "triggering effect." On December 29 1967 this self-styled "amateur psychic" predicted in Chicago's *Sun-Times* that Edward Kennedy's career would be damaged by a drowning accident. In part he wrote: *"I see tragedy involving water around Ted Kennedy."* Eighteen months later (June 25 1969) Mary Jo Kopechne died after Senator Kennedy's car plunged from a bridge at Chappaquiddick.

Asked, after the event, how he had received this information so far in advance de Louise said, "It happened while a photographer was taking shots of me. He asked me to look into a prop crystal ball – and I agreed, regarding it as a joke. But when I looked into the glass I was shaken to see a newspaper headline containing the name TED KENNEDY – and the word DROWNS. This was followed by an image of a young woman with her hair streaming in the water. It left me in no doubt that a woman associated with Senator Kennedy would die in a river or lake."

The Sicilian-born Joseph de Louise had begun his working life as a Chicago hairdresser. Customers began to gossip about the accurate personal predictions he was wont to make while blow-drying and styling. In November 1967 a radio station invited him to go to air with some predictions. In his first appearance de Louise warned that a "sizable bridge" would collapse somewhere in the United States within three weeks, causing many deaths.

On December 15 West Virginia's Silver Bridge gave way at rush hour, killing 93 people.

In February 1969 de Louise warned that a jetliner would crash southwest of Chicago. "I see the number 330 – but I'm not sure if that's the time or the flight number," he wrote. On September 9 a passenger jet collided with a trainer plane 174 miles south of Chicago, killing 89 passengers. The accident happened at 3.30 p.m.

The ability to foresee disasters of this kind is not of course confined to people who identify themselves as clairvoyants. The files of university parapsychology departments contain innumerable cases of pre-reported dreams and waking visions whose content has been validated by subsequent events.

The profound mystery lies in *how* such visions of the future can possibly have occurred. Theorists offer a wealth of possible answers. One popular explanation invokes Einstein who said that time, like space, is curved. When we experience precognition we can perhaps be likened to fish in a bowl, seeing reflections from the curving glass in front of our noses.

Some parapsychologists believe that the simultaneous impact of globally reported events on the minds of billions of people may somehow create an "Odic Force" which somehow reverberates backward in time – creating precognitive dreams, hunches and waking visions. The reverberations may also enter the subconscious minds of writers, prompting them to create books or stories which unconsciously mirror future happenings.

Quantum physicists would of course argue with the notion that information can move "backward" in time. Particle experiments have repeatedly demonstrated that *effects* can be viewed before *causes*.

Next to Jules Verne one of the most consistently prescient writers in the English language was a former merchant seaman Morgan Robertson (1861-1915). In the year before his death Robertson published a book *Beyond the Spectrum* which describes a war between the United States and Japan. In the narrative, hostilities break out in **December**, when the Japanese launch a sneak attack on an American naval base in Hawaii. In real life, 27 years after the book appeared, Japanese planes bombed Hawaii's Pearl Harbor, triggering America's entry into World War II. The date of this attack was **December** 7, 1941. In Robertson's 1914 story the Americans strike their opponents with sun-powered weapons which kill in a blinding flash: a possible precognitive reference to the atomic bomb.

In magazine articles Morgan Robertson several times described himself as a "semi-automatic" author. He was convinced that whenever he sat down to write, someone else took over. The novel that earned him his greatest fame was *Futility*, published in 1898 by M.F. Mansfield and Company. This purported work of fiction describes in quite breathtaking detail the fate of the *Titanic* – as yet unbuilt and unconceived – which would sink with enormous loss of life 14 years after the book was published.

Robertson's fictional liner, the *Titan* (launched 1898) and the real-life *Titanic* (launched 1912) share similarities which seemingly exceed all credible bounds of coincidence.

- Both vessels were British.

- Both were described as "unsinkable."

- Robertson called his liner "the largest craft afloat and the greatest of the works of men." The *Titanic* was the largest craft afloat.

- Top speed of both ships was 24 knots.

- *Titan* was 800 feet long; the *Titanic* 882 feet.

- Both the imagined ship and the real ship had three propellers.

- *Titan* had 24 lifeboats; the *Titanic* 20. Lifeboat capacity on both vessels was described (after their respective sinkings) as inadequate.

- *Titan* carried 2,000 passengers; the *Titanic* 2,200.

- *Titan* sank on a mid-April night after grazing an iceberg in the Atlantic. The *Titanic* sank on the night of April 14 1912 after grazing an iceberg, also in the Atlantic.

- The damage to both ships was at starboard side forward.

Morgan Robertson was not alone in foreseeing the sinking. On April 7 1912 an American writer, Mayne Garnett, published a short story, "The White Ghost of Disaster", in New York's *Popular Magazine*. The story described a gigantic passenger liner with too few lifeboats striking an Atlantic iceberg. As would happen in subsequent reality a nearby ship failed to respond to the stricken liner's distress rockets. In a subsequent interview with the magazine Garnett revealed that he had based his story on a vivid dream he had experienced while traveling on the *Titanic*'s sister ship *Olympic*.

The British author W.T. Stead, who had dreamed for many years that he would die in icy water, produced two fictional works that prefigured the *Titanic* disaster. The first – a short story published in 1886 in the *Pall Mall Gazette* – centered on a liner which sank in the Atlantic. As would occur with the *Titanic* 26 years later there were too few lifeboats and many passengers died. In 1892 Stead revisited his dark obsession in a novel *From the Old World to the New* – describing an immense liner which struck an Atlantic iceberg and sank. A nearby vessel, the *Majestic*, rushed too late to the rescue. Captain of the fictional *Majestic* was E.J. Smith. Two decades later a real-life E.J. Smith became captain of the *Titanic*.

In March 1912 President William Taft invited Stead to speak at an international peace conference – sending him a free ticket aboard the *Titanic*. Stead overcame his fear of water and accepted. He was one of the 1,517 who drowned.

Robert Jahn, Dean of Princeton University's School of Engineering and Applied Science, was so intrigued by premonitions and what they might reveal about the nature of consciousness that in 1979 he founded a scientific organisation to study them. The PEAR laboratory (Princeton Engineering Anomalies Research) conducted numerous rigorously controlled tests to ascertain the reality or otherwise of precognition. The PEAR scientists call their work "remote perception". Experiments – involving prediction of target sites *before* they were thrown up by random number generators – have shown probabilities against chance ranging from one million to one through to one trillion to one. PEAR's view is that "scientific research has shown that information about the future can be shared with the present."

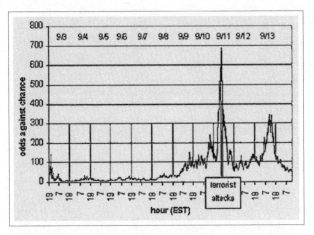

On September 11 2001, random number-generators positioned around the planet began to feed extraordinary waves of data into a Princeton University server. The machines, supposedly driven only by chance, drove the graph to an unprecedented peak of 700. Had these robots somehow registered the horror felt by millions at the World Trade Center's destruction? Graph courtesy PEAR (Princeton Engineering Anomalies Research).

To discover whether humanity's combined consciousness can be measured PEAR installed 34 random number generators around the world. The group wanted to see whether data from these machines (which they call EGGs) could be affected in any way by the reactions of the human race to major global events. In September 2001 the researchers received a profoundly significant answer.

On 9/11 the EGGs – purportedly robotic and driven only by chance – suddenly began to feed an extraordinary stream of data into the dedicated server in Princeton, New Jersey. The graph, as the above figure demonstrates, rose to an unprecedented peak on that terrible day in world history. Normally the graph registered between 0 and 100. But it leapt to 700 on the day terrorists struck America. In a fashion the scientists do not pretend to understand, the random number generators appeared somehow to have registered the empathy and grief of millions.

"One way to think of these startling correlations," wrote coordinator Roger Nelson, "is to accept the possibility that the instruments have captured the reactions of a global consciousness beginning to form. The network was built to do just that – to see whether we could gather evidence of a communal shared mind in which we are participants, even if we don't know it… Perhaps the best image is of an infant slowly developing awareness."

As with other great humanitarian crises the horror of the terrorists' actions was foreseen – in one case by TV scriptwriters who imagined they were creating fiction. A scene in the series pilot of *The Lone Gunmen* (televised early 2001) depicts a hijacked jetliner flying toward New York. It contains this exchange:

HIJACKER 1: Your flight's going to make an unscheduled stop.

HIJACKER 2: Corner of Liberty and Washington, Lower Manhattan.

PRISONER (turning to his father): World Trade Center. They're going to crash it into the World Trade Center.

The tragedy of 9/11 had been signaled in words, paintings and on videotape long before the atrocities occurred. In June 2001 a 30-year-old Lancashire psychic appeared on the BBC's *Kilroy* program to describe a distressing nightmare she had had about an attack on America. Valerie Clarke told host Robert Kilroy Silk:

I had this dream a while ago and I thought it was a bombing at the World Trade Center. In my dream I was at the World Trade Center wandering the streets. I was in some sort of barricade when the building blew up. At the same time this plane went down behind it. In my dream I wasn't sure if the plane had gone into the building.

Following the terrorist attacks the BBC interviewed the young mother again. She said:

"That dream haunted me for a long time. When I finally saw the destruction of the Twin Towers on television it gave me a sick feeling in my stomach. But it wasn't a shock. I'd been expecting it."

After the terrorists struck, several record distributors were forced to remove compact discs from the market. Their cover art (prepared long before 9/11) bore too graphic a resemblance to actual events.

The Dream Theater group's CD *Live Scenes from New York* had been scheduled for release on September 11 2001. It was withdrawn. The cover depicted New York (including the Twin Towers) ablaze. Mike Portnoy, the band's leader, said, "I can only say it's a horrible coincidence that we obviously could never have foreseen. The timing of the release of the CD happening on the very same day as this tragedy is merely an incredible coincidence."

Newspapers reported that the Californian rock group The Coup had also planned a September 2001 release for its album *Party Music*. The cover, printed the previous June, pictured the musicians in the foreground with a blazing Trade Center, smoke billowing into the blue sky behind them. New artwork was hastily substituted. Another album, *Time to Explode*, performed by the Inner City Hustlers, had been released in July 2001. On its cover were burning buildings resembling the Twin Towers.

Also removed from public view was a downloadable video game, *Trade Center Defender*, in which the player was invited to shoot down jets which hijackers were trying to crash into the Twin Towers. If the player failed the towers collapsed in flames.

"Clairvoyant" Churchill

WINSTON CHURCHILL was renowned for flashes of foreknowledge which saved his associates' lives on several occasions during World War II.

In 1941 the great British leader gave a dinner for four of his ministers at 10 Downing Street. As the soup course was being served he abruptly rose from the table and hurried to the kitchen, where a butler, a cook and a maid were working. He ordered the three to go to the air raid shelter, immediately. The bewildered workers did as they were told.

Soon after Churchill had resumed his seat an air raid warning sounded. The first bomb exploded at the rear of 10 Downing Street, demolishing the kitchen. When the all-clear sounded the kitchen staff thanked Churchill for saving their lives. Reportedly the butler asked, "But how did you know the bomb would fall on the kitchen, sir?"

"Just an instinct," Churchill replied.

Later that year, after inspecting a gun crew in action, the prime minister returned to his staff car. The driver opened the door on the side where Churchill customarily sat – and was surprised when he swept past and opened the door on the other side.

Minutes later, as the car sped through the darkened streets of blitzed London, a massive blast from an unexploded bomb shattered the window beside Churchill's usual seat, tearing a hole in the fabric. If he had been sitting in his customary place he would undoubtedly have been killed, opening the way for Britain's powerful appeasement lobby to make peace with Hitler.

Lunar Visions 1865, 1870

When the French company J. Hetzel published Jules Verne's novels *From the Earth to the Moon* and *Around the Moon* few readers regarded them as anything more than entertainments – albeit inspirational ones. Not until 100 years after the second book's publication did observers realize that these yellowing, dusty volumes had held an extraordinary mirror to future events.

In the first of the novels, set in the United States at the end of the Civil War, a band of gun enthusiasts decide to fire a cannonball at the moon. Michel Ardan, the most daring member of the group, has a better idea. He proposes that they design a vehicle in which men – himself included – will travel through space. And here the uncanny confluence between Verne's text and subsequent reality begins:

Jules Verne's Moonship, pictured in the French first edition
of his novel *From the Earth to the Moon* (1865.) The book
contains numerous uncanny glimpses of the future – including
the surnames of Verne's lunar voyagers, which pre-echo the
names of NASA astronauts aboard *Apollos 11* and *8*.

- In the novels and in real life the United States was the first nation to send men to the moon.

- To test their prototype ship Verne's would-be space voyagers launch it with a cat and squirrel aboard – retrieving it from the ocean when the flight is over. One century later, NASA's experimenters launched monkeys into space – also recovering their capsule from the sea.

- Verne's frock-coated enthusiasts considered 12 possible launch sites, finally choosing Florida over Texas. Their site was close to what would become the Kennedy Space Center. NASA's moon-team weighed up seven sites – then, like their fictional predecessors, rejected Texas for Florida.

- The Verne craft's shape and size closely resembled that of *Apollo II*. Like *Apollos 8* and *II* it was built from aluminum.

- Verne's ship used retro-rockets, as did the *Apollo* spacecraft.

- Verne's ship was launched in December and was recovered from the ocean by a US Navy vessel. *Apollo 8* was launched in December 100 years later and was retrieved from the sea by a US Navy ship.

- The cannon used to launch the Verne capsule was named *Columbiad*. *Apollo II*'s command module was *Columbia*.

- Both the fictional and the real spacecraft were manned by three astronauts. And the name confluences continue. Verne's voyagers were **Ardan**, **Barbicane** and **Nicholl**. *Apollo 8*'s crew were **Anders**, **Borman** and **Lovell**. *Apollo II*'s crew comprised **Aldrin**, **Armstrong** and **Collins**. With one letter substituted and one added, Ardan becomes an anagram of Anders. Nicholl, with an S substituted for H, becomes an anagram of Collins.

Verne's voyagers shiver and stamp as their flimsy moonship
penetrates the cold deeps of space. Illustration from 1872 English
edition of *From the Earth to the Moon*.

The Telephonoscope (1869): a prediction of widescreen cable TV by prescient French author-illustrator Albert Robida, a contemporary of Verne.

- Verne's fictional astronomers set up a telescope to watch the moon journey unfold. NASA used a telescope at Johnson Space Center to track its astronauts. When an explosion rocked *Apollo 13*, 200,000 miles from Earth, the Johnson telescope registered the near-disaster.

- *Apollo 13*'s escape velocity was 24,000 m.p.h. Jules Verne's ship escaped Earth's gravity at 25,000 m.p.h.

- Verne's craft reached the moon in 97 hours 13 minutes. *Apollo* took 97 hours 39 minutes.

-· Verne's pipe-smoking, champagne-quaffing lunar travelers followed a flight plan prepared in Cambridge, England. NASA's astronauts flew to a plan prepared in Cambridge, USA.

- Both the fictional and real-life spaceships carried compressed food.

- Verne's ship lost oxygen, froze up and was unable to land. After an explosion *Apollo 13* also leaked oxygen, prompting Mission Control to call the landing off.

- Both Verne's and NASA's travelers used a slingshot technique to fling themselves back to Earth.

A comparably prescient contemporary of Verne was the French author and illustrator Albert Robida. Decades – and sometimes generations – before they were invented this nineteenth century visionary illustrated his novels with graphic depictions of widescreen TV sets, computers, sophisticated warplanes and cities strangled by pollution.

Robida's warnings about the sinister potential of scientific progress were published in an era when other authors were lauding technology as the savior of humankind. In a pictorial novel, *The War of the Twentieth Century*, he produced the first modern vision of technological warfare ever published. The book predicted the havoc that would be created by missile-armed submarines, tanks and the yet-to-be-invented airplane, laden with bombs. The novel also forecast military use of chemical and bacteriological weapons.

Robida also predicted, alone among his contemporaries, that industry in the twentieth century would chemically pollute earth, water and crops, threatening the survival of life on Earth. In the novel *La Vie Electrique* he drew distressing pictures of industrial waste, belching from futuristic factories, killing wildlife and poisoning the atmosphere and water. A character complains, "Our air is dirty and rank... our rivers carry purees of the most deadly bacilli... our streams swarm with pathogenic ferments."

Readers enjoyed these action-crammed books, but took none of their gloomy prognostications seriously. Robida fell into obscurity. Not until the late twentieth century did a small number of collectors rediscover his works and their remarkably accurate depictions of our tainted times.

Precognition is difficult to prove. But when a correct and detailed forecast, conscious or otherwise, appears in print, the task can become a little easier.

In November 1936 the astrological magazine *Oblo's Almanac* published these words: "Trouble occurs with an airship. Measures must be taken to avoid crash by lake with loss of life up to 40 souls."

On May 6 1937 the airship *Hindenburg* exploded into flames, killing 33 people. It crashed on Lakehurst New Jersey.

Herbert Greenhouse's book *Premonitions* was published in New York in 1971. One chapter, purporting to be a "History of the Future", says, "Russia and the US send a fleet of ships to Mars in 1989. *Phobos*, the Martian satellite, has disappeared, much to the bewilderment of astronomers." This was a prophecy made through a fog, as not every element was true. Nevertheless the book had accurately identified the year, 1989, in which the Russian space probe *Phobos* would vanish in mysterious circumstances above Mars.

Driven by Dreams, To Desert a Ghost Ship

A RECURRING DREAM in which a gaunt figure whispered warnings of disaster prompted a passenger to quit the Australian liner *Waratah* several days before she disappeared.

The man who deserted the doomed ship was an engineer, George Sawyer, who, with 211 other London-bound voyagers, boarded the luxurious Blue Anchor vessel in Sydney in June 1909.

An experienced traveler who had gone on 16 major voyages, Sawyer sailed aboard *Waratah* to Melbourne and Adelaide and across the Indian Ocean to Durban. But there he went to the Blue Anchor Line's office and demanded to be transferred to another ship. As the office manager subsequently confirmed, Sawyer was initially unwilling to give a reason for his request.

But when company officials accused him of creating unnecessary inconvenience, the embarrassed engineer admitted that he had based his decision on a series of dreams. Since the *Waratah* left Australia, he said, his sleep had been disturbed by visions of "what seemed to be the corpse of a man" exhorting him to get off the ship or die.

He had not previously given much thought to omens, he said – but the nightmares had been so frightening that nothing would persuade him to return to the *Waratah*.

Next day the liner left Durban without him. A week later it vanished.

The Aberfan Premonitions

Constance Milden, 47, was working in her kitchen in Plymouth, England, when she was suddenly shocked by what she would later describe as "a terrible waking dream." Her eyes were wide open. But all she could see was a vision of horror: an avalanche of coal hurtling down a steep slope. Directly in the path of the black avalanche stood a little boy. He was transfixed, seemingly unable to move – and Constance Milden was sure he would die. Beside the boy stood a young man in a peaked cap.

Constance was so shaken by this strange daydream that she related it that night to the members of her church circle. The nightmare meant little to her fellow congregationists – but the following morning it made sinister sense. At 9.15 a massive deposit of coal waste slid down a mountainside overlooking the Welsh mining village of Aberfan. It killed 144 people, among them 128 children. Most were buried alive. When Constance Milden saw the disaster on TV news she recognized the little boy, who had survived. He was talking to a young man in a peaked cap – one of the rescuers.

This precognitive vision – and press reports of other foreglimpses of the avalanche – prompted a group of Oxford University researchers to advertise for anyone who also had received intimations of the tragedy. Dr J.C. Barker, consultant psychiatrist at Shelton Hospital, Shrewsbury, issued a similar appeal. More than 400 people replied. Some claimed to have heard voices warning about Aberfan. Others described dreams, days or weeks before the coal-slide, in which they watched desperate parents, drenched by pouring rain, digging desperately into the slurry with their bare hands.

Perhaps the most moving example of prescience was described in the British weekly *News of the World*. Reverend Glannant Jones told the newspaper that a local child, 10-year-old Eryl Jones (no relation), had dreamed of her own death in the coal-slide two weeks beforehand. "She was a dependable child, not over-imaginative," the clergyman said. "A fortnight before the disaster she said to her mother, 'Mummy, I'm not afraid to die.' Her mother asked, 'Why do you think of dying and you so young?' Eryl replied, 'I shall be with my schoolmates Peter and June.'

"The day before the coal slid down the mountain Eryl told her mother she had had a dream in the night. 'I dreamed I went to school and there was no school there,' she said. 'Something black had come down all over it.'"

The coal-waste engulfed Aberfan's junior school, killing everyone inside. Eryl was buried in a communal grave – her schoolfriend June on one side and Peter on the other.

Dr Barker was so overwhelmed by the number of testimonies he received that he established the British Premonition Bureau, to which people could write describing dreams or waking visions that seemed to presage future disasters. By cross-matching the data in these reports Barker hoped he might be able to issue useful warnings before the foredreamed mishaps occurred. His idea was copied in Europe, Australia and the USA – but in every case the new premonition bureaus were rendered ineffective by lack of funds and staff.

Obsessed – by a Maniac's Sinister Shadow:
Jack the Ripper

The hideous murders committed by that most enigmatic of assassins, Jack the Ripper, have reverberated across three centuries. This sadistic killer, believed by some to have been a surgeon or a particularly skilled butcher, unleashed his rage against piteous London prostitutes in the summer and fall of 1888. Despite strenuous police efforts he was never caught. And although virtually all other criminals of his era are long forgotten the Ripper still casts a sinister shadow into the present day. Historians, retired policemen, authors and forensic experts continue to sacrifice years of their lives trying to establish who the killer was: naming diverse "culprits" ranging from a distinguished artist to Queen Victoria's grandson. But more than a century after his grisly rampage the Ripper's true identity remains unknown...

Buck's Row, Whitechapel.
August 31 1888. 4.10 a.m.

IT WAS THE FINAL morning of summer. Already an autumnal chill was in the air. Constable John Neil, trudging his beat through the narrow foul-smelling streets of East London's slums, was feeling tired. He had had a busy morning and was looking forward to the end of his shift and a hot breakfast at home beside the kitchen fire.

Suddenly he skidded, just managing to avoid a painful plunge onto the cobbles. He had stepped into something slippery. By the glow of his lantern he saw that he was standing in blood. Momentarily he imagined the ooze had spewed from one of the meat carts that plied to and from the local slaughterhouses. This had happened to him before. But then, in the half-light he saw the dark flow's origin. At the entrance to a mean courtyard lay a woman whose throat had been slashed open from ear to ear. Her blood was still slowly bubbling onto the ground.

Reflexively Constable Neil felt for a pulse. The wrist was cold. The woman's eyes were wide, staring. She was dead, all right.

Neil ran into the courtyard. Perhaps the killer was still about. But the yard was empty. He called for help. A colleague, on duty in a nearby alleyway, came running.

Twenty minutes later the body was in a morgue attached to the workhouse on Old Montague Street. Inspector Spratling of the London Metropolitan Police examined the murder victim. A bruised and possibly broken jaw suggested the assailant had punched her before cutting her throat. Morgue attendants cut away the filthy blood-soaked clothes.

Spratling gagged. The abdomen had been sawn open; internal organs removed.

White-faced and sick the inspector remarked to a reporter, "Only a madman could have done this." At the inquest the police surgeon Dr Rees-Llewellyn would tell the coroner, "I have never seen so appalling a case. She was dissected in a manner that only a person skilled in the use of a knife could have achieved. I believe that person… to have been left-handed."

London's halfpenny newspapers reacted to the crime with unfeigned horror. "No murder was ever more ferociously and more brutally done," said *The Star*, going on to describe the killer as "the Devilish Dissector."

Police quickly identified the victim as Mary Ann Nicholls, a 43-year-old mother of five children, all of whom had been snatched away by a husband who deserted her for another woman. Lonely and grindingly poor, Mary had "fallen into the grip of gin." To find pennies enough to pay night by night for her rented bed she had been forced to work as a prostitute.

Countless women, trapped in what one social reformer called "the Hell of East London", suffered privations similar to Mary's. Whitechapel and the area around it housed more than 900,000 people who were either crammed into teeming hovels, or were homeless and, in winter, at risk of freezing to death on the streets. For most, the only sources of income were either the sweatshops, in which 14-hour days were the norm, the cruel slaughterhouses whose stench hung thickly over every house, or prostitution, which (relatively) paid best.

By night "gentlemen" young and old would visit East London for sexual encounters that were cheap and quick. Many of these men carried syphilis and gonorrhea home to unsuspecting wives.

But the greatest burden of misery was endured by the East Enders themselves. Their clothes and bodies were reekingly filthy. Water was in such short supply that personal cleanliness was impossible. Babies, lying malnourished in makeshift cots, faced myriad hazards. They risked infection not only from debilitating disease but from the very water their mothers used to clean them. One of the commonest causes of death in infants was gangrene caused by rat-bite. The mortality rate across all levels of the population was so high that mortuaries were overwhelmed. Many families were forced to keep a loved one's corpse in the house until the day of the funeral. Too often it was a pauper's funeral.

Above this resounded the screams of pigs, sheep and cattle being crudely bludgeoned or knifed to death in the open slaughterhouses which dominated the slum landscape. Samuel Barnett, vicar of St Jude's Church, Whitechapel, called for these "abominable institutions" to be closed down. In a letter to a London newspaper he expressed his "concern for the moral consequences, especially to the children of the poor, of this open peep-show of cruelty to animals."

To all this squalor the man soon to be known as Jack the Ripper added an additional burden of horror.

At 6 a.m. on September 8 1888, not far from where Mary Ann Nicholls was murdered, a market porter found a second prostitute's sickeningly mutilated body. It was lying in the yard of a house at 39 Hanbury Street.

Dark-haired and blue-eyed, 47-year-old Annie Chapman was less than five feet tall. She liked to dress colorfully. The distraught porter told detectives the first he had seen of her was a pair of brightly striped socks peeping from beneath her bloodied skirt. Dark Annie, as her friends called her, had been strangled then disemboweled. Pelvic organs were stripped away; intestines draped over the right shoulder. A few pitiful possessions – a square of cloth and two combs – were arranged neatly and tauntingly at her side.

Annie, a promiscuous alcoholic, had abandoned her husband, children and cosy West London home six years earlier. When her money ran out she drifted into Whitechapel, where a bug-ridden overnight bed could be rented for two pence or less. Distressed friends told police that Annie was never a prostitute in the full meaning of that word. She had tried to earn an income by selling small bunches of flowers and embroidered handkerchiefs. Only when business was slow had she resorted to selling her body. The night before she died, said a fellow tenant, the lodging house keeper had turned Annie out into the street, telling her not to return before she had earned money enough for her night's board. Weak and coughing blood she had gone off looking for a client. Annie had suspected, said the friend, that she might be suffering from tuberculosis. The autopsy confirmed that fear.

At the inquest into Annie Chapman the coroner, Wynne E. Baxter said:

"The injuries, removing the pelvic organs with one sweep of the knife, have been made by someone who had considerable anatomical skill and knowledge. There are no meaningless cuts. It was done by one who knew where to find what he wanted, what difficulties he would have to contend against, and how he should use his knife so as to abstract the organ without injury to it. No unskilled person could have known where to find it, or have recognized it when it was found. For instance, no mere slaughterer of animals could have carried out these operations. It must have been someone accustomed to the post-mortem room… It is my opinion that the murder instrument was… a narrow thin knife with a blade between six and eight inches long… the kind of knife used by slaughtermen and surgeons for amputations."

The dual murders were considered too much for Whitechapel CID to handle.

Scotland Yard's Central Office took over the case, appointing Detective Inspectors Frederick Abberline, Henry Moore and Walter Andrews, backed by a team of subordinate officers. From the morning the second corpse was found East London was thick day and night with hundreds of policemen on the beat. They were ordered to question – and if necessary arrest – anyone at all who behaved suspiciously.

Basil Thomson, in his book *My Experiences at Scotland Yard* (1923), recalled that the Metropolitan Police had sweeping powers to solve the murders. They could – and did – investigate "every pawnshop, every laundry, every public house and even every lodging house in a huge area of the city." Police distributed 80,000 handbills, conducted unannounced house-to-house searches and questioned hundreds of sailors, British and foreign. Acting on tip-offs from the public, police arrested and questioned 76 butchers and slaughterers – all to no avail.

According to a widespread rumor, the Ripper was a policeman himself. Surely only a member of the constabulary could possibly have committed the crimes undetected. Another popular theory, promulgated by the nascent tabloids, was that the Ripper was a distinguished surgeon who had caught syphilis from a prostitute. Rendered insane by the disease he was now visiting a terrible revenge on every whore he could find. Doctors quickly learned never to carry their black bags openly through the East End. It was a sure way to invite violence.

At the time of the killings the theatrical version of Robert Louis Stevenson's *Dr Jekyll and Mr Hyde* was enjoying great success in the West End. This story of a gentle physician by day who became a murderous monster at night did nothing to abate the public's newfound suspicion of surgeons. A letter-writer to the *Times* urged that the play be closed down until the killer was caught.

Annie Chapman's murder was followed by three weeks of peace. Unnerved Londoners allowed themselves to speculate that the maniac might have suicided or fled.

But he had not finished yet. At one o'clock on the foggy morning of September 30 Louis Diemschutz, a caretaker at the Men's Educational Club, drove his ponycart into the yard behind his employers' Whitechapel premises. He noticed "what looked like a large bundle of rags lying against a wall." By the light of a match he saw that it was a woman, soaked in blood.

Diemschutz screamed for help. Constable William Smith ran to the yard from his beat nearby. He shone his lantern on the woman. Her throat had been cut. The body was still warm: an indication that the killer might be close by. Smith alerted colleagues, but the murderer had escaped.

The victim was 45-year-old Elizabeth Stride – also known as "Long Liz." As her nickname suggested she was considerably taller than most Londoners of the era. Scotland Yard detectives established that she was of Swedish descent and had been married to an Englishman, John Stride, who died in 1884. Elizabeth had then followed a familiar downward path. She was frequently jailed for drunkenness – and prostituted herself whenever she needed money for her nightly lodgings. The autopsy showed that her shoulders were bruised – suggesting that the murderer had slammed her to the ground and held her there while he slit her throat.

It was obvious to the detectives that the killer had been interrupted in his work. He had not had time to disembowel his prey.

But the Ripper would not be cheated of his frenzied plan. Less than an hour later he struck again. At 1.45 a.m. Constable Edward Watkins, patrolling his beat in Mitre Square, made a chilling discovery. In the south-west corner of the warehouse-flanked area a woman was lying on her back, her clothes hoisted around her waist. Several days later the still-shocked policeman would tell the coroner, "Her throat was cut and her bowels protruding. The stomach was torn up. She'd been ripped to pieces like a pig in a market – with her entrails flung in a heap around her neck."

The police surgeon testified that the uterus and left kidney were missing.

The victim was Catherine Eddows, aged 46, mother of three children. The night before she died police had arrested her for drunken misconduct. They locked her in a cell at Bishopsgate police station. Then, fatefully, in the early hours of the morning, a duty sergeant deemed her sober enough to be released onto the street.

Fourteen hours after Catherine's death a witness, Joseph Lawende, went to Scotland Yard. He told detectives that while leaving the Imperial Club at about 1.35 a.m. he saw a woman wearing clothes resembling the police description which would be published later that day. She was standing at the entrance to Church Passage on Mitre Square, talking to a young blonde-mustached man in dark clothes and wearing a deerstalker hat. Lawende said he had not seen the woman's face but was reasonably certain from her demeanor that she was a prostitute. The description of Catherine's companion was not information of the first order. London in 1888 teemed with young men sporting blonde mustaches.

The Ripper rested for several weeks. As each day passed without another murder Londoners became increasingly hopeful that the nightmarish rampage was over. But then, on Friday November 9 the madman killed again. His final victim was Irish immigrant Mary Jane Kelly, a pretty 25-year-old blonde. She was two decades younger than her savaged predecessors.

Described by friends as plump, kindly and pleasant-natured, Mary had lived for three years with Joseph Barnett, a fish porter. The couple tended to drink excessively – often to the degree that they had no money left to pay the rent. In consequence they continually performed "midnight flits" – moving to a fresh lodging house every few weeks. In mid-October they hired a room in Miller's Court on Whitechapel's Dorset Street. In this seedy hovel their defacto marriage ended. According to the couple's friends Barnett had long objected to Mary's habit, whenever she needed cash, of selling herself on the streets. He did not want a prostitute as a wife. He genuinely loved Mary and hoped she would bear his children one day. It was his view, often loudly expressed, that they should live on the money he earned at the fish market.

When Mary declined to abandon her part-time profession Barnett flew into a rage and left her. He had no idea that she was pregnant.

Mary and her erstwhile "husband" were as usual behind in the rent. On the morning of Friday November 9 Thomas Bowyer, a lodging house employee, knocked at the door to demand payment. There was no reply. Bowyer reached in through the shattered window and pulled the curtain aside. Sprawled across the bed he saw what he described as "the work of Satan." Bowyer ran to fetch a policeman. The young constable who was first on the scene told a reporter, "When my eyes became accustomed to the dim light I saw a sight which I shall never forget to my dying day."

In his report the attending police surgeon Dr Thomas Bond fixed the time of Mary Kelly's death at between 1 and 2 a.m. He described the scene thus: "The body was lying naked in the middle of the bed, the shoulders flat... The whole of the surface of the abdomen and thighs was removed... The arms were mutilated by jagged wounds and the face hacked beyond recognition... The viscera were found in various parts: the liver between the feet, the intestines by the right side and the spleen by the left. The throat had been slashed with such ferocious force that the tissues were cut all the way down to the spinal column."

Dr Bond added that when he and a fellow surgeon tried to reconstruct the torn corpse they found that "the heart had been cut out and taken away."

The savagery of this crime – unprecedented even by the Ripper's warped standards – sparked panic in London. Whitechapel's piteous hordes of prostitutes faced a particularly terrible dilemma. They did not dare to venture out at night to earn coins for their night's lodgings – and yet, without money they would be evicted from those lodgings, "to walk", as one newspaper put it, "on dark streets in which a ravening lunatic prowls."

Relatively fortunate at this time of hysteria were those prostitutes living in the safety of brothels. The number of these sanctuaries was swiftly diminishing, however. Spurred by the demands of the Social Purity Movement and the requirements of the Contagious Diseases Act, police in the previous 12 months had shut down more that 200 "bawdy-houses" in East London. These closures, in the words of one social reformer, "rendered thousands of women homeless, hence vulnerable to attack."

Police questioned witnesses to Mary Kelly's final hours and made several arrests. But nothing stuck. They could identify no suspect against whom they could build a convincing case.

Scotland Yard's failures prompted outraged editorials in the popular press. One weekly quoted Queen Victoria as allegedly having told her prime minister, "This new, most ghastly murder shows the absolute necessity for some very decided action. All these streets and courts must be lit and our detectives improved. They are far from what they should be."

The Times was rather more sympathetic toward Scotland Yard:

> *"The murders, so cunningly continued, are carried out with a completeness which altogether baffles investigators. Not a trace is left of the murderer, and there is no purpose in the crime to afford the slightest clue. All that the police can hope is that some accidental circumstance will lead to a trace, which may be followed to a successful conclusion."*

This was an accurate and fair assessment. Even in our twenty-first century, with its abundance of psychological profiling, DNA testing and other forensic aids serial killers are notoriously difficult to catch. The Scotland Yard of 1888 was unequipped to solve such crimes of stealth. Even fingerprinting was an undeveloped art.

The *East London Observer* remarked, "The murders are singular for the reason that the victims have been the poorest of the poor. No adequate motive in the shape of plunder can be traced. The excess of effort that has been apparent suggests that the crimes are the work of a demented being."

Some detectives believed the Ripper had murdered at least 11 women. But Scotland Yard's official stance was that there had been only five: Nicholls, Chapman, Stride, Eddowes and Kelly. The killings of streetwalkers before and after these victims died had also been psychosexual in nature. However, in the opinion of most investigators they had lacked the "signature" and surgical expertise seen in the murders of the central group.

From the time of the second killing onward, analysts professional and amateur besieged newspapers and the Metropolitan Police with ideas about who, and what manner of person, the Ripper might be. One theory that would achieve wide popularity was espoused in a letter to the *Times* by a Dr Edgar Sheppard. "I see him as being of the upper class and an earnest religionist," he wrote, "...a person who acts believing that he is extirpating vice and sin."

Until 1914, when the Great War temporarily halted speculation, Jack the Ripper was the subject of numerous books and flimsy penny dreadfuls – most authors claiming that they had solved the mystery at last.

London's Metropolitan Police service had its own suspect list. In an official report Sir Melville MacNaghten, head of the Criminal Investigation Department, named his favored three:

- Montague Druitt, a 31-year-old barrister whose notorious mental instability had destroyed his career. Druitt often expressed regret that his family had forced him to study law when he would have preferred to become a surgeon. Several weeks after Mary Kelly was ferociously mutilated, Druitt's body was found floating in the Thames.

- Kosminski, an immigrant Polish tradesman who detested women and was officially known for his violence against them. Police records assert that he had "strong homicidal tendencies." In 1889 he was committed to a lunatic asylum. Inspector Donald Swanson, officer-in-charge of the Ripper case, insisted at the time of the killings and long into his retirement that this man was undoubtedly the culprit.

- Michael Ostrog, a Russian-born thief and confidence trickster who had suffered many mental breakdowns resulting in committal to asylums.

- Unofficially Macnaghten also admitted to suspicions of Dr Francis Tumblety, an American quack doctor who was arrested for gross indecency one week after the final murder. He was bailed at a high price and absconded.

Detective Inspector Frederick Abberline, who had worked on the case almost from the beginning, was unimpressed by Macnaghten's ideas. In Abberline's view the principal suspect was George Chapman, who was hanged in 1903 for murdering his wife. To Abberline, however, even this notion was no more than theoretical. Speaking as chief inspector shortly after the execution he said: "You can state most emphatically that Scotland Yard is really no wiser on the subject today than it was 15 years ago."

Official attempts to find the Ripper pale beside the efforts of the legion of self-appointed investigators who have worked on the case ever since. During the twentieth century and into the twenty-first forensic pathologists, retired policemen, sociologists, journalists, historians and practitioners of numerous other disciplines have spent years of their lives vying to find the "real" Jack the Ripper. They continually produce a maze of mutually contradictory conclusions. A sampling:

The Insane Prince Albert

In this scenario, which became popular during the 1970s, Prince Albert Victor, grandson of Queen Victoria, is infected with syphilis while visiting brothels in the East End. As the disease develops to its tertiary stage his mind snaps. In a murderous rage he rampages through the East End, wreaking his revenge upon prostitutes.

When police arrest him after he mutilates his fifth (or possibly eleventh) victim they are shocked to learn that he is a member of the Royal Family. The unfortunate matter is hushed up. Minders are appointed to keep a strict watch on Albert, never allowing him near the East End again. The Ripper murders stop. Their princely perpetrator dies of syphilitic complications in 1892.

Skeptics object that Albert was made Duke of Clarence in 1891 – scarcely an honor the queen would bestow on an unhinged butcher. Private diaries of the time portray him as a gentle and considerate chap. And Royal records show that he died of influenza during the 1892 epidemic. But all this, of course, could be part of the coverup…

The Lover's Lesson

A particular target of authors' suspicions was the fish porter Joseph Barnett, defacto husband of the Ripper's final victim Mary Kelly.

The flimsy case against Barnett, which police pursued only briefly, was that he committed the first four Ripper murders in the hope of terrifying Mary into obeying him. Motivated solely by the desire to show Mary how perilous a prostitute's life could be he began a rampage through the ranks of ladies of the night.

But although she was frightened and began to suggest they quit Whitechapel Mary remained adamant that she would never give up her source of additional income. This was a blow to Barnett's pride. And he was even further humiliated when he lost his job at the market. Mary was now the sole breadwinner: a situation he found intolerable. In a liquor-fueled rage he killed and mutilated the woman he had loved.

Detectives considered the rumor but were unimpressed. As one contemporary journalist put it, "The plot of the play was strong, but the principal actor was unsuited to the part."

The Gruesome Gang

Trevor Marriott, a British detective, devoted the first 10 years of his retirement to "proving conclusively" that neither Prince Albert nor American doctor Francis Tumblety had committed the Ripper's crimes.

Among many convincing indicators of Albert's innocence was the fact that the Royal diary showed he was not even in London at the time of the murders. And Francis Tumblety? He was known for his homosexual tendencies. "People with such leanings would surely kill members of the same sex," said Marriott.

In a 1994 lecture at the University of Ulster the detective deemed it far likelier that the killings were the work of a like-minded group of lunatics. "At the core of my doubt that there was only one killer is the fact that two of the bodies were found within 12 minutes of each other," he said. "If a lone offender had been responsible for that first murder and was disturbed, as has been suggested, he'd have been in a great hurry to leave the area. It seems highly unlikely that a solo murderer would have lingered to dispose of a second victim."

The Cruel Colonel

The British crime writer Tom Slemen and his friend, criminologist Keith Andrews, announced in April 2001 that they had found new evidence identifying the Ripper.

He was a military man from Gloucester, Colonel Claude Conder, they said.

In an interview with the *Gloucestershire Echo* (April 13 2001) the two men claimed that their clues included "cryptic messages carved on the victims' bodies" in ancient languages which Conder knew from working as an archeologist in the Middle East.

Tom Slemen told the newspaper, "Jack the Ripper was a brilliant 39-year-old British intelligence officer, archeologist, writer, mapmaker and trained killer. The man Keith and I know to be the Whitechapel murderer has lain in Cheltenham Cemetery for 91 years. His name was Claude Reignier Conder. He was born in Cheltenham and had many relatives there He was not suspected of being the Ripper at the time of the killings and even so-called 'Ripperologists' will not have heard of him."

The researchers said that the nineteenth century Metropolitan Police Chief Sir Charles Warren, who was in charge of the hunt for the Ripper, was a close friend of Colonel Conder. Warren knew Conder was the killer, but took the secret to his grave when he died in 1927.

During the 1860s Warren and Conder had served together in the Royal Engineers. Both archeologists, they excavated hundreds of Middle East sites – and wrote an internationally successful book about their discoveries. A crucial link to the Whitechapel murders was a trove of rings and ornaments they removed from King Solomon's Temple in Jerusalem.

The prostitute Annie Chapman stole several of these treasures from Colonel Conder's London house. She was a friend of the other four women who would become the Ripper's victims – and all cooperated in selling the booty.

The outraged Conder hunted the women down and exacted a dreadful revenge. Tom Slemen said, "He was a trained killer who specialized in close surveillance of the enemy and swooping, using ancient techniques. He would watch the routines of the patrolling soldiers for hours, then attack silently and from behind under the cloak of darkness. The victim's throat was slit before he could make a sound. These deadly skills came in very useful in 1888."

Colonel Conder retired to Cheltenham where in 1910 he suffered a stroke that would prove fatal. Tom Slemen said, "The Ripper took almost three weeks to pass away from a cerebral embolism that left him paralyzed and in a state of terror.

"Who knows what vengeful specters haunted the deathbed of a man who took the lives of five women in a sinister and brutally horrific way?"

The Self-Incriminating Artist

In 2003 the bestselling crime novelist Patricia Cornwell published a deeply researched book, *Portrait of a Killer: Jack the Ripper – Case Closed*.

The culprit, Cornwell claimed, was the 28-year-old impressionist painter Walter Sickert who was in East London at the time of the killings – and in the early twentieth century produced a macabre series of paintings depicting murdered prostitutes. In her study of the case the celebrated writer spent $4 million. She bought 30 Sickert paintings (some at $70,000 apiece)... paid forensic scientists to scour his painting table ... juxtaposed his images with morgue photos of the victims... and found clues in the artist's early history. Sickert, she discovered, had a psychological profile typical of many serial killers. His father had been abusive. He grew up to be a nervous, compulsive person who washed his hands incessantly. His mental disorder might have been exacerbated by an early trauma. A great-nephew revealed that as a child Sickert underwent painful surgery for a fistula on his penis: an operation thought to have left him sterile. Thrice-married, Sickert was never able to father children. His sexual disability might have exploded into a murderous rage against women.

The book, during whose production the author flew an entire team of forensic experts to Britain contains what some see as compelling proof that Sickert was guilty. But as with all Ripper exposes, not everyone is convinced.

Letters from Hell

ON SEPTEMBER 27 1888 – 19 days after the murder of Annie Chapman – London's Central News Agency received an envelope addressed to The Boss.

Inside, written in red ink, was the following letter:

25 Sept, 1888

Dear Boss,

I keep on hearing the police have caught me but they wont fix me just yet. I have laughed when they look so clever and talk about being on the right track. I am down on whores and I shant quit ripping them till I do get buckled. Grand work the last job was. I gave the lady no time to squeal. How can they catch me now? I love my work and want to start again. You will soon hear of me with my funny little games. I saved some proper red stuff in a ginger beer bottle over the last job to write with but it went thick like glue and I cant use it. Red ink is fit enough I hope ha.ha. The next job I do I shall clip the lady's ears off and send to the Police officers just for jolly wouldn't you. Keep this letter back till I do a bit more work then give it out straight. My knife's so nice and sharp I want to get to work right away if I get a chance.

> *Good luck.*
> *Yours truly,*
> *Jack the Ripper*

Don't mind me giving the trade name.

Scrawled horizontally in the ink-stained letter's margin were the words:

wasnt good enough to post this before I got all the red ink off my hands curse it. No luck yet. They say I'm a doctor now. Ha.ha.

The news agency's manager sent the letter to Scotland Yard. Soon afterward a card postmarked October 1 and in the same handwriting arrived:

I wasn't codding dear old Boss when I gave you the tip. Youll hear about saucy Jackys work tomorrow double event this time number one squealed a bit couldn't finish off. Had no time to get ears for police. Thanks for keeping last letter back till I got to work again.

Jack the Ripper

Detectives were divided about whether the two letters might be genuine. The "double event" threatened in the second communication had certainly occurred, with the deaths of Elizabeth Stride and Catherine Eddowes on September 30. It was possible the card had contained a prediction by the murderer – but in the light of the October 1 postmark it was equally conceivable that a hoaxer had written the message after the killings occurred. Scotland Yard took a chance – and posted facsimiles of the letters to every newspaper and police station in the hope that someone would recognize the handwriting.

The idea backfired. Hundreds of hoax letters, all signed Jack the Ripper, began to pour into police headquarters. But other missives were characterized by the tantalizing possibility that they might be genuine. A chilling example was received in mid-October by George Lusk, chairman of the Mile End Vigilance Committee. It was bloodily wrapped around what appeared to be part of a human kidney:

From hell

Mr Lusk

Sor,

I send you half the kidne I took from one woman prasarved it for you. Tother piece I fried and ate it was very nise I may send you the bloody knif that took it out if you only wate a whil longer

Signed

Catch me when you can

Mister Lusk

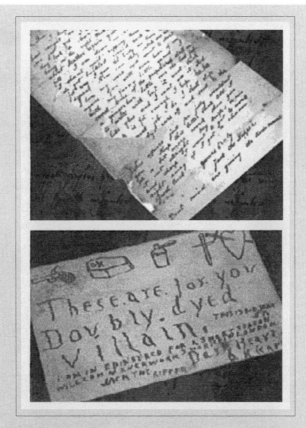

At the height of the horror-murders that terrified London, police received hundreds of letters purportedly written by Jack the Ripper. Only a handful (including the above) were considered possibly genuine.

Hoping that the kidney might merely have been bought at a butcher's shop the distressed Lusk, accompanied by one of his committee members, took it to the London Hospital where they sought forensic help from a Dr T. Openshaw. Initially the doctor presented his finding verbally: a naive mistake, as reporters immediately rushed off to sensationalize what he had said. In self-defense he then released a short written statement. The specimen, Openshaw said, was a left kidney taken from an adult human and preserved in spirits. It had belonged to someone with Bright's Disease.

At the inquest into Catherine Eddowes the police surgeon testified that she too had been afflicted with Bright's Disease:

The fiend at work. A contemporary illustrator's probably
erroneous notion of what Jack the Ripper might look like.

a powerful indication that the kidney mailed to George Lusk might have
been hers.

Several days after his report was published, Dr Openshaw received
this letter at the London Hospital:

*Old Boss you was right. It was the left kidny I was goin to hopperate
agin close to your ospitle just as I was goin to dror my nife along
of er bloomin throte them cusses of coppers spoilt the game but
I guess I will be on the job soon and will send you another bit of
innerds.*

Jack the Ripper

O have you seen the devle
with his mikerscope and scalpul
a looking at a kidney
with a slide cocked up

The writer of the two kidney-related letters appears to have been barely literate. This may well have been the case. But if he was in fact the Ripper, his misspelt and clumsily punctuated correspondence might simply have been an attempt at deception, arguably perpetrated by an insane upper-class Englishman with degrees in literature and medicine.

The identity of the crazed kidney-sender is just one more enigma to reflect upon in the mirror-world of mystery surrounding Jack the Ripper.

Did British Agents
Execute Hess?

When Rudolph Hess, Deputy Fuehrer of the Third Reich, parachuted into Scotland seeking peace talks at the height of the London Blitz, both Hitler and Churchill labeled him a madman. But declassified evidence now suggests that the leaders knew about Hess's mission beforehand – and regarded it very seriously. Hess's journey was, in fact, a turning point in twentieth century history, directly influencing the outcome of the conflict. Convicted as a war criminal, Hess spent the final 42 years of his life in Spandau prison. Some historians believe British authorities so feared the impact of the secrets he might reveal if ever he were released that they had him strangled in his cell...

Lanarkshire, Scotland.
May 10 1941. 11.05 p.m.

L ONDON WAS ABLAZE. David McLean, a Scottish plowman, sat in his chilly cottage listening to the bombs fall and to the calm voice of a BBC newsreader describing the devastation. It sounded like the worst Luftwaffe attack yet. He wondered how much longer England could hold out.

The bulletin was interrupted by a loud noise from outside. It was a plane, very close by. A plane whose engine seemed to be cutting out. And seconds later, the jarring din of a crash. A downed Spitfire? Surely not here, in this dark stretch of countryside so far from the fighting. He went outside, taking a pitchfork just in case.

The aircraft was clearly visible, near the boundary fence, burning. McLean broke into a run. Perhaps there were people still alive. But long before he reached the wreckage he was confronted by a tall man with hands held high above his head. In heavily accented English the stranger introduced himself as Alfred Horn. He had run out of fuel and bailed out. "It is essential I see the Duke of Hamilton immediately," he said. "I have an important message for him."

The plowman pointed his pitchfork at the purported Mr Horn's chest. "Come in for a cup of tea," he replied. "Then we'll see what we can do."

Just before midnight a Home Guard truck rattled to a halt outside David McLean's cottage. An elderly captain and two privates took the parachutist into custody. By this time the man, obviously insane, was claiming he was Rudolph Hess, Deputy Fuehrer of the Third Reich. Nobody believed him for a moment – but he was an enemy pilot nonetheless and had to be imprisoned until Higher Authority could be notified. The Home Guardsmen took the pilot to a local scout hall where they locked him up until the army could take over. At 2 a.m. soldiers arrived to transport him to Marycliff Barracks.

Under interrogation the pilot, a fit-looking man in his late 40s, reiterated his assertion that he was Rudolph Hess. He had flown here with the full knowledge and approval of the Fuehrer to broker peace between Germany and Britain. The real enemy, he said, was the Soviet Union. This was the menace the two nations should be fighting together, rather than trying to destroy each other. Ideally, the pilot said, he would welcome an audience with King George VI. But failing that, it was imperative that he see the Duke of Hamilton at once.

Ramblingly the German explained that he and Hamilton had met at the Berlin Olympics in 1936. They had become very friendly. The duke would understand how important it was that they speak as soon as possible.

To the parade of officers, steadily escalating in rank, who were invited to the interrogation room the pilot's assertions sounded like madness. The notion of the Deputy Fuehrer bailing out of a Messerschmitt over Scotland was only a degree less likely than Hitler himself dropping by. But the prisoner certainly resembled the Rudolph Hess they had seen in press photographs and cinema newsreels. The commanding officer nervously decided he had better advise someone high up. Very high up. He rang the office of the prime minister, Winston Churchill, and spoke to a senior aide. On balance, the commander said, he tended to believe that this fellow might be telling the truth. Particularly odd, he felt, was the crashed Messerschmitt, which his men had now inspected. It carried no bombs or weapons of any kind. Following this conversation the commander also alerted the Duke of Hamilton whose estate was half an hour's drive away.

Churchill, on this Sunday morning, was at Ditchley Park in Oxfordshire. He immediately took personal control of the incident, first calling the commander back to hear more about the interrogation, then ringing the Duke of Hamilton with an order to fly down from Scotland immediately, bringing a photograph of the mysterious German.

When the duke arrived Churchill glanced briefly at the snapshot a corporal had taken – and nodded. It certainly looked like Hess. Right age, right eyebrows, right facial bone structure. What manner of trick or folly was this, then? Did this idiot genuinely have Hitler's backing? Or, as seemed more probable, had he lost his mind?

In a memoir the duke recalled that Churchill then sent him away. His house guests, the prime minister explained, awaited him in Ditchley's private cinema. "Hess or no Hess, I'm off to see the Marx Brothers," he said, and strode from the room. Churchill's dismissive attitude toward the arrival of Rudolph Hess would persist throughout the war. Despite Britain's desperate plight in 1941 he had no intention of striking any kind of bargain with Hitler's odious regime.

The Fuehrer seemed equally anxious to repudiate Hess. The Nazi propaganda machine reported that Hitler was shocked by his deputy's "treachery" and could only suspect that he had lost his mind. Should Rudolph Hess ever dare return to the Reich he would be executed.

Far from being granted an audience with the king, Hess was consigned to oblivion. He spent the rest of the war locked up in high-security Scottish, Welsh and English prisons – even sojourning briefly in the Tower of London. Britain's wartime newspapers – and their readers – largely forgot him. In 1946 Hess was tried with other Nazi criminals at Nuremberg – only escaping execution on the grounds of insanity. Sentenced to life imprisonment he spent the subsequent four decades at Spandau. In 1987, aged 93, he allegedly suicided by hanging himself.

But the history of Rudolph Hess was neither as straightforward nor as simple as that. It now seems certain that the leaders on both sides of the war were lying when they said they'd had no prior knowledge of Hess's peace mission. It must be conceded, however, that Churchill had lied with the noblest of intentions.

In 1941 Britain's wartime prime minister was being forced to fight on two fronts: against the Nazis abroad and against a powerful lobby of appeasers and defeatists at home. Many members of Britain's ruling class were convinced that a détente with Germany was not only possible but desirable. Peace with Hitler would safeguard their properties and their profits.

Churchill, who distrusted Hitler and abhorred his genocidal policies, would have no truck with the peace movement. While he was leader Britain would pursue a policy of total war on Nazism.

To the peace lobbyists it was obvious that Churchill would have to be replaced by a more malleable prime minister.

Augsburg Germany, May 10 1941, 5.45 p.m.

Although few people realized it at the time, the Hess mission – and the farce into which it deteriorated – would prove pivotal to the survival of democracy. If the Deputy Fuehrer had not made gross navigational errors combined with naive blunders, the outcome of his visit might have been "successful" enough to change world history.

The comedy of errors began when the 47-year-old politician took off from a private runway at the Messerschmitt factory in a twin-engine ME-110.

The plane was unarmed and carrying extra fuel. Although Hess flew through heavily guarded airspace toward enemy territory no German fighter or anti-aircraft unit tried to stop him.

Hess sincerely believed that in flying to Scotland he was responding to an invitation from the Duke of Hamilton who, he imagined, was an activist for peace. However, declassified documents have revealed that he was the victim of a sophisticated trick. Months earlier, Britain's SOE (Special Operations Executive) had begun to intercept secret letters sent to the duke by Hess's private secretary, spelling out proposals for an armistice. The British agents had replied, forging the duke's signature and suggesting a confidential meeting at his Scottish estate.

The audacious hoax was designed to destabilize Hitler. The duke's role in it (when he discovered that he had a role) would be to do exactly what the SOE told him.

The smuggled letters at the heart of the deception told Hess that the airstrip near the duke's mansion, Dungavel House, would (in defiance of blackout restrictions) be lit up for him on the night of his arrival. The number two man in Nazi Germany would have a dream run into Scotland.

As he crossed England's northern coast Hess must have felt confident that all was going well. Three Spitfires, scrambled to check on him, made no hostile move. And when two Czech Hurricane pilots intercepted the lone Messerschmitt 20 minutes later, they too received orders not to fire.

Hess undoubtedly felt ever more welcome as he flew on toward the Firth of Clyde. But then everything began to go wrong. In the blackout, where not even the glimmer of a house light was visible, he lost his way. He turned and tried again to find the duke's brightly illuminated airstrip. But the blackness below was Stygian and featureless. Uneasily aware that his fuel was running low, Hess flew on aimlessly, seeking any light anywhere that might guide him to a landing place. But his time ran out. When the fuel gauge needle registered empty he abandoned the Messerschmitt and parachuted into the darkness below.

Analysts still speculate about the major players' reactions at this point. It seems reasonably certain, however, that with his intelligence plot partially unraveled Churchill knew he had been plunged into a perilous game. The plan had been to control Hess from the moment he landed on Scottish soil. British agents intended to use him to lull Hitler into believing Britain was secretly discussing peace – thus freeing Germany to attack her treaty partner Russia. Now that Hess had become a wild card in military custody, Churchill realized he would have to get to him first. If the appeasers won the race they would begin to exert political and public pressure for genuine peace talks with Hess. An Anglo-Nazi "friendship", the prime minister knew, could only end with the treacherous Hitler invading Britain.

Providentially Churchill was able to neutralize Hess in time. A month later Adolf Hitler, like Napoleon before him, made the direst mistake of his blood-drenched career, by invading the Soviet Union. Hitler hurled an army of three million men against his erstwhile ally Stalin. That winter Russian resistance and the bitter weather stopped the Germans outside Moscow – the beginning of the doom of the Third Reich.

Until M15's documentation is released in 2017 the full story of the Hess mission will remain unknown. But nobody questions the central fact that embattled Britain's brilliant lies and trickery helped in some degree to persuade Hitler to fight on two fronts. It was the Nazis' disastrous failure in Russia that helped turn the war's tide against Hitler – a result for which, in some degree, he could thank his blundering deputy Rudolph Hess.

In the Hess case, Britain pursued a textbook policy of deception and disinformation. And the trickery seems unlikely to have ended with defeat of the Axis Powers. During the 1980s British spokesmen publicly deplored the Soviet Union's "inhumane" policy of opposing Hess's release from Spandau. He was an old man, they argued, and could do no further harm.

But in truth, freedom for Hess was the last thing Britain wanted. He was privy to secrets which could harm the national interest, even 42 years after the war. Better he remain a prisoner. Or die.

In his book *Who Murdered My Father?* Ruediger Hess claims that when Russian attitudes thawed and his parent's release seemed imminent, Britain exercised the death option. Two SAS soldiers infiltrated Spandau and executed the geriatric prisoner. There is evidence that Ruediger may be right. An autopsy on Rudolph Hess found marks on his neck suggestive of strangulation rather than suicide.

The President's Secret Telegram

PRESIDENT FRANKLIN D. ROOSEVELT shared Winston Churchill's view that Nazism posed a threat not only to Britain but to the United States, which had not yet joined the war.

The president was in regular contact with the British prime minister – and was particularly interested in what the interrogation of Rudolph Hess might reveal.

On May 15 1941, five days after the Deputy Fuehrer parachuted into Scotland, Roosevelt sent the telegram below:

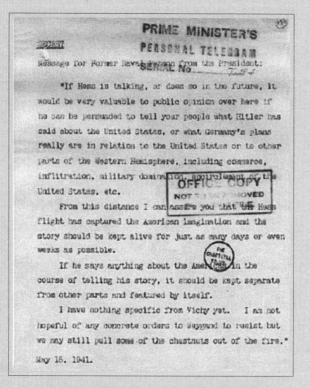

In a secret (now declassified) telegram to his courageous friend Winston Churchill, President Roosevelt seeks information about the defecting deputy-Fuehrer Rudolph Hess.

SECRET

Message to Former Naval Person from the President:

If Hess is talking, or does so in the future, it would be very valuable to public opinion over here if he can be persuaded to tell your people what Hitler has said about the United States, or what Germany's plans really are in relation to the United States or to other parts of the Western Hemisphere, including commerce, infiltration, military domination, encirclement of the United States, etc.

From this distance I can assure you that the Hess flight has captured the American imagination and the story should be kept alive for just as many days or even weeks as possible.

If he says anything about the Americans in the course of telling his story, it should be kept separate from other parts and featured by itself...

* * *

On December 7 1941 Japanese bombers attacked Pearl Harbor. America was at war.

Who Was Hess?

RUDOLPH HESS, central figure in one of World War II's greatest unsolved mysteries, was born to prosperous parents in Alexandria Egypt on April 26 1894.

He did not set foot in Germany until he was 14.

At the outbreak of World War I he volunteered for the army, eventually becoming a pilot flying the Kaiser's early warplanes.

Hess was deeply affected by Germany's defeat and the humiliating terms imposed upon her by the treaty of Versailles. In 1920 he heard Hitler speak at a Munich beer hall and immediately joined the Nazi party. He was the sixteenth member. Hess rose swiftly through the party, beginning as Hitler's personal secretary (in which role he helped write *Mein Kampf*). In April 1933 he became Deputy Fuehrer. In this principally ceremonial role he showed fanatical devotion to Hitler and was notorious for blindly obeying all his commands.

Hess was not a man who made independent decisions. Among Nazis he was known as something of a lapdog who always sought the Fuehrer's permission first.

Hitler, say German historians, would undoubtedly have known that his deputy was flying to Scotland to negotiate peace.

Mystery of the Shadow
on Mars

Almost half of the probes fired from Earth to Mars have been lost. But none of these costly failures has baffled space scientists more than the disappearance of the Russian spacecraft Phobos 2. On March 27 1989, moments before its communication systems blacked out, Phobos transmitted two mystifying images back to ground control. The first showed what appeared to be a gigantic cylindrical object; the second a shadow 15 miles long which the intruder was apparently casting on the Martian surface. And that wasn't the end of it. In September Britain's Channel 4 televised further photographs from the aborted mission: images almost too bizarre to be believed…

*P*HOBOS *1* AND ITS COMPANION *Phobos 2* were the most sophisticated and expensive space vehicles the Soviet Union had built. The ships were packed with advanced European technology and powered by solar panels. They were principally programmed to analyze the composition of their namesake Martian moon Phobos and to study the surface of Mars itself.

Both probes disappeared before they had completed their tasks.

Phobos 1, launched on July 7 1988, fell silent on September 2. An official announcement blamed the failure on a software error which had turned the spacecraft's solar panels away from the sun, thus depleting the batteries.

Russia's hopes now rested on *Phobos 2*, which had been launched five days after its sister-probe. During its long voyage to Mars-space the vehicle transmitted large quantities of data about the sun. By late March it was ready to begin the mission's final phase – releasing two landers onto the surface of Martian moon Phobos. One was a mobile "hopper"; the other a stationary platform.

However, before the Russian controllers could command *Phobos 2* to perform these tasks it began to transmit stark pictures. The images bewildered some of the watching scientists and filled others with awe and consternation.

The spaceship's camera had photographed a cylindrical object of immense size hovering above Mars. The cylinder was subsequently estimated to be about 1.2 mile wide and 14 miles long. Its sides, as pictured, were perfectly parallel, with rounding at both ends: suggestive, some controllers said, of a cigar.

Moreover the cylinder was casting a *shadow* on the surface below – a shadow 25 kilometres long.

Seconds after this image reached Earth *Phobos 2* ceased transmission. According to the Russians it was neither seen nor heard from again.

NASA's official commentary on the foregoing events mentions neither the cylinder nor its shadow. The release simply reads, "The mission ended when the spacecraft's signal failed to be successfully reacquired. The cause of the failure was determined to be a malfunction of the onboard computer."

In its October 19 1989 issue the British scientific journal *Nature* offered more detail. Just before it was lost, the report said, the spacecraft was spinning – due either to a computer malfunction or to an "impact event" by an unknown object.

Britain's Channel 4 revealed much more of the story. Following a media conference given by the Russian scientists who had conducted the *Phobos 2* mission the station televised a picture of the cylinder above the Mars moon. The report (also shown in Australia and Canada) went on to show other extraordinary images received by Russian mission control.

Dr John Becklake of the London Science Museum appeared in the newscast to comment on a set of high-resolution infrared photographs taken by the doomed *Phobos 2*. The shots showed a grid, almost mathematical in its precision, at Hydaspis Chaos beneath the surface of Mars. Dr Becklake said:

"This city-like pattern is 37 miles wide and could easily be mistaken for an aerial view of Los Angeles... We have some lines on the surface of Mars in the infrared, which means it's heat and it's not visible... As for what it is, I don't know and the Russians aren't telling us."

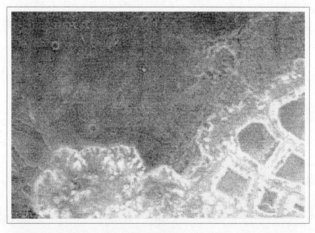

A "grid-pattern" beneath the surface of Mars. NASA, without comment, released this infrared image in March 2002, among a large batch of other pictures. The release came 13 years after Russia's doomed *Phobos 2* spacecraft transmitted an almost identical "grid" photograph. Courtesy NASA.

The genuineness of the Soviet photographs was seemingly validated 13 years later. On February 19 2002 America's *Mars Odyssey* spacecraft, using infrared film photographed a similar (or the identical) "grid image" in the Hydaspis Chaos area. NASA released the picture – amid a large batch of others – on March 1 2002.

In December 1999 Marina Popovich, who had been one of the Soviet Union's most celebrated test pilots, presented Western journalists with copies of *Phobos 2*'s "cylinder" photograph. The picture, she said, had been given to her by Alexei Leonov, first man to walk in space and also a high official in Russia's space program. The Soviet authorities had by this time become secretive about the photograph, but she had managed to smuggle her copy out. "This picture is only information for thinking," Marina Popovich said.

Dr James Harder, professor emeritus at Berkeley agreed. "It could be an artifact of *Phobos 2*'s camera... some kind of moonlet... or what it apparently looks like, some kind of UFO," he said.

And the mysterious Martian grid? The Canadian Broadcasting Corporation's nightly news hour *The National* presented a particularly thoughtful analysis several months after the *Phobos 2* event, showing and speaking of "a sharply defined rectangular area interconnected with a lacework of perfectly straight 'canals' much like city blocks." The picture-analyst continued, "Since no corresponding surface features appeared in visible light the infrared photo was interpreted as a heat signature of underground caverns and 'canals'. They were unusual in their extreme geometrical regularity, suggesting underground formations of artificial origin."

Of the "shadow" photograph the analyst said, "This depicted in visible light a convex elliptical shadow on the Martian landscape. The azimuth [overhead] solar inclination prevented shadow-casting by Martian features, implying a shadow thrown by something overhead in orbit. As no corresponding object was visible in the photo, whatever cast the shadow had to be above the 300-mile-plus orbit of the *Phobos 2*.

"This implies a huge orbital object in order to cast a visible shadow, complete with umbra and penumbra areas."

Fifteen years after *Phobos 2* vanished, NASA's Mars Rover was making daily discoveries – even finding evidence that a rock depression had held a salty sea which might once have supported life.

The mysteries of Mars are only beginning to unravel. At any time now, the planet may yield up revelations that are not only stranger than we might imagine – but stranger than we *can* imagine.

The Strangler Who Stole His Victims' Names
Edward Joseph Leonski

The year was 1942: one of the darkest periods in World War II. Large convoys of American troops were landing in Australia to help repel an imminent Japanese invasion. Melbourne was the base for 15,000 US soldiers. Browned-out by night, her streetlamps switched off and car headlights narrowed to slits, the city was filled with foreboding. And a sudden spate of horrific murders made the atmosphere infinitely worse. On the city's darkened streets a maniac was sadistically beating then asphyxiating women he had randomly accosted. "The Brownout Strangler", as the newspapers called him, proved to be a 24-year-old GI who was quickly caught, tried and hanged. But it was not until decades after his death that two writers discovered a profound mystery surrounding the murders. Inexplicably the killer's surname was woven deeply into the names of his victims...

Albert Park, Melbourne.
May 3 1942. 7 a.m.

FOR HARRY GIBSON it was the same routine every morning. Up at 6 o'clock and at work an hour later, ready to hose down the footpath outside Albert Park's waterfront hotel. Almost always there'd be a mess to flush away – but in the past few months he had been finding a lot more of it than usual. People were drinking too much nowadays. Worry about the war – that'd be the reason.

As the high-pressure stream swirled into the gutter Harry peripherally noticed a movement in the recessed doorway of a nearby drycleaning shop. It was a soldier – an American soldier – rising from a stooping position. He'd been there all night, probably, sleeping off a binge. The GI brushed himself down and strode briskly away.

Harry, his task complete, rewound the hose. Then something – he couldn't explain what – prompted him to stroll the few steps to the drycleaning shop. What he saw in its entranceway almost gave him a seizure. Sprawled on the concrete was a woman, partly naked. Her eyes were blackened, face caked with blood, clothes torn with what appeared to have been monstrous force. She lay at his feet, unmistakably dead.

Harry Gibson ran to a telephone box and rang police headquarters at Russell Street. Homicide detectives and a police surgeon were at the scene within 15 minutes. They established that the woman, in her late 30s or early 40s, had been savagely beaten by someone of great strength and then strangled to death. Robbery had not been the motive. The victim's purse, containing coins to the value of more than £1, lay bloodied beside her.

In their subsequent investigation police found that the woman had lived under a series of aliases. They eventually identified her as Ivy Violet McLeod, an accomplished singer who often appeared at charity concerts. She had been 40 years old. The killing – clearly the work of a maniac, a sadist or both – created great public unease. Melbourne was a sleepy city bordering on the provincial. Murders of such ferocity were virtually unknown.

Six days later the unease turned to terror, when a second violently battered body was found. This time the discoverer was a nightwatchman, Henry McGowan, who first came across a woman's handbag abandoned in a lane – and then, at 4 a.m., found the victim on the steps of Morningside House in the city thoroughfare of Spring Street. To police the killer's signature was almost instantly recognisable. The young woman, brutally beaten, clothes ripped frenziedly away, had been strangled with immense pressure. Marks made by large fingers were visible on her skin.

A strange coincidence now confronted the homicide investigators. As in the case of Ivy McLeod the victim's real name proved difficult to establish. Like her predecessor in death she had used a series of aliases. Only with the help of press publicity were detectives able to confirm that she was 31-year-old Pauline Thompson, a mother of two and the wife of a policeman in the country city of Bendigo.

Pauline, pretty and good-natured, had been working as a typist by day and as a radio station's receptionist by night. In this wartime era of manpower shortages it was not unusual for a woman to hold two jobs. And she almost had a third, because she worked professionally as a singer as well. On the day she died Pauline told her husband she had an evening off and would attend a fund-raising event at the Music Lovers' Club.

She left the event early. The last recorded sighting of her was just before midnight when she left a city hotel where she had been drinking with an American soldier. Witnesses saw her hurrying off into teeming rain.

After Pauline Thompson's death several women approached police to say that a muscular GI had ferociously attacked and tried to kill them. Could it possibly be, they asked, that this man was the Brownout Strangler? In one incident the man had became violent in a woman's flat, but fled when her screams brought neighbors running. He left behind a regulation-issue army singlet.

Fall in Melbourne was cold and rainswept. Darkness was falling before six o'clock. With the air raid regulations forbidding lights in the streets, women became frightened of walking from the office to the railway station or tram stop. Some began moving in convoys. Others quit their jobs and fled to relatives in the countryside.

The exodus quickened after May 18 1942. At 7 a.m. on that day an Australian soldier, Private Donald Wallace, found an umbrella and hat on the perimeter of the US Army Barracks at Camp Pell. Shortly afterward, in a slit trench, he discovered a woman's throttled and battered corpse.

The Brownout Strangler's third victim was identified as Gladys Hosking, a 40-year-old librarian at Melbourne University. A popular and accomplished singer, she had performed in university operas and was also prominent in a YWCA choir. In her life's last hours she left work with a friend, Dorothy Pettigrew. Both lived close to the university.

Again, police appealed in the press for witnesses. The result was helpful. Several people said they had seen Gladys Hosking sharing her umbrella with an American soldier. He did not seem threatening – and she was happy and talkative. But the most promising testimony came from Private Noel Seymour, a young Australian soldier. He said he had been standing guard over trucks on the perimeter of Camp Pell when he heard a noise and switched on his flashlight to check. The beam illuminated a US soldier, slipping under a railing. The GI, plastered with yellow mud, explained that he had spent a day's leave with his girlfriend and had slipped and fallen while returning to camp. Suspecting nothing, the Australian guard grinned and waved his fellow soldier on. It was not until the next day that he learned about the body in the trench.

This was enough for Melbourne's homicide investigators. Convinced the killer must be one of the 15,000 American soldiers based at Camp Pell, they asked US authorities for all the help they could give in tracking him down. Commander-in-chief General Douglas MacArthur immediately ordered that all soldiers at the camp be confined to base. This enabled the Australian police to walk witnesses through the camp in the hope that they might identify the GI who attacked them. For a time it seemed that the detectives' theory about the culprit's identity might be wrong. But the breakthrough came when the uncle of a woman who had narrowly escaped death identified the soldier responsible: the pleasantly fresh-faced Edward Joseph Leonski, 24, of the 52nd Signal Battalion. In a subsequent lineup the man's niece also identified Leonski. Further confirmation came from Private Seymour, who said Leonski was the mud-covered soldier he had encountered on the night of the third killing.

Confronted by the damning evidence against him the young GI confessed. He was charged with the murders, handcuffed to a bedrail and placed under armed guard in the military camp's stockade.

Edward Leonski should have been tried under the laws of the State of Victoria, of which Melbourne is the capital. But the US military was so appalled that one of its members had committed such vicious crimes against an ally's citizens that it sought the Australians' permission to hold a court martial. The military tribunal was conducted in Melbourne's Criminal Court.

Leonski pleaded insanity. A defense witness testified that before joining the army the accused man had been arrested – but not charged – with trying to strangle a young woman in Texas. Psychiatrists called by the prosecution insisted that Leonski, although dangerous, was sane. The tribunal found him guilty of the three murders and sentenced him to death. General Douglas MacArthur personally confirmed the sentence on November 4 1942.

On November 9 Edward Joseph Leonski was marched to the gallows in Melbourne's Pentridge Prison. Guards reported that he was cheerful, calm and singing to himself just before he died: "It's a lovely day tomorrow… Tomorrow is a lovely day."

* * *

IN THE EARLY 1980s, four decades after Edward Leonski's execution, two Melbourne screenwriters began separately to research his story.

Each of these men discovered eerie coincidences surrounding the case: mysterious flukes of chance which had gone unnoticed by the newspapers of the time – and by the authors of books about the nightmare killings.

The first writer to start work on the Brownout Strangler case was Cliff Green, who created the acclaimed screenplay for Peter Weir's *Picnic at Hanging Rock*, the magic-steeped story of a group of schoolgirls who vanish from a school camp. For financial reasons *Babyfaced Killer*, the film Green was commissioned to write, failed to eventuate. But not before he had unearthed two fascinating facts: facts I have presented without comment in the foregoing text.

Cliff Green told me: "The record shows that Leonski accosted his three victims at random. It's pretty amazing, therefore, that every one of them happened to be a singer. Pauline Thompson had worked professionally as a vocalist in Bendigo. Gladys Hosking sang in amateur opera productions and was a member of a YWCA choir – and Ivy McLeod also sang at concerts."

Even odder, said Green, was the coincidence of the aliases. "Ivy McLeod and Pauline Thompson had used such a variety of false names that when their bodies were found police had difficulty identifying them." Fellow writer William Nagle's screenplay *Death of a Soldier* was made into a film in 1986. Two elements of the Leonski tragedy fascinated him: the role of detective Bluey Adams – and the uncanny coincidence linking the killer to his victims.

"Adams's hunches were legendary throughout the Victorian police force," Bill Nagle told me. "And in the Leonski case he excelled himself. Adams hadn't been assigned to the murder investigation. But one night he just happened to be sitting in a hotel where Leonski was showing off to friends. The young soldier downed a concoction of beer, whiskey and sauce, then walked on his hands along the bar. Bluey Adams turned to a colleague and said, 'That bloke's as mad as a hatter. And look at the strength in those hands. They're strangler's hands. That's the Brownout Murderer.' Adams begged the homicide men to look at Leonski. Several days later his advice, based simply on a hunch, was proved correct."

But to Nagle the most chilling – and incredible – aspect of the affair concerns the names of the killer and the women he strangled.

When the victims' names are arranged in the order of their deaths they include letters which, when combined, sequentially spell the name LEONSKI. With a pencil stub and pad Bill Nagle demonstrated the point:

The victims – Mc**LEO**d, Thompso**N**, Ho**SKI**ng

The Brownout Strangler – **LEONSKI**

Mystery of the Missionary
and the Men from Nowhere
Alien Intrusions

In June 1959 an Australian priest, Reverend William Gill, stood on a tropical beach with 38 other witnesses and gazed up at an extraordinary spectacle. Hovering over the sea was a cluster of glowing circular craft. Atop the closest, which stood stationary above the shallows, was a railed "observation deck." Standing on it were four men (or what appeared to be men) performing a task of some kind. The next evening the craft astonishingly appeared again. On this occasion Reverend Gill waved – and one of the visitors reciprocated, setting off a prolonged period of waving between the skyship and the people below. This Close Encounter of the Third Kind would soon be internationally celebrated. Investigators described it as the first time credible observers had reported the presence of humanoid beings aboard an apparently alien vessel. It would not be the last…

NOBODY AT THE REMOTE Anglican mission in Boianai, Papua New Guinea, had the faintest notion of what was going on. There seemed to be no logical explanation for the brilliantly lit objects (some called them "lanterns") which for weeks now had been appearing by night in the tropical sky. Inexplicable too were the noises that rolled across the normally quiet sea: explosions so loud that they woke people from their sleep. And who could even begin to explain the large sparkling light that Father Gill in early April had twice watched hovering above Mount Pudi?

Eventually the teachers, medical staff and students living at the mission would receive an answer to their questions. An answer of sorts. All of these uncanny phenomena had been no more than an overture: a preparation for a series of events that would electrify the world.

The performance (so described because it was a seemingly deliberate display) began at 6.45 p.m. on June 6 1959.

Father William Booth Gill finished dinner and stepped out of the front door of the mission house. He immediately noticed a dazzling light in the western sky. It was at a higher elevation than Venus, which also was visible – and resembled the light he had seen over Mount Pudi two months before. But this one was moving across the ocean, seemingly toward the mission.

In his landmark interview with Melbourne lawyer and UFO investigator Peter Norris, Father Gill remembered calling out to one of the mission's teachers, Steven Moi, "Come and look at this!" The young man ran down to the beach followed by his wife Nesi and another teacher. Before long 39 people were gathered on the sand.

It was now apparent (witnesses said in a signed statement) that the light was a solid object of some kind. As it slowly descended, the observers saw that it was a circular craft, glowing blue, with "portholes or panels" and "something like legs" attached to its broad base. At the top was something resembling a "railed deck." Other circular objects, similarly glowing, were visible higher and further away.

The principal craft came to a halt at about 300 feet above the shallows. Impossibly it stood stock-still in the air.

Father Gill recalled, "We all saw movement. A man appeared on the deck. He was joined by three others. They were engaged in some kind of activity whose nature we couldn't understand. One or two of the men would leave, then return, then go off again for no perceived reason…"

At intervals a thin shaft of electric-blue light shone upward from the ship's deck, illuminating the low cloud cover. Father Gill said, "The men seemed to be lit not only by the reflection of this light upon them but by a sort of glow which completely surrounded them, as well as the craft. The glow didn't touch them, but there seemed to be a space between their outlines and the light."

Bedroom invader? An "abductee's" drawing of a
creature which, he claims, removed him from bed and
subjected him to a painful examination.

In his statements, diaries and letters to colleagues Father Gill described the movements of the smaller objects as "erratic" – confusingly advancing, receding and changing direction. At times they would "swing back and forth like a pendulum," he said. "One object moved off and appeared to descend to the village. Everyone thought it was going to land and went running down the beach. But it swooped up and over the mountains, turning red as it disappeared."

The encounter lasted for almost three hours. At 9.30 p.m. the principal disk moved away at enormous speed, casting a halo of blue light on the clouds and changing color from red to blue and green before vanishing.

So breathtaken were the observers on the beach that no one departed. The entire crowd waited, watching the sky, half-hoping and half-fearing that something more might happen. Their patience was rewarded. At 9.46 p.m., as recorded in Father Gill's notes, the glowing disk returned and hovered until 10.30. This time no occupants were visible. At 11.04 p.m. heavy rain began to fall, driving the witnesses inside.

The following evening (June 27) the circular craft, or one similar to it, appeared again. In a prepared statement Father Gill gave to Peter Norris and myself, he described the event:

Saturday 27/6/59

Large U.F.O. first sighted by Annie Borews (a medical assistant) at 6 p.m. in apparently same position as last night, only seemed a little smaller... I called Ananias and several others and we stood in the open to watch it. Although the sun had set it was still quite light for the following 15 minutes.

We watched figures appear on top – four of them – no doubt that they are human... Two smaller U.F.Os were seen at the same time, stationary. One above the hills west, another overhead.

On the large one two of the figures seemed to be doing something near the center of the deck – occasionally bending over and raising their arms as though adjusting or "setting up" something (not visible).

One figure seemed to be standing and looking down at us. I stretched my arm above my head and waved. To our surprise the figure did the same. Ananias waved both arms over his head then the two outside figures did the same. Ananias and self began waving our arms and all four now seemed to wave back. There seemed to be no doubt that our movements were answered. All mission boys made audible gasps (of either joy or surprise, perhaps both).

As dark was beginning to close in, I sent Eric Kodawara for a flashlight and directed a series of long dashes towards the U.F.O. After a minute or two of this the U.F.O. apparently acknowledged by making several wavering motions back and forth. Waving by us was repeated and this was followed by more flashes of flashlight, then the U.F.O. began slowly to become bigger, apparently coming in our direction. It ceased after perhaps half a minute and apparently came no further.

After a further two or three minutes the figures apparently lost interest in us for they disappeared "below" deck. At 6.25 p.m. two figures reappeared to carry on with whatever they were doing before the interruption.

In his interview with Peter Norris, Father Gill recalled how he and his companions shouted to re-attract the men's attention – beckoning to them to land on the beach. But the occupants did not respond.

At 6.30 p.m. Father Gill calmly went inside for dinner!

When he returned at 7 p.m. the principal UFO was still present, but seemingly smaller. All the observers walked to church for Evensong. When they returned at 7.45, cloud cover was heavy and the disk was no longer visible. The people of Boianai Mission would not see their glowing humanoid visitors again.

However, at 10.40 p.m. everyone's sleep was shattered by what Father Gill described as an "earsplitting explosion" which seemed to have originated just outside a mission-house window.

Shortly after the sightings the Reverend William Gill made a scheduled return flight to Australia on church duties. His visit gave investigators the chance to assess him and his voluminous documentation of the Boianai incidents. Everyone who met the missionary was impressed by his quiet integrity. He was still clearly bemused by all that had befallen him and his flock – and sought no notoriety or gain, other than to try to ascertain what he had seen.

Dr Donald Menzel, a Harvard University astronomer and dedicated UFO debunker, announced (without visiting Boianai or interviewing witnesses) that they had all obviously been looking at the planet Venus. In his book *The UFO Experience* Professor J. Allen Hynek corrected Menzel – pointing to Gill's own written statement, that he had seen the planet which occupied a distinctly separate part of the sky.

The Royal Australian Air Force sent two officers to interview Father Gill. At that time, like its contemporaries in the US, Britain and Europe, the RAAF was heavily engaged in discrediting witnesses and trying to shake their belief in what they had experienced. Father Gill recalled – characteristically without rancor – that the officers "talked about stars and planets and then left."

But the Gill encounters were not so easily dismissed. Importantly there were multiple witnesses who offered strikingly similar accounts. Even more significantly it became apparent in the weeks following the visitations that they had occurred during a "flying saucer flap" involving scores of isolated settlements across Papua New Guinea. Investigators were able finally to catalog more than 600 of these sightings.

Peter Norris, tough-mindedly skeptical president of the Victorian Flying Saucer Research Society, summarized the Boianai case favorably. The Gill reports, he said, constituted the most remarkable testimony of UFO activity ever given to civilian investigators. The society evaluated the Gill documents as "unique" because, for the first time, credible observers had reported the presence of humanoid beings associated with UFOs.

"Look at Us – We're Here!"

Dr Menzel and his fellow flying saucer disparagers had an easier time in the 1950s than they would have enjoyed today. Technology, in the form of videotape and digital cameras, now enables witnesses to produce proof – or at least tentative proof – of what they saw.

A particularly dramatic case of mass verification occurred on July 11 1991 when thousands of tourists poured into Mexico City, recommended as the ideal place to view the pending eclipse of the sun. Many visitors brought video cameras to capture the event. They also captured something they had not expected.

As the solar disk darkened, a variety of anomalous objects – domed, circular, oval, cigar-shaped – began to swarm through the sky above the city. Literally hundreds of people, from home movie amateurs to professional TV cameramen, caught the extraordinary scene on videotape. The UFO invasion was screened by television stations around the world. The phenomenon lasted for weeks beyond the eclipse and attracted television crews from the United States, Japan and Europe.

One tape, shot at night by a police officer in Atlixo, shows a circular craft, clearly under intelligent control hovering at roughly 1,000 feet. Bigger than a football field, it is ringed with yellow lights. Police chief Miguel Cruz commented, "The lights look exactly like a ship's cabin windows."

Even Joseph Fernandes, Mexico's most celebrated UFO debunker, was impressed. After years of telling witnesses they had seen nothing more than Jupiter or weather balloons he conceded that many of the images shown on TV were unexplainable. The footage that first caused him to change his mind showed two bright-red globes performing sharp-angle turns above a mountain. "I will admit that no ordinary aircraft would be capable of these maneuvers," he said.

Almost 13 years later (March 5 2004) UFOs posed again for Mexican cameras. The photographer this time was a reconnaisance officer aboard an air force plane assigned to monitor drug-traffickers. While cruising at 11,000 feet through a late evening sky above Campeche the pilot suddenly realized he had company: a small number of dazzlingly bright objects whose number rapidly increased. Eventually surrounding the aircraft (as tape analysis later showed) were 16 brightly shining UFOs of varying sizes.

The Mexican government, which is less inclined toward secrecy than America and her allies analyzed the 15-minute videotape then released it to newspapers and Mexico's biggest TV network, Televisa. The footage shows the objects swarming rapidly around the aircraft. Lieutenant Mario Vasquez, the infrared equipment operator said, "These images are genuine, completely real. There's no way they could have been faked or altered."

To officials – and later to reporters – the pilots and crew offered detailed and separate testimonies. They said the encounter began when three disks appeared beside the jet. *But the moment the crewmen switched on their camera, eight more objects popped into view*.

It was difficult to avoid the conclusion (anthropomorphic though it may seem) that the UFOs *wanted* to be seen – and wanted their presence recorded.

This was not at all unusual. In a large proportion of the thousands of sightings I have investigated, the same rule – which I call the Father Gill syndrome – has applied. By means of spectacular behavior, or marks left on the ground, or subliminal messages, UFOs seem often to *invite* us to observe them. The French physicist Jacques Vallee had a theory about this.

Humanity, he surmised, is being conditioned; slowly trained to look outward and beyond its own petty planetary concerns.

In 1985 the Australian Broadcasting Corporation invited me to conduct a one-hour national talkback program on UFOs. I invited listeners to describe not only their sightings, but to recall how those experiences came about. More than half the callers claimed they had received some kind of prior warning that they would see something anomalous. One woman said:

"My sister and I were walking one evening in hilly countryside near our house. Suddenly, as we later agreed when we compared notes, our skins began to prickle strangely. Then something prompted us to look up – and we saw dome-shaped objects among the stars. We were both convinced we'd been told to look."

Another caller said:

"I was driving along a deserted country road in Western Australia when I had to slam on the brakes. A large branch was lying across the road. When I got out to shift the branch my attention was attracted by something weird. It was a large oval craft sitting in a paddock, ringed with strangely colored lights and surrounded by a kind of mist. I got out of there as fast as I could. I've often wondered whether that branch was placed on the road deliberately... and whether for some unknown reason I'd been singled out to see what I did."

In 1978, when I was writing for Rupert Murdoch's national daily, *The Australian*, a reader, Mrs Gail Glanville, kindly sent me a photograph of a peculiar aerial object which she had taken in Gosford, New South Wales. The UFO was large and egg-shaped with two bright panels on its underside. Two of my photographer friends on the newspaper, Mike Arthur and Andrew de la Rue, submitted the picture to 150 magnifications. Mike reported, "There's no way this could be an insect on the lens or a flaw in the emulsion. In magnification all details remain clearly delineated."

Perhaps more significant than the UFO itself was the manner in which its photograph came to be taken. Mrs Glanville told me:

"I was driving through the countryside with my husband – and at the time nothing could have been further from my mind than odd things in the

sky. But suddenly something very powerfully prompted me to tell him to stop the car. I got out and took two pictures of the landscape and clouds – why, I didn't really know. I had no idea I'd photographed anything extra. But when we had the film developed one of the shots showed the object. The other, although I'd taken it under identical conditions, was blank."

Three of the most dramatic UFO photographs ever taken were accidentally captured by a New Zealand man, Lou Blackburn, on October 27 1979. Accidentally, that is, on his part. The object seems to have steered itself directly toward the spot where he was standing.

SKY JEWEL At dawn on October 27 1979 New Zealander Lou Blackburn took photographs of a friend's new fishing boat at Motunau Beach. He was unaware until the slides were shown months later that his camera had three times captured a UFO, clustered with iridescent lights, moving above the water.
Lou Blackburn

Lou, an amateur photographer, had simply intended to take snaps of a crayfishing boat his friends Norman and June Neilson recently bought. He was unaware the camera had snared images of a craft ringed with lights until three months later when the crayboat photographs were projected at a Neilson family slide show.

Lou took the shots at sunrise. Using a 35mm Olympus camera he photographed the Neilsons' crayboat as it moved out of the tidal river mouth at Motunau Beach. The boat, the dark sea and the burgeoning sun were the only things he saw. Because they lived in a remote area the Neilsons had to wait until December to have the film processed. In January, using a projector, they had their first real look at the pictures of their new boat.

June Neilson told me, "A friend was first to see the UFO. He asked, 'What's that cluster of diamond-colored lights in the sky?' And we've been wondering ever since."

Photographic experts ruled out any possibility the images could be a hoax. One report said, "This is a genuine photograph taken of a UFO under existing cloud formation." Investigators deemed the pictures "scientifically significant". The reason: the shots were taken 19 miles south of Kaikoura Strait which, 10 months earlier, was the scene of one of the world's most-publicized UFO cases.

The drama began on December 21 1978 when pilots John Randle and Vern Powell claimed their *Argosy* freighter plane had been buzzed by five UFOs over the Clarence River. Powell, a pilot of 25 years experience, described one as "a brilliant white light, like an arc lamp, and moving at tremendous speed. Later it changed to a red light."

The anomalies were tracked on radar by the air traffic control towers in both Wellington and Christchurch. Controllers watched for more than an hour as the five objects dogged the plane. One UFO, registered on Wellington radar and seen by ground observers, stopped dead in the sky and remained motionless for 30 minutes (echoing the behavior of he circular craft that stood stock-still above the shallows at Boianai).

The Melbourne TV station then known as Channel 0 asked one of its senior reporters, Quentin Fogarty, who was vacationing in New Zealand, to hire a plane and film crew and recreate the events the pilots had described. The channel's news department saw it as a good silly-season filler.

Three days later Quentin told me, "All we'd expected to do was reconstruct what happened in December. Instead, about 40 miles out of Wellington, the objects started coming at us. Dave Crockett started his camera and filmed them.

"I got the powerful feeling they were in control and were aware we were taking pictures."

Throughout the flight Wellington and Christchurch radar relayed warnings to Fogarty's pilot, Captain Bill Startup, that he was in danger of colliding with fleets of glowing "unknowns." When he returned to Melbourne Quentin said several of the objects which had buzzed the plane were immense and saucer-shaped with clearly visible domes. Others were round or egg-shaped with rings of light moving around them at fantastic speeds. One was as big as a four-story house.

Dr Mike Deakin, senior lecturer in mathematics at Monash University, also studied the film, making measurements of frozen frames. TV producer Leonard Lee took the film to the United States for testing by the optical physicist Dr Bruce MacCabee. Dr MacCabee made digitized prints of some frames. One of these computer pictures shows a glowing triangle in the black early morning sky. Another reveals an oval shape with a dome-like protuberance. A third depicts a circular object traveling at immense speed. On a single film frame it describes a near-perfect figure 8.

When the news plane landed after its first flight Mrs Crockett, shaken by the experience, chose to stay on the ground. Quentin Fogarty and his colleagues, showing considerable courage, ordered the *Argosy* up again to take more film.

I arrived early at Channel 0 Melbourne to see the first rough videocassettes of the footage flown in from Christchurch and to hear Quentin's commentary. At one point of his report he said, "We've just heard from Wellington radar that we've got one behind us... it's a bright white and green light... we've just been informed by Christchurch radar that there are six UFOs in front of us... This gets the old adrenalin flowing... I can say for sure we have a firm convert here... we've now heard from Wellington radar there's another one behind us. Let's hope they're friendly."

The Fogarty-Crockett film aroused international interest. The BBC bought it and described it in a newscast as "a world-first". The footage was shown also on America's CBS. Predictably it inspired a hail of ridicule from "experts" who had neither traveled aboard the plane nor rigorously examined the filmic evidence – but simply knew such an event could never have occurred.

During the *Argosy's* flights the Royal New Zealand Air Force was placed on standby. Officially the force did all it could to debunk and minimize the affair. When Dr Bruce MacCabee tried to charter *Argosy* to recreate its strange odyssey the owners refused. The air force, they explained, had "requested" that no further UFO flights be made.

Bruce MacCabee joined a study group of 17 scientists headed by Professor J. Allen Hynek, former astronomical consultant to the US Air Force. The team included a plasma physicist, an electronics consultant, a biophysicist and an optical physiologist. They subjected the footage to massive computer analysis.

Several months later Professor Hynek, the former professional skeptic, called a press conference in New York to describe the film as "the first verified UFO sighting." He added, "No sensible explanation has been offered for this phenomenon. It is certainly not a hoax. This film and the evidence accompanying it raise UFOs above buffoonery to a scientific level."

Close Encounters of the Sinister Kind

Not all intruders are as apparently harmless as those who tracked the *Argosy* or waved to the watchers at Father Gill's mission. Many "contactees" claim to have experienced extreme trauma during encounters with aliens. In most countries support groups have been established to help these people cope. Often, however, circumstances will oblige a sufferer to endure the nightmare alone. One such situation was described to me by a correspondent George Hodgekiss:

"Shortly after my 60th birthday I retired from a fairly stressful line of work and began to look around for something quite different. I accepted a job minding an oil rig on the edge of the Gibson Desert. I imagined I would be able to enjoy the peace the desert brings – but it didn't entirely turn out that way.

"The first in a series of troubling events occurred on May 21 1986. I'd turned off the generator and was standing by the gas stove looking out at the clear stars when I saw a huge bright light. At first I imagined it was a convoy of trucks coming my way. As my only contact with people was through the pilots who flew in supplies I was pleased – and put on coffee for the drivers. But when I came back the light had disappeared. In its place was a brilliantly lit box, about the size of a removal van. It hovered above the desert for a while, then faded and vanished.

"Between May and October that light appeared frequently and in various forms. Sometimes it was balloon-shaped and at others like a beam. Often it was accompanied by a deafening roar, like a power-drill. One night a formation of flashing lights in the shape of a cube hung over the camp. When I tried to chase them in my Nissan Patrol I found the battery had gone flat.

"The next evening something in the shape of a square hung over the camp. It was so white and bright my eyes ached when I tried to look at it.

"At this point for some reason the diesel engines and generator went into overload. The diesels weighed over 15 tonnes and were mounted on a steel skid. They'd bounce up and down as though something very powerful was shaking them.

"All this activity, whatever it was, played havoc with the birds and animals. When I was walking around, birds would simply drop dead in my path. And I saw night-hawks, which have amazingly acute eyesight, fly straight into the side of a drill. In October, when my six months were up, I returned to Perth with a great sense of relief."

In June 1992 the Massachusetts Institute of Technology hosted a conference of health professionals who had psychiatrically examined people making claims of alien contact. They had found the vast majority of these people (drawn principally from the ranks of those who had reported abduction) to be sane. Delegates could suggest no conventional medical explanation for what seemed to be happening.

One of the people attending the conference was the social scientist Keith Basterfield, a working member of the organisation UFO Research Australia. Before studying the evidence presented at the conference he had tended to disbelieve the testimony of purported abductees. But following his return to Adelaide he established a telephone hotline to help people who believed they had been victims. One caller, a psychology graduate, told the psychologists working with Basterfield that she had until recently felt little interest in UFOs and had read virtually nothing on the subject. She said her views changed radically when "something" lifted her from her bed and subjected her to an unpleasant ordeal.

With what seemed to be characteristic understatement she told the psychologists:

"I woke up one morning and told my husband that an interesting thing had happened overnight. I'd found the room filled by a brilliant blinding light. I was then lifted up into the light, getting the feeling meanwhile that I shouldn't be afraid.

"Next I was lying on a table surrounded by strange beings. I got the mental impression they were saying, 'This will be uncomfortable but not painful." Then I felt something probing my stomach – and I sensed they were going to take eggs from an ovary. They told me not to be frightened and said, 'You're going back now, but you won't feel this really happened.' Next thing I knew I was wide awake in bed, remembering everything.

"I never believed for a moment that the experience was a dream. It was stark and very real."

Keith Basterfield told me that some victims fear for their sanity. "But psychologists working with UFO researchers are helping these people come to terms with whatever it might be that has happened to them."

Some people seeking the hotline's help reported having their first experiences in early childhood. One was a Queensland man who recalled being kidnapped by arcane beings when he was between four and six years old. The aliens were blue-gray in color with large heads and eyes and no visible ears. While talking to the boy telepathically they placed him on a low table then moved a box the size of a cigarette pack across his body. "Then they inserted something up my nose," the man said. "It was painful. Throughout my life I've associated this experience with seeing a blue light outside the window."

Mysteriously missing time was a major theme in many cases. A Finnish couple, Ben and Helen K., set out from Rockhampton in central Queensland at 11.35 p.m. to drive to Gladstone. They were bemused on arrival to find that 40 minutes had passed and that neither had the faintest memory of the towns they had passed through. However they did remember seeing "an unusual green light". Something odd had also happened to their 1971 Valiant sedan. It had unusual marks on the bonnet and was covered with a film of odorless oil.

A similarly tantalizing "time-loss" was experienced by two young men, P and H, while driving near Port Lincoln, west of Adelaide. "We saw a light in the sky, then we entered a kind of endless space," one said. "During this time I can vaguely remember walking into a big room and seeing some kind of being. Then we were back in the car – and it was hours later."

"Some reports of abductions are similar to descriptions of near-death experiences," Keith Basterfield said.

UFO Burns: Victims Sued America

IN 1982, THREE PEOPLE who claimed they had suffered radiation injuries from a flame-belching UFO sought $20 million compensation from the US Government.

The Administration denied all knowledge of the event.

The scarred, sick victims were a 51-year-old grocery store owner, Betty Cash, her employee Vicki Landrum, 57, and grandson Colby, age seven.

Their ordeal began on a pine-wooded back road near Huffman Texas on December 29 1980. After eating an evening meal at a roadhouse they were headed home with Betty at the wheel. At about 9.15 p.m., they reported, a large glowing object emitting flames from its base appeared above the treetops ahead. It appeared to be descending swiftly and Betty accelerated, hoping to speed past before it landed.

But she was too late. The bright blue UFO, diamond-shaped and about 15 times the car's size, was now so low that its cone of flame blocked the road ahead. Betty came to a halt about 260 feet from the object, which she subsequently described as "making a beeping sound", looking like aluminum and "lighting the road brighter than day." She was surprised that the forest crown had not caught fire, but she could see in the bright light that the upper leaves had turned brown.

She put the car in park, then with her friend got out for a closer look. Vicki quickly returned to comfort the terrified boy – but Betty, consumingly curious, dared to walk closer. She had no doubt that the peculiar object was an aircraft of some kind – one that seemed to be in trouble. She began to wonder whether she should try to get help. This was when she first noticed that the brightness had begun to burn her skin.

She hurried back to the car, whose handle was so fiery it burned her flesh. Using a jacket sleeve to protect her fingers she opened the door, steadied herself on the dashboard and climbed back into the sedan's now-stifling interior. When investigators later checked the car they found that Betty's fingerprints had become permanently embedded in the dash.

Betty closed the window against the heat and switched the airconditioning to Cold. As she cowered with her companions, wondering what to do next, the diamond-shaped object began slowly to ascend. When it was clear of the trees an astonishing thing happened.

A swarm of black military helicopters, filling the sky with shattering noise, suddenly appeared and surrounded the UFO. In their legal testimony the women said the helicopters gave the impression of being escort aircraft.

As the enigmatic craft, still ringed by helicopters, moved away over the trees Betty tried to restart her car. After great difficulty the engine came to life and she was able to head home. Several times along the way the trio spotted the glowing UFO again, dogged by its estimated 23 helicopter companions.

They were not the only witnesses. An oilfield worker, Jerry McDonald, noticed the display from his back garden. An off-duty Dayton, policeman L. Walker, and his wife, who were driving home from Cleveland also saw the aerial procession. He identified the helicopters as Chinooks. This tallied with investigators' later analysis of drawings separately made by Betty Cash and the Landrums. The 'copters, their pencil pictures suggested, were large double-rotor CH-47s, accompanied by what appeared to be fast single-rotor Bell-Hueys.

Betty dropped her passengers at their house, then drove on to her own home where a friend and her children were staying. The friend was shocked by Betty's appearance. Her skin was a blazing red, suggestive of someone who had lain in tropical sun all day. Her neck was grossly swollen and blisters had appeared on her eyelids and mouth. She woke frequently during the night to vomit. Colby and his grandmother suffered symptoms similar but less severe – probably because they had spent less time outside the car. Nevertheless all three were so sick that they were eventually admitted to hospital, where specialists tried unsuccessfully to ascertain what had happened to them. The best guess was that they had suffered radiation burns, but no one could be sure.

In the years that followed Betty was repeatedly hospitalized, several times for intensive care. She lost more than half the hair on her head. Continuous skin eruptions left her with permanent scars. Vicki and Colby suffered similar skin troubles, along with deteriorating eyesight. Vicki also lost hair from her head. When it eventually grew back it was of a different texture.

All three victims incurred such enormous medical expenses that in 1982 they approached their senator, Lloyd Bentsen, who arranged a meeting with government lawyers at Bergstrom Air Force Base. The army assigned Lieutenant Colonel George Serran to investigate. He reported that although he was convinced of Cash and Landrum's sincerity he could find no evidence that military helicopters had been in the area at the time. No bases in the area could have produced such a large number of Chinooks.

John Schuessler, deputy director of America's Mutual UFO Network, also studied the case. He detected no radioactivity at the encounter site – but did find an area of melted asphalt.

When the US military sympathetically but firmly refused any compensation, CAUSE (Citizens Against UFO Secrecy) stepped in. New York attorney Peter Gersten filed a $20 million lawsuit on the three victims' behalf. After hearing "expert" evidence from NASA and the air force, army and navy, US District Court judge Ross Sterling dismissed the case. He was satisfied, he said, that no craft similar to that described by Cash and Landrum was under the control of any US Government agency.

But the judge might have been wrong. In the decades following the Cash-Landrum incident many other witnesses reported seeing black helicopters in company with UFOs.

Churchill, Stalin in "Flying Saucer" Search

THE LEADERS of Britain and the Soviet Union were so alarmed by military and civilian UFO sightings that they established secret projects to discover what was going on.

In 1952 during a rash of UFO reports British Prime Minister Winston Churchill sent his advisers this memo:

"What does all this stuff about flying saucers amount to? What can it mean? What is the truth?"

Churchill was promptly briefed with a report from a shadowy scientific panel, the Working Party on Flying Saucers. Established in 1951 in conjunction with the Defence Ministry the group was chaired by the developer of radar, Sir Henry Tizard. Its findings were comforting: all UFO sightings were explicable by misidentifications of earthly aircraft or such natural events as meteors or the weather.

Whether Churchill was reassured by this, history does not record. But it is known that several months after he wrote his memorandum the Royal Air Force issued an order banning all personnel from discussing sightings with anyone not from the military. In London's *Observer* (November 21 2001) writer Paul Harris commented:

"In trying to underplay sightings Britain was following the lead of the United States, which had conducted several studies into its own UFO sightings and adopted a policy of official secrecy. When the British report was presented a top CIA scientist traveled over to the meeting to make sure the conclusions of America's closest ally fitted in."

Dictator Joseph Stalin (as described in greater detail earlier) was equally disturbed by the UFO mystery. In 1948 he ordered that secret research projects into the phenomenon be established at no less than four military establishments and seven universities. Their brief was to determine the nature of flying saucers and to establish the degree (if any) to which they were a threat to Russia.

Stalin's scientific advisers were generally disinclined to believe that the craft were of terrestrial origin: at least as we understand that term. Optimistically the dictator ordered that UFOs be captured and their technology studied to give the USSR a technological edge over its enemies.

There is no evidence that a working UFO ever fell into Soviet hands. But there are clues which seem tentatively to suggest that the United States might have been luckier.

The Day John Lennon Died Twice
Mystery of Coincidence

Beatle John Lennon once remarked that he attracted coincidences "like a magnet." Eerily, these flukes of chance kept recurring to the day of his death. Just seven minutes after an insane gunman murdered Lennon on a New York street, a second John Lennon died in the celebrated singer's home city of Liverpool. Psychologist Carl Jung described such synchronicity (his name for coincidence) as "the most powerful natural force" in the universe. In Jung's view, synchronicity, mysterious in its workings, often alters the course of history – and has the power to shape our lives.

ON DECEMBER 9 1980 (Liverpool time) a deranged assassin gunned down former Beatle John Lennon on New York's 72nd Street. Media outlets around the world paid tribute to Lennon, recognizing him as one of the century's most important composers of popular music.

But the *Liverpool Echo*, principal newspaper in the singer's 574,000-population home city, added something more.

Initially unnoticed in the paper's Lennon-dominated page of classified death notices was a small advertisement marking the demise of a *second* John Lennon. This 56-year-old man, a kitchen porter at a Liverpool hostel, had also died on December 9 – just seven minutes after the murder of his famous namesake. His name was real – not adopted.

Before long, mathematicians were being asked to calculate the odds against two John Lennons, both Liverpool men, expiring within minutes of each other on the same date.

In the words of a Russian proverb, "Women know that cherries will always crowd together in a cherry pie."

The Austrian biologist Paul Kammerer managed to give scientific weight to this old saw. During the 1920s, with exemplary patience, he spent seven to eight hours daily sitting on park benches, scrupulously noting the age, sex and type of clothing of passersby, along with the shapes of their umbrellas, bags and parcels. When he analyzed his tables he found that they showed the classic *clustering* patterns familiar to everyone from gamblers to actuaries.

Repeatedly over the months, Kammerer's graphs identified dense clusters of coats of the same color, shoes of the same shape and pedestrians of roughly the same age. In his resulting scientific paper (which Einstein praised as "by no means absurd") Kammerer wrote, "The recurrence of identical or similar data in contiguous areas of space or time is a simple empirical fact which coincidence... cannot satisfactorily explain."

Death Takes a Vacation

ON SEPTEMBER 1 1946 the *New York Times* published a brief report headlined OBIT EDITOR OFF, DEATHS STOP. The story read:

"Mrs Mildred West, whose duties on the *Alton Evening Telegraph* include the writing of obituaries, has been taking a week's vacation.

And for the first time in the memory of her fellow workers on the newspaper a week has passed with no deaths being reported in this city of 32,000.

Normally 10 deaths occur on average every week."

The Awesome Apollo Coincidence

Some synchronicities, however, are so breathtakingly extraordinary that it seems impossible to dismiss them as mere "empirical facts."

In 1994 the British scientific journal *Nature* published a letter from Andrew Scott, pointing out strange links between the *Apollo II* moon landing (1969) and the three Shoemaker-Levy comet fragments which crashed on Jupiter (1994):

- Comet fragment #1 struck Jupiter on the same day as *Apollo II* was launched, 25 years earlier.

- Comet fragment #2 hit Jupiter 25 years *to the minute* after *Apollo II*'s astronauts landed on the moon. (This fact was also noted by Arthur C. Clarke, author of *2001: A Space Odyssey*.)

- Comet fragment #3 collided with Jupiter almost exactly 25 years after *Apollo II* lifted off from the lunar surface.

Few coincidences – at least those we know about – resonate on so cosmic a scale. Through the years hundreds of readers have kindly sent me letters describing synchronicities in their lives. These experiences are always small, but fascinating nonetheless. In 1996 Pam Green wrote from Sydney, "My ex-husband's date of birth was July 3, 1959 – a fact whose significance you'll appreciate shortly. After we broke up, remaining friends I'm happy to say, I was on my own for a couple of years. Then I met a man with whom I really clicked. On our first date I discovered to my surprise that he was in the same line of rather specialized business as my ex-husband, though they didn't know each other. We're now sharing our lives – but it was only after we'd been together for a few months that I learned something which quite astonished me. He, too, was born on July 3, 1959. So he's the same age as my husband and in the same profession. It almost feels as if, while I'm starting a new life, some force is trying to haul me back into the old one…"

Dennis the Menace X 2

An eerie echoing of dates and names occurred in 1951 when two cartoon characters, each named Dennis the Menace, simultaneously began their careers on opposite sides of the Atlantic Ocean. Britain's Dennis appeared (and still does) in the comic paper *Beano*. America's Dennis started life as a syndicated newspaper strip.

It was several weeks before the Americans and the Britons became aware that their newly minted Dennises had namesakes.

The comic strips' creators were then confronted by the most stunning coincidence of all. The two characters had made their debuts on the same day: March 12 1951.

* * *

Another case in which a name created synchronous echoes was described by the French physicist Jacques Vallee. During the 1970s he became interested in a Los Angeles cult, the Order of Melchizedek, named after a minor biblical prophet.

Hoping to find references to Melchizedek, Vallee visited a public library, without success. Several days later he took a cab to Los Angeles airport and on arrival asked the female driver for a receipt. She tore a slip from her book and signed it *M. Melchizedek*. Vallee was impressed by the coincidence, but surmised that the surname might be common among certain migrants. On returning home he checked the massive multi-volume Los Angeles telephone directory.

It listed only one Melchizedek: his cabdriver.

In recalling this experience Vallee imagines a situation in which a librarian has to decide between two methods of storing books – either alphabetically or as a jumble. If she chooses the latter system she might ensure that each randomly arranged volume has a beeper fitted to its spine. It will respond to a signal by making a sound to advertise its position. Possibly, says Vallee, this is a rough simulation of how the universe operates, with beepers sometimes responding to our signals and creating what we understand as coincidences.

But he concedes that it's only a theory.

Many synchronicities involve the seemingly pointed linkage of words to an event – as in the case of John Steinbeck's burning books. A truck loaded with several thousand copies of the author's latest novel flipped over and burst into flames after it was struck by a bus running out of control. The novel's title: *The Wayward Bus*.

Lennon's Line of Nines

JOHN LENNON was convinced, with some justification, that the number 9 played a peculiarly synchronistic role in his life. In media interviews he returned repeatedly to the subject.

- Lennon was born on October 9, as was his son Sean.
- Brian Epstein first saw The Beatles perform at The Cavern (nine letters) on November 9 1961.
- The Beatles signed their first recording contract with EMI on May 9 1962.
- The group's debut recording *Love Me Do* was numbered 4949 on Parlophone.
- Lennon wrote three of his songs, *Number 9 Dream*, *Revolution 9* and *One After 909* at his mother's house, 9 Wavertree Road, Liverpool. He believed this address had favorable aspects ("Wavertree" and "Liverpool" each have nine letters).
- He met Yoko Ono on November 9 1966.
- The numerical coincidences continued to the time of his death and beyond. The gunman Mark Chapman shot Lennon in New York on December 8 1980. But the five-hour time difference meant it was December 9 in Liverpool.
- An ambulance took the singer's body to the Roosevelt (nine letters) hospital... on 9th Avenue.

Electrifying Odds

In 1989 a chain of coincidence involving a nursing sister and her two adult daughters extended across three American cities.

The synchronous events were set in motion when Gloria Patterson of Baltimore was woken by thunder and pounding rain. Unable to sleep she switched on a bedside lamp and television set. Lightning then struck the house, popping the lightbulb and shorting the TV.

Distressed, Mrs Patterson rang her elder daughter Mary in Phoenix. She was shocked to learn that Mary's house also had been struck by lightning. A TV and video recorder had been ruined – and a fireball was hovering around a skirting-board socket.

Mother and daughter chatted for a while, then said goodnight.

As Mrs Patterson was settling back to sleep she received a call from her other daughter Susan in Bel Air. The young woman reported that lightning had just struck her chimney, scattering bricks across the sittingroom.

Lightning seemingly refuses to leave some people alone. Roy Sullivan, a US park ranger, had continuous millions-to-one brushes with shocks from the sky. *The Guinness Book of Records* chronicles his high-voltage history:

In 1942 a lightning bolt sheared off his big toenail. In 1969 lightning removed his eyebrows.

The following year it seared his shoulder – and a bolt in 1972 set his hair ablaze. Sullivan was struck again in 1973, 1976 and 1977. But when he died in 1982 lightning was not to blame.

An extremely odd lightning coincidence befell Jennie Roberts while she was vacationing with her husband on Queensland's South Stradbroke Island in October 1991.

She was sunbathing on a rubber mattress when she was struck by a surge of power that entered her body through her watchband and burned a trail to her toes. The rubber mattress saved her life.

The lightning also burned a hole through the book Jennie Roberts was reading. Its title: *The Dead Zone*, by Stephen King. The book's cover shows a man being struck by lightning.

Case of the Dumbstruck Donor

A coincidence that focused laser-like on the three people involved was chronicled by *The Times*, UK, on December 31 1998. Vladimir Gusiyev (a pseudonym) was in the habit of walking his dog every morning before leaving for work. He began to notice a pretty young woman who proceeded regularly in the other direction, taking her infant son to a nursery.

Vladimir plucked up courage to talk to the woman, who seemed happy to tell him she was divorced. They began to keep company – and soon married.

From the beginning mutual friends remarked on the little boy's striking resemblance to Vladimir. The local optometrist even pointed out that the child suffered a minor eye defect similar to his stepfather's. It was this final jigsaw-piece of information that prompted Vladimir to consider a wild possibility.

The previous year he had donated sperm at a fertility clinic. His wife had told him that months before the separation her former husband had agreed that she be artificially inseminated.

Vladimir dared to wonder whether his stepson – offspring of a woman he had met randomly in the street – might be his own natural child.

A DNA test confirmed that his hunch was correct.

* * *

Another interesting example of synchronous relationships can be found in William Manchester's *American Caesar* (1978). He reveals that three principal figures of World War II – Prime Minister Winston Churchill, President Franklin D. Roosevelt and General Douglas MacArthur – were all descended from a Mrs Sarah Belcher of Taunton, Massachusetts. General MacArthur just happened to be an eighth cousin of Winston Churchill and a sixth cousin, once removed, of FDR.

Close By – When 3 Presidents Were Shot

BY A FLUKE of chance, Abraham Lincoln's son Robert was at the scene when three presidents fell victim to assassins.

- He was present on April 15 1865 when his father, wounded by John Wilkes Booth's bullet, lost his struggle for survival.
- On July 2 1881 Robert Lincoln was with President James A. Garfield at Washington's Baltimore and Potomac Railroad Station when Garfield was gunned down. He was at the stricken president's side within seconds.
- On September 6 1901 President William McKinley was attending the Pan-American Exposition in Buffalo when a gunman fatally wounded him. Robert Lincoln was on a train arriving in Buffalo when the shooting occurred. He hurried to comfort the president, who died eight days later.

More than a century after Abraham Lincoln's death, students of synchronicity began to point out the strange pattern of coincidences that seemed to link him to assassinated President John F. Kennedy.

- Lincoln was elected to Congress in 1846; Kennedy in 1946.
- Lincoln was elected president in 1860; Kennedy in 1960.
- Both men were strongly concerned with civil rights.
- The wives of Lincoln and Kennedy lost children while living in the White House.
- Both presidents were shot in the head, from behind, on a Friday, with their wives at their side.
- The car in which Kennedy died was a Ford Lincoln. Lincoln was shot in Ford's Theater.
- John Wilkes Booth, who killed Lincoln, was born in 1839. Lee Harvey Oswald, who killed Kennedy, was born in 1939.
- Both assassins were known by their three names – each set of which comprises 15 letters.
- Booth ran from the theater and was caught in a warehouse. Oswald ran from a warehouse and was caught in a theater.
- Both assassins were killed before they could be tried.
- Shortly before Lincoln died he was in Monroe, Maryland. Shortly before Kennedy was shot he was visiting Marilyn Monroe.
- Both presidents were warned of danger. Lincoln's secretary, who was named Kennedy, begged him not to go to the theater. Kennedy's secretary, who was named Lincoln, implored him to stay away from Dallas.
- Both men were assassinated by Southerners.
- Both men were succeeded by Southerners.
- Both successors had the surname Johnson.
- Lincoln's successor, Andrew Johnson, was born in 1808. Kennedy's successor, Lyndon B. Johnson, was born in 1908.

The Magical Notepad

A synchronicity of names which Carl Jung might have described as significant and life-shaping is described by the American writer Stephen Diamond in his book *What the Trees Said* (1971). The author recalls how, with only $10 in his pocket, he spent an idyllic weekend with a girlfriend in San Francisco. It was, he says "a strange and wonderful meeting of body and mind… under the watchful eyes of the eucalyptus trees."

Anxious to obtain a notebook to record his experiences, Diamond went to the local drugstore, but left empty-handed. Walking back to the house he noticed a paper notepad lying face-down on a pile of old clothes and books. He picked up the pad and tore off the first few pages which were caked with mud. The rest of the 200 sheets were clean and ready to use.

It was a doctor's pad. At the top of each page was printed the name STEPHEN DIAMOND, MD.

Writer Stephen Diamond was shaken by this coincidence of names. "I took it as a sign," he says, "a road-marker which seemed to indicate that I was on the right track in that search for healing and the essence of my former self..."

The Uncanny Visitor

Jeffrey Simmons, chairman of the British publishing house W.H. Allen, had long been fascinated (largely as a bystander) by cases of synchronicity. In 1950 he encountered the phenomenon on a powerfully personal level. The experience inspired him to send a letter to the author Arthur Koestler, who published it in *The Times*. A copy was subsequently lodged in the files of the Society for Psychical Research.

Jeffrey Simmons said:

"My purpose in writing is to put on record for you something that happened to me which is in many ways more puzzling than anything similar I have read about.

"I have been a publisher for 25 years. During this time I have had occasion only once to pulp a book. For a time after the war a subsidiary company of ours published some Tarzan *books in paperback. As near as I can recollect the year was perhaps 1950. A letter reached me from a... very irate lady who wrote that she had always regarded the* Tarzan *books as suitable for children, but she was disgusted to discover that they were filled with descriptions of sex and flagellation – and how dare we publish such filth?*

"The explanation for this outburst was that the Tarzan *books were produced for us by a small printer – who also happened to print books which by the standards of the time were considered pornographic.*

"He had mistakenly bound the pornography in the Tarzan *covers and vice versa. He... suggested that we pulp the books and he would print new ones.*

"I asked our production manager whether he knew a firm that could do the (pulping) job. He said he did not, adding that he had never needed to pulp a book during his 40 years in publishing.

"By an unusual chance a young boy from our warehouse was delivering a message to the production manager at that very time. He told me he lived in Battersea and that there was a firm called Phillips Mills, of which I had not then heard.

"Using the production manager's telephone I asked our switchboard operator to look up their number and telephone them for me.

"She replied, 'Their representative is here.'

"I thought at first that she was joking – but in fact the Phillips Mills representative had walked in literally seconds before I spoke to the operator.

"He was an old man and told me that my office was on his beat. Apart for a short time when he was ill he had passed this office every day for years, but had never before called in. I asked him what had made him call in now. He said he did not know; something just told him to do so. Incidentally, he never called again, as far as I am aware.

"The amazing implications of this (string of coincidences) will not be lost on you. Telepathy can explain why the man called in, but in order for it to have operated he had to be passing at the very instant I wanted him, having just heard of this firm – on the one and only occasion I needed him.

"Was this preordained? At the very least there was some extraordinary chain of circumstances working in my favor. But why should it be so for something so seemingly unimportant? After all it would have made no material difference if I had had to telephone Phillips Mills and their representative had visited me the following week.

"If there are helpful forces operating in unimportant matters, might they not also be operating, unknown to me, in important cases? How much control do we have over our own destiny?"

Carl Jung suggested that curious coincidences of this kind might be the work of a "Cosmic Joker": a being, or force, whose sole motivation is to make sport with our lives. But some physicists believe that the explanation of synchronicity may lie within ourselves. Might it be, they ask, that our human consciousness continually *creates* the reality surrounding us – and that coincidences are therefore no more than the physical products of our thoughts?

Curious Case of the Mirror-Image Murders

STRANGE SIMILARITIES between two murders, committed 157 years apart, have intrigued British police.

Birmingham detectives noticed the coincidences when they glanced over yellowing crime files during an office clearout. The antique records showed that the rape-strangling of a young woman near the village of Eddington in 1817 was identical in numerous details to a killing at the same spot in 1974.

In both cases a man named Thornton was arrested, tried and acquitted.

So many other synchronicities linked the two cases that the detectives compiled a dossier. Its principal points:

• The body of the first victim, 20-year-old Mary Ashford, was found in long grass on **May 27** 1817.
• On **May 27** 1974 the body of Barbara Forrest, also 20, was found 390 yards from where Mary died.
• The young women are thought to have shared the same birthday.
• Both had died at approximately the same time of day.
• On the eve of their murders, both had visited a friend's house to change before going to a dance.
• From 8 p.m. until midnight on May 26 1817 Mary danced and drank with a young bricklayer, Abraham Thornton. Afterwards he walked her home.
• From 9 to 11 p.m. on May 26 1974 Barbara danced at the parish hall, built within yards of the hall where Mary had spent her final evening.
• Hours after Mary was found, Abraham Thornton was arrested and charged with murder.

- Hours after Barbara was found police arrested a man also named Thornton, with whom she had worked at a charity accommodation home.
- In August 1817 the first Thornton appeared at Warwick Assizes Court and was acquitted on all charges.
- In March 1975 the second Thornton faced a judge in a Birmingham court – and was also acquitted on all charges.

Crime Queen Died –
with Her Own Tale Untold:
Agatha Christie

When the bestselling crime novelist Agatha Christie mysteriously disappeared, newspapers worldwide speculated that she had been abducted or committed suicide. More than 15,000 volunteers scoured countryside surrounding the vanished writer's house. Hundreds of police across Britain and Europe followed a tangle of trails and questioned numerous witnesses, but could find no key to the case. After 11 days during which her husband came under increasing suspicion of murder, Agatha Christie was found at last. From this point however, the puzzle only deepened. Christie adamantly refused to tell anyone, relatives and detectives included, what had befallen her or where she had been. Almost half a century after her disappearance Agatha Christie died. Her secret was buried with her…

THE MARRIAGE OF Colonel Archibald Christie and his wife Agatha was not a happy one. He was a much-decorated flying hero of World War I: a stern, no-nonsense military man who tended to speak in monosyllables. Agatha, by contrast, was a romantic creature, described by one friend as "sensitive and imaginative, with a hunger for affection that she too seldom received."

Agatha, born in Torquay, England, to a wealthy and loving American father and his English wife, married Archibald on Christmas Eve 1914. While he fought with distinction in the Royal Flying Corps she served as a nurse. It was during her assigned time in the dispensary that she acquired the knowledge of drugs and poisons that would benefit her so richly as a writer.

In 1919 Agatha and her husband announced the birth of their daughter Rosalind. By this time Archibald had left the Flying Corps to work for a London firm of financiers.

Many marriages founder on the rocks of monetary argument – and it was financial difficulties that helped sunder the Christies. In their case however the problem was not too little cash, but too much. In 1920, while recovering from an illness, Agatha produced her debut detective novel *The Mysterious Affair at Styles*. She sold the book to the first publisher she approached. It was such a commercial and critical success that she proceeded at white heat to write more.

By the time the couple celebrated their tenth wedding anniversary Agatha's novels were selling in phenomenal numbers, making her an ever-richer woman. Archie, by contrast, was receiving a merely adequate salary in the city. He was a proud unbending man. Friends sensed that he was having difficulty coping with his wife's extremely public prosperity.

The money went to Agatha's head and she wasted thousands on ill-advised investments and purchases. But she had always been a generous soul – and she never ceased to press gifts and luxuries on her spouse. Archie, the kind of man who would rather be the condescending giver than the humble recipient, began to spend much more of his time on the golf course.

In 1926 the couple – or more accurately Agatha – bought a 12-bedroom mansion amid sweeping formal gardens in Sunningdale Berkshire. Visitors envied the Christies for their seemingly idyllic lives. It was apparent to few that there was a worm in the apple. Archibald Christie was now spending most of his spare time outside the house. He had become deeply and romantically involved with Nancy Neele, a member of the golf club.

Agatha found out. On the morning of December 3 1926 she angrily confronted her errant husband. He admitted the affair – and in the heat of the row demanded a divorce which would free him to marry his lover. Moreover he would spend that weekend with Nancy.

Agatha never revealed to anyone how distressed she was when her husband slammed out of the house. But the servants were in no doubt about the deep hurt she was feeling. Wealthy and lionized though she was, she remained a fragile and emotionally vulnerable person. Two maids and a gardener were the last people to see her that night. She went upstairs to kiss her sleeping daughter, then packed a few possessions in a bag, went out to her four-seater Morris car and drove away into the winter darkness.

When she was absent from breakfast next morning the servants raised the alarm. Archibald Christie, remorseful about his harsh words and fearful that his wife might have harmed herself, hurried home.

Local police quickly found the car, abandoned at a chalkpit only half a mile from the house. Its ignition was switched on, the front wheels suspended perilously over the edge of a 115-foot drop. On the back seat were a fur coat and several other items of clothing. However there was no sign of the missing woman. If Agatha had suicided she hadn't done it here.

With three rival police forces in the south of England competing to find her, and European police on alert, the disappearance of Agatha Christie dominated the daily news. In what was possibly the biggest missing-person hunt in British history hundreds of uniformed officers, aided by more than 15,000 volunteers, scoured the Surrey Downs. They were under official instruction to look for a body. Police divers spent numbing hours searching the bottom of Silent Pool, a dark deep lake in which several locals had sunk to their deaths. The missing writer had used this bleak stretch of water in one of her novels: drowning a character in its Stygian deeps.

Investigators had good reason for surmising that Agatha might be dead. Before she vanished she had written several confusingly contradictory letters. In one, to her brother-in-law, she claimed she was off to Yorkshire for a vacation; but in another, to local police, she said she feared for her life.

As hours of effort fruitlessly passed, police attitudes began to harden toward Archibald Christie. The fact that he was seeing another woman had attracted their suspicions from early in the investigation. Detectives now regarded him as a prime murder suspect and were granted permission by a magistrate to tap his phones and covertly follow him wherever he went. All the evidence pointed to Christie. He stood to inherit a considerable sum from his wife's will: a will she would certainly have changed when divorce proceedings began. Christie might well have seen this as a last window of opportunity to strike.

The colonel did little to help himself in the courts of police and public opinion. He blundered through the crisis, making statements that ranged from the inept to the seemingly detached. He told the *Daily Mail* that his wife had actually spoken to him in the past about the possibility of disappearing – observing that the sensation it would create might give her usable "atmosphere" for a novel. It was typical of Agatha's "theatrics", he suggested, that she should leave her car dangling dramatically above a chalkpit.

None of these observations played well with the British public. In the minds of many there was every possibility that Archie Christie was a killer. Newspapers, after all, were darkly hinting as much. It all made perfect sense: the other woman; the fortune he had surely hoped would soon be his. Why didn't the police arrest him at once?

The unfortunate Christie's accusers were eventually proved wrong. On December 14 a head-waiter took steps to save the colonel's diminishing reputation. The man rang police from the hotel where he worked: the Hydro, in Harrogate Yorkshire, to say that an attractive red-haired woman who had booked in several days earlier was – almost certainly in his view – the missing author. Several guests who had pored over her pictures in the newspapers agreed.

Police, a swarm of reporters and photographers in their wake, rushed to the hotel, which was 250 miles from the Christies' mansion. Detectives interviewed the woman who was registered under the name Teresa Neele. The coincidence was too great. "Neele" was the surname of Colonel Christie's lady-friend. Moreover, "Teresa", as one newspaper pointed out, was an anagram of "teaser" – a playful linguistic joke typical of Agatha Christie.

A police car ferried Archibald Christie to the hotel. To his immense relief he was able to step out of the shadow of the gallows by identifying "Teresa

Neele" as his wife. He later confided to friends that while his concern for Agatha's welfare had been paramount, he had been haunted also by a more selfish fear. Had she never been found, the circumstantial evidence might have placed a noose around his neck.

From the moment he saw his wife again, Archibald Christie became the protective husband he should have been all along – forbidding the milling journalists to venture anywhere near Agatha – and answering their questions about what might be ailing her with a shrug and the single word, "Amnesia."

With press cars in pursuit Agatha and Archie traveled by taxi to her sister's house in Cheadle, Cheshire. When they arrived the family turned the press away again. The next day, papers published a range of "sour grapes" stories for which Agatha Christie never forgave them. More than one writer echoed Archie's suggestion that she might cynically have staged her disappearance to gather material for a forthcoming novel. Others accused her of concocting a publicity stunt.

Some of these unfriendly articles were transparently designed to flush Agatha out. In defending herself, the editors hoped, she would be forced to explain what really had happened. She was too intelligent to take the bait, but the papers speculated anyway:

- She had intended to kill herself by driving her car at high speed over the chalkpit's edge – but her resolve had failed her at the last moment.

- She had, as her husband suggested, suffered an amnesia attack, "waking up" en route to the hotel, where she unconsciously – and poignantly – chose her rival's surname as a pseudonym.

- She knew precisely what she was doing – and had staged the disappearance in a desperate bid to win her husband's sympathy and bring him home.

- Some confidantes of the Christie family (one journalist reported) believed there was a far stranger and more sinister reason for the vanishing: a reason which, if known, would have shocked Britain.

Three years after Agatha Christie became the focus of one of her nation's most tantalizing mysteries Archie won his divorce and married Nancy Neele. At age 40 Agatha, too, remarried, becoming the wife of an archeologist, Sir Max Mallowan. The partnership was happy. She traveled with her new husband to sites around the world, using some of the settings in her novels.

However, the public remained insatiably curious about what had befallen her in December 1926. Before agreeing to grant any journalist an interview the novelist habitually extracted a promise that "The Question" would not be asked.

The attack then came from another quarter. On the fiftieth anniversary of that bizarre series of unexplained events in Berkshire Warner Brothers released a film, *Agatha*, starring Dustin Hoffman and Vanessa Redgrave. A disclaimer appeared in the opening credits, but an incautious moviegoer might forgivably have believed that the movie was revealing the true story behind the disappearance. Agatha Christie, to whom personal privacy had always been of paramount importance, took the studio to court to prevent the film from being shown. The judge found against her.

During her long professional career Agatha Christie wrote 80 novels which in English and other languages sold an extraordinary two billion copies – more than Shakespeare. However the book which the world was particularly impatient to read was her promised autobiography which, she had decreed, could only be published posthumously. After she died in January 1976 the autobiography duly appeared. But nowhere within it was the smallest reference to those 11 days of mystery.

Agatha even left her daughter in the dark. In 1984 Rosalind authorized Janet Morgan to write a searching study of her mother's life. Morgan discovered a great deal. But on the issue of the disappearance she conceded defeat:

"Gaps remain in this story. No one knows why Agatha fled on the night of December 3. We simply do not know what she planned to do – if indeed she had any plans at all."

The Strange Secret of
Sirius C

In 1995 two French astronomers announced that they had recorded "perturbations" around Sirius, one of the stars closest to Earth. These disturbances, they opined, could indicate the presence of a third star in the Sirius system. If such a sun exists its discovery will reverberate far beyond astronomy. The reason lies in the 5,000-year-old teachings of a West African tribe, the Dogon, whose ancient maps, drawn on a host of artifacts, actually show twin suns orbiting Sirius. Only one of these suns (dwarf star Sirius B) is presently known to us. But according to Dogon lore the second satellite sun is there also. Its existence was revealed to the tribe long ago by "people from the sky". If this third star is found and photographed, it will confront us with a profound question: are the Dogons' ancient tales mere myths, or an accurate description of a visitation from the stars?...

THE FRENCH ANTHROPOLOGIST Dr Marcel Griaule was loved and respected by the people of the West African Dogon tribe. After he had lived among them for 16 years, sharing their caves and hillside huts, they conferred upon him a privilege never previously offered to an outsider.

At dawn one day in July 1947 the four highest priests woke Griaule and led him on a two-hour walk to the Dogon people's most sacred place. Here the holy men revealed to him the history of the Dogon: a saga which had begun in antiquity more than 5,000 years before.

Griaule at first was confident that he was hearing nothing more than myth. The Dogons' description of a "visitation" at what they called "the beginning of time" by the *Nommo* (fish-like beings from the sky) seemed to bear little relation to reality. But then the priests began to illustrate their chanted narrative by scratching pictures in the sand with sticks. Griaule recognized the formal representations immediately. They appeared on a range of tribal artifacts, ranging from carved statues and woven blankets to masks and pottery.

Now, however, he was being offered a new interpretation of what the patterns signified. The *Nommo*, said the priests, had revealed that they came from a world far away – a world whose sun was brightly prominent in the night sky. The star's name was *Sigi Tolo*. Orbiting it were two lesser suns. The first, *Po Tolo*, was named after a tiny grain. This small white star – the heaviest object in creation – was composed of a dense metal called *sagala* and orbited the principal star once every 50 years. The third star in the system, only one-quarter as dense as its orbiting companion, was called *Emme Ya* (the sun of women).

In turn *Emme Ya* was orbited by a planet: the world from which the *Nommo* had journeyed to Earth, arriving amid flame and thunder.

Griaule's research had suggested years earlier that the Dogon were of Egyptian descent and had lived in Libya for a time before settling in Mali. The priests' drawings of the visiting fish-beings strongly resembled images in the cultures of Babylonia, Sumer and ancient Egypt. Like the merfolk of Western legend the *Nommo* were amphibians who, the priests claimed, could only survive for a short time on land before being forced to retreat underwater.

Also intriguing to the anthropologist were the tribe's star maps, with their two satellites, invisible from Earth, orbiting a large sun. It was obvious to him that the sun depicted in these charts must be Sirius, bright in the clear African sky.

Griaule wrote to Paris requesting an astronomical atlas. When the volume, battered and stained, arrived weeks later, he was disappointed. Sirius was alone in its solar system. It had no satellites. So much for the Dogon stories? Perhaps. But recognizing that the book, presumably taken from his employers' library shelf, was out of date Griaule ordered something more modern from a Paris bookstore. After a further month of waiting his patience was rewarded. The recently published atlas revealed that Sirius, 8.6 light-years from Earth, did indeed have an orbiting companion – but only one, not two as in the Dogon legend. This dense dwarf star moved in a 50-year elliptical orbit around its mother-sun, as the priests, quite astonishingly, had described.

The dwarf also fitted the Dogon description of a star that rotated on its axis and was white and enormously heavy. Griaule, isolated in Western Africa though he was, laboriously acquired further books and journals. They confirmed that the facts about Sirius B had not been known or understood until the early decades of the twentieth century.

Could it be possible, he wondered, that the tribe's knowledge of the dwarf star predated modern astronomy by thousands of years?

Griaule's anthropological research took a new direction. In 1950, with his scientific colleague Germaine Dieterlen, he published the paper *A Sudanese Sirius System*. It created few ripples.

In 1956 Dr Marcel Griaule died in Paris of a heart attack. He was 58. The Dogon tribespeople showed their respect by staging a prolonged funeral tribute. Nine years later Griaule's book *Le Renard Pale* (The Pale Fox), co-authored with Germaine Dieterlen, was published in France. The two authors devoted much of the work to a detailed analysis of the Dogon's mystifyingly accurate astronomical "beliefs". They asked how a tribal society could possibly possess such sophisticated insights into the mechanics of a neighboring solar system – and how that society had managed to acquire complex knowledge of the nature and behavior of dwarf stars.

Griaule, quoting from copious and meticulous notes, also disclosed what the members of this remote hill tribe had told him about our own neighborhood. Saturn ("the body of limiting place") had rings around it. Earth's moon was barren and waterless. Jupiter had four large moons. Our sun's planets, just like the satellite stars of Sirius, moved in elliptical orbits. The Milky Way was a spiral galaxy of stars.

Marcel Griaule's posthumous work was published only in French. It attracted little attention beyond his own country. But 10 years after the book appeared, Griaule was famous.

In 1966 the distinguished academic Robert Temple happened by chance to read Griaule's original paper on the Dogon tribe. Temple, a Fellow of the Royal Astronomical Society and a member of the British School of Archaeology, was impressed by the Frenchman's painstaking scholarship. He began his own research into the Dogon and their ancient traditions which dovetailed so uncannily with modern discoveries.

In 1976 Temple published a book, *The Sirius Mystery*, which surmised that the *Nommo* were extraterrestrials who came to Earth from a planet in the Sirius system. They made contact with the Babylonians, the Egyptians and the forerunners of the Dogon, sharing their astronomical knowledge with the three civilisations.

Temple's argument stirred a wasps' nest of skepticism. Chief among the critics was the astronomer Carl Sagan who insisted that the mystery of the Dogons' allegedly ancient knowledge was easily solved. It was likely, he said, that tribal priests between 1925 and 1935 had spoken to visiting European missionaries who brought them up to date on Western astronomy's latest findings. The priests had then incorporated the data – from dwarf stars and their density through to orbits – into their religious tradition.

Robert Temple counter-attacked – publishing evidence in the form of a letter from the Superior of the White Fathers in Mali that *no missionaries* had visited the Dogon before 1949. And it was two years earlier – 1947 – that the tribal priests had shared their astronomical insights with Dr Griaule.

Temple's supporters produced further arguments. Was it really feasible, they inquired, that Europeans in possession of the latest astronomical knowledge would rush to Africa to share it with a tribe of hill-dwellers?

And if indeed this had happened, how had the Dogon found time to incorporate the Sirian star charts into traditional artifacts ranging from pottery and statues to ceremonial masks? In any case many of these artifacts were centuries old.

On BBC TV's *Horizon* program Dr Griaule's colleague Germaine Dieterlich dismissed the skeptics' attempted debunkings as absurd. Marcel Griaule had not been a science fiction writer. He was a serious anthropologist who in scholarly fashion had sought to share what he learned during 16 years among the Dogon. And Robert Temple had simply built on Griaule's work.

The debate stalled. Neither side had indisputable facts enough to win it.

But within the tribe's tradition itself lay hope of an eventual resolution. The Dogon maps, supported by tribal lore, specifically indicated that Sirius was orbited by two stars. So far, Western astronomers had not detected, let alone photographed, the purported second satellite of Sirius.

If the presence of that third sun were proved, no skeptic would be able to claim that the Dogon had heard about it from a missionary.

In 1995 two French astronomers produced findings which may lead to a solution of the Sirius enigma. In the journal *Astronomy and Astrophysics* David Benet and J.L. Duvent published an article, Is Sirius a Triple Star?

They said they had measured perturbations in the Sirius system which could be explained by a third sun, Sirius C, orbiting the mother star. They theorized that this as-yet hidden body is a red dwarf, only about 0.05 per cent the mass of Sirius B.

Should the astronomers be proved right, the Dogon's 5,000-year-old belief in *Emme Ya*, the sun of women, will be scientifically validated.

And open-minded observers will then be entitled to ask how a tribal society, without texts or telescopes, obtained its information.

Author "Saw" Mars Moon – Without a Telescope

THE DOGON were not alone in enjoying an inexplicable knowledge of the cosmos.

In his novel *Gulliver's Travels* (published 1726) Jonathan Swift offered a moderately detailed description of the two moons of Mars.

The book appeared at a time when no one knew the Martian satellites existed – and when no telescope on Earth would have been powerful enough to detect them.

Not until 1877 – 151 years after Gulliver – did the US Naval Observatory astronomer Asaph Hall observe the moons, which would become known as Phobos and Deimos.

Swift's narrative describes how Laputan scientists have…

"…discovered two lesser stars or satellites which revolve about Mars, whereof the innermost is distant from the centre of the primary planet exactly three of its diameters, and the outermost five; the former revolves in the space of ten hours, and the latter in twenty-one and a half; so that the squares of their periodical times are very near the same proportion with the cubes of their distance from the centre of Mars, which evidently shows them to be governed by the same law of gravitation that influences the other heavenly bodies."

Swift somehow got the number of moons right. He accurately positioned them close to the planet. And their orbital periods (10 hours and 21.5 hours) were not a light-year distant from the moons' actual orbital times of 7.6 and 30.2.

The French author Voltaire was possibly copying Swift when in 1750 he wrote *Micromegas* – the tale of a visitor from space who alerts humankind to the existence of the Martian moons.

The fictional extraterrestrial hails from a planet orbiting Sirius.

The Eye in Clarke's Sky

In 1968 the science fiction author Arthur C. Clarke experienced a leap of astronomical insight comparable to Jonathan Swift's vision of Mars.

In chapter 35 of his novel *2001: A Space Odyssey* Clarke describes his protagonist, astronaut Bowman, discovering an eerie landmark on the Saturnian moon Japetus. It is an oval shape, brilliantly white, which seems almost to have been painted on the moon's surface.

As he drops closer the astronaut sees the ellipse as a vast empty eye (a black dot in its center) staring up at him. The dot subsequently proves to be one of *2001*'s celebrated monoliths.

Clarke's actual words were: "…he had half convinced himself that the bright ellipse set against the dark background of the satellite was a huge, empty eye, staring at him as he approached. It was an eye without a pupil, but nowhere could he see anything to mar its perfect blankness.

"Not until the ship was only fifty thousand miles out, and Japetus was twice as large as Earth's familiar Moon, did he notice the tiny black dot at the exact centre of the ellipse."

In 1979 Voyager I transmitted the first photographs of Japetus to Earth. Clarke's friend, astronomer Carl Sagan, who was then working with the Jet Propulsion Laboratory, sent him a print of one photo, with the note "Thinking of you."

Stunningly the picture showed a large white eye-shaped oval on the surface of Japetus. At the centre of the eye was a small black dot.

Clarke recalls this event in the preface to his 1982 novel *2010: Odyssey Two*.

At the time *2001* was published, Jupiter's moons were no more than pinpoints of light in the most powerful telescopes.

Sabotaged? Horror of the Hindenburg

Adolf Hitler regarded the immense airship Hindenburg *as the perfect propaganda tool. To the distress of the craft's idealistic designers he swathed its fins in swastikas, used it to dominate the skies above the 1936 Berlin Olympics and sent it on leaflet-dropping exercises across the Reich. When the* Hindenburg *exploded into flames while landing in Lakehurst, New Jersey, the Nazis went to extraordinary lengths to explain the tragedy away as an "act of God." But many analysts believe there were sinister secrets behind the zeppelin's destruction: secrets which to the present day have never been revealed...*

THE PROVERB "HE WHO sups with the Devil needs a long spoon" had bitter significance for Dr Hugo Eckener. As the nationally popular principal of Germany's Zeppelin Company he was politically naive enough to accept money from Hitler's regime to finance his pet project the *Hindenburg*: the largest, most luxurious airship ever designed.

It was a decision he would regret lifelong.

Eckener's firm, founded during the 1880s by the celebrated aeronautical engineer Count Ferdinand von Zeppelin, had launched fleets of successful dirigibles over the decades. But to the Nazis the *Hindenburg* (named after a German national hero) was the most glittering prize of all. They unstintingly poured public money into its construction – and then, when it was complete, moved with unseemly haste to collect their dues.

To Hugo Eckener's dismay Hitler's henchmen insisted on emblazoning the massive craft with swastikas and flying her into every corner of Europe to demonstrate Germany's burgeoning might. From the moment she was launched the *Hinbenburg* was not only a swaggering symbol of National Socialism but its willing handmaiden. When Hitler invaded the Rhineland she appeared over every major German city, dropping leaflets urging a YES vote in the referendum justifying the attack.

And when the airship sailed above Berlin's Olympic Stadium in August 1936 older British visitors were unpleasantly reminded of the bombs that had whistled down from zeppelins over London in the Great War.

Hugo Eckener, never a tactful man, made no secret of his displeasure that the *Hindenburg* was being misused to promote a political party – and a party he despised at that. He was particularly unhappy about the fact that the United States government, generally mistrustful of Hitler, was refusing to allow the Zeppelin Company to buy an American product it sorely needed: a product which theoretically would make the *Hindenburg* immeasurably safer for passengers and crew.

From the drawing board onward, Zeppelin engineers had planned to fill their airship's lift-bags with helium gas, rather than the flammable hydrogen other dirigibles used. The United States was the only nation on Earth producing helium in commercially usable quantities. American authorities, fearing that the new, unstable Reich might use helium for military purposes, banned its export.

Dr Eckener was obliged to have his airship redesigned for hydrogen – and to take drastic precautions to minimize the risk of fire. One of these was the inclusion of a smoking room, insulated by walls a foot thick. It would be the sole spot aboard the *Hindenburg* where passengers could light up. The tightly sealed area was pressurized to prevent hydrogen seeping in.

One expert observer described the multitude of precautions as an example of "ideal but probably unnecessary" engineering. Lesser dirigibles,

CHANGES IN CAR PARKING RULES — PAGE 5   WEATHER: *Cold Westerly Winds, Occasional Showers*

LAST WEEK'S NET SALE—223,520 DAILY

The Sun
NEWS ~ PICTORIAL
With Which Is Incorporated The Morning Post

HEADACHES
IT MAY BE YOUR EYES
COLES & GARRARD

No. 4565   Registered at the G.P.O. Melbourne, for transmission by post as a newspaper.   Melbourne: Saturday, May 8, 1937   (48 Pages and 4 Page Supplement)   1½d.

33 Killed In Airship Explosion
Hindenburg Falls In Flames In U.S.

START of the Hindenburg's second return flight to Europe. The ground crew is using props to raise the airship.

MAJORITY of 64 SURVIVORS
BURNED and INJURED
Sun World Cable

NEW YORK, Friday.—The German airship Hindenburg, with 36 passengers and a crew of 61 was totally destroyed by an explosion when she arrived at Lakehurst airport from Germany last night. Thirty-three persons are believed to have perished in the fire which followed the airship's crash. So far 19 bodies have been recovered.

Of the 64 who escaped alive, 20 were passengers. Most of them were seriously injured and burnt.

Captain Lehmann, a former master, who was a passenger, was critically injured. The present master (Captain Preuss) and his second-in-command, (Captain Kampf) escaped, but were badly burnt.

A terror-stricken crowd watched the disaster, which, by a coincidence, occurred on the eve of the anniversary of the sinking of the Lusitania.

A storm preceded her arrival at the airport. As she approached the hangar a burst of flame enveloped her stern. A terrific explosion fol-

lowed and she crashed, a blazing mass, to the ground.

Only three children were on board. They escaped injury.

The flames were not extinguished until midnight, but the embers were so hot that it was impossible to complete the search for bodies.

Three women were on board. Their fate is unknown.

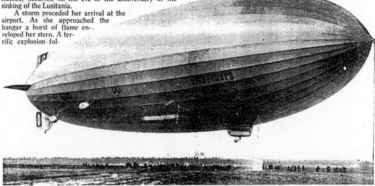

THE ILL-FATED DIRIGIBLE HINDENBURG LANDING AT LAKEHURST, New Jersey (U.S.A.) on the completion of her last trip before that which ended in disaster on Thursday night. Water ballast is being dumped as the huge airship is manoeuvred towards a U.S. Navy mooring mast.

all hydrogen-filled, had been plying the planet's often lightning-riven skies for years. Their overall safety record was impeccable. In an era when it could be perilous to cross the Atlantic in an airplane, zeppelins were seen as the bright future of passenger travel.

And the *Hindenburg* was the queen of them all.

Almost as long as the *Titanic* and as high from fin to fin as a 13-story building, the airship offered standards of luxury previously undreamed of. For the first time aboard a dirigible, passengers could enjoy a hot shower. In the diningroom travelers chose from a large variety of vintage wines and ate gourmet meals from gold and blue porcelain. They could then listen to music or watch plays in the entertainment area, or retreat replete to warm and spacious cabins.

But what most passengers found unforgettable were the stunning views from the windows of a promenade deck 200 feet long. Poets were inspired to describe the experience of sailing serenely above sparkling oceans, mountains and dark German forests. Hugo Eckener, who had been a successful writer before he succumbed to the siren song of the zeppelins, described his beloved *Hindenburg* thus:

> *"It is like one of those opalescent butterflies which fascinate as they flutter in the summer sunshine, but seek a sheltered corner whenever a storm blows up. Often, when people greet it enthusiastically as it appears in the heavens I have felt as if they believed they were seeing in it a sign and symbol of a lasting peace…among people."*

Just in case anyone failed to comprehend these sentiments Eckener subsequently wrote:

> *"If airships are used for political purposes it will be the end of airships."*

The Reich's propaganda minister Dr Joseph Goebbels was displeased. At a press conference he made a "declaration of banishment", saying, "Dr Eckener has alienated himself from the nation. From this time newspapers may no longer mention his name nor publish his picture." However the regime did not remove the independent-minded Eckener from his post at the Zeppelin Company. In extreme disfavor though he was, he remained an indispensable part of the Reich's airship program.

On 6 May 1936 the *Hindenburg* made the first passenger flight from Germany to North America. Passengers, paying less than the price of a first-class ticket on the Queen Mary, lauded the gigantic aircraft's comfort and stability. "Everything was so still," wrote one traveler. "… It was like standing in an upper story of a hotel and looking out of the window at the street below. And no one, not even those with the most delicate of stomachs, became airsick. Simply there was nothing to cause it. One of the crew showed us how he could stand a pencil on end – and no matter how long we watched it never fell over."

As months passed, the trans-Atlantic flights became almost commonplace. They inspired a poetic reaction in some observers. One American journalist wrote, "The airship, silent and strange, slipped like an enormous fish through the ocean of cloud above us."

Others had more practical concerns. On April 8 1937 a Katherine Rauch of Milwaukee sent a letter of warning to the German Embassy in Washington:

"Please inform the Zeppelin Company that they should open and search all mail before it is put on board prior to every flight of the Hindenburg. The zeppelin is going to be destroyed by some bomb…"

Whether the letter was prescient or merely alarmist we will never know.

On 3 May 1937 the huge aircraft set out on what was by now another routine flight from Frankfurt to the United States. Only half the berths were occupied: 36 out of a possible 72. The poor bookings were considered in the trade to be the result of increasing political tensions in Germany.

On 6 May, when the *Hindenburg* was moving above the pine woods at Lakehurst, New Jersey, she was running 12 hours late. The commander, Captain Max Pruss, had encountered strong headwinds along the way. While waiting for them to die down to enable him to land safely, he had sailed over New York, treating his enchanted passengers to views of the Empire State Building, a baseball game and the Statue of Liberty. This was described by a Zeppelin Company guest, writer Leonhard Adelt, as "resembling a tiny porcelain figure."

At 4 p.m. over Lakehurst, Pruss, in the control gondola, received a weather report: "Gusts now 25 knots." It was still not the right time to land. He signaled to Charles Rosendahl, the air station's commander, that he would continue to wait for calmer weather. Pruss steered his craft toward the coast, then headed north along New Jersey's bleak spray-shrouded beaches. Most of the passengers were delighted. This was additional entertainment for no extra cost. They stared down awestruck at the wild nature below: swirling fogs and crashing waves whose raw ever-changing majesty no mere painter could have captured.

At 6.12 p.m. it was time for the *Hindenburg* to buckle down to business. Commander Rosendahl signaled Captain Pruss, "Conditions now considered suitable for landing." Pruss turned back toward Lakehurst but did not seem to be in a hurry. At 7.10 Rosendahl intensified his message: "Conditions definitely improved. Recommend earliest possible landing."

Before that happened, however, there was important work to be done. Captain Pruss straightened his ship by emptying 2,400 pounds of ballast water onto the ground, unintentionally drenching several outraged spectators. The massive zeppelin was now ready to descend.

In a small shed next to the gigantic Number One Hangar a young announcer, Herbert Morrison, was describing the scene for his audience on Chicago radio station WLS. In subsequent years some of these listeners would say they remembered hearing Morrison's historic broadcast direct from Lakehurst. But in fact he recorded his famous commentary on large metal disks for later broadcast. Morrison said:

"Here it comes ladies and gentlemen – and what a sight it is, a thrilling one, just a marvelous sight. It's coming down out of the sky pointed toward us – and toward the mooring mast. The mighty diesel motors roar, the propellers biting into the air and throwing it back in gale-like whirlpools... This great floating palace can travel at such a speed with these powerful motors... The sun is striking the windows of the observation deck on the eastward side and sparkling like glimmering jewels against a background of black velvet..."

At 7.25 p.m. the crew dropped ropes to allow workers below to tow the ship into position. The *Hindenburg* now hovered about 290 feet above the airfield.

"It's practically standing still now. They've dropped ropes out of the nose... and they're being taken hold of down on the field by a number of men. It's starting to rain again... The back motors of the ship are just holding it, just enough to keep it from... It's burst into flames!

It's on fire and it's crashing! It's crashing terribly! Oh my! Get out of the way, please! It's burning, bursting into flames and falling on the mooring mast... this is terrible! This is the worst catastrophe in the world... There's smoke and flames now and the frame is crashing to the ground, not quite to the mooring mast... Oh, the humanity – and all the passengers screaming."

Passenger ticket for a 1936 *Hindenburg* flight.

According to witnesses the flame in the first few seconds had been blue and small. But then it had exploded into a bright yellow fire which crumpled the airship's rear, revealing twisted metal – metal that continued to float above the landing field. Passengers and crew began to jump for their lives.

Some broke limbs. Some were crippled. Many died, both on the ground and in the furnace above. Ground crewmen instinctively ran as the gigantic pyre came crashing down. During the 27 seconds of the disaster some spectators remained standing. Others spreadeagled themselves, faces pressed into the earth, fearing that a fuel explosion would engulf the airfield.

The statistics published next day listed 34 dead. Captain Pruss survived. A cabin boy had escaped death when a water tank exploded above his head, drenching him. If the *Hindenburg* had been carrying her normal complement of passengers the death toll would undoubtedly have been higher.

In Germany Hitler immediately broadcast a message of sympathy to the victims and their families – describing the fire as "an act of God." This bland assertion, made before the smallest investigation was attempted, was to be the unswerving Nazi line. Dr Goebbels instructed newspaper editors that their coverage must emphasize the "accidental" nature of the tragedy. The possibility of sabotage must not even be hinted at. Any editor whose publication suggested that there might be effective opposition to the National Socialist regime would be courting a charge of treason.

Surviving victims, lying in the Paul Kimbell Hospital near Lakehurst, suffered no such inhibitions. One guest-passenger on the *Hindenburg*'s death flight had been Ernst Lehmann, a zeppelin pioneer and distinguished German pilot. Fatally burned, his body swaddled in bandages, Lehmann in his last hours told his friend, airfield commander Charles Rosendahl, that he was certain someone had planted "an infernal machine" (a time bomb) aboard the airship. He had heard something that sounded like a small explosion seconds before flames engulfed the craft.

Sabotage: The Secrets

TWO GERMAN CITIZENS known for their detestation of the National Socialist regime were on the *Hindenburg* during her May 1937 flight to Lakehurst.

Other known anti-Nazis were aboard – but Joseph Spah and Erich Spehl recommend themselves to sabotage proponents – and the FBI – as having had the greatest motive and opportunity to strike.

• Spah, a vaudeville acrobat, was traveling home to his family in the

United States after a three-month European tour. His Alsatian dog Ulla, which he had bought as a present for his three children, was in the cargo hold amid an assortment of other animals and birds, all in wicker cages. Unescorted passengers were forbidden to enter this area, but Spah, a person of considerable charm, talked crew members into letting him visit his "lonely" pet whenever he pleased.

In this vulnerable section of the airship Spah would have had ample opportunity to plant an explosive and a timing device. Spah survived the crash. FBI agents questioned him but could find insufficient evidence to make an arrest.

- Equally under a cloud in the eyes of American and German investigators was the young crewman Erich Spehl. Known for his uncommunicative and secretive nature Spehl had long been a fearless private critic of the dictatorship. As one of three riggers aboard the airship he enjoyed unrestricted access to the axial walkway. He could easily have attached a miniature time bomb to a gasbag's outer skin. The tiny eruption would have been all that was required to destroy one of the most potent icons of Hitler's power.

Spehl died in the blaze. But if indeed he was the culprit it seems most unlikely that he deliberately sacrificed his own or anyone else's life. If unexpectedly bad weather had not delayed the airship's landing she would have been sitting in her gigantic hangar, with nobody aboard, at the moment the time bomb exploded.

Captain Pruss is also widely believed to have blamed a saboteur for the crash. On his return to Germany he was warned and fell silent. The painfully burned Hindenburg captain owed his life to a German-Jewish physician who had fled the Third Reich and established a practice in New York. When Pruss asked for his bill the doctor replied, "In an emergency of the German people there is no charge for my services." Air Minister Hermann Goering had the grace to send the physician a note of thanks.

For their own reasons neither the American nor the German government wanted to give much weight to talk of sabotage. Among theories put forward at the two nations' official inquiries was the suggestion that the disaster had been sparked by St Elmo's Fire. This is the static electrical charge which in stormy conditions can surround such elevated objects as weathervanes. Perhaps, an expert told the American hearing, a support wire had snapped, tearing open a hydrogen cell whose leaked gas was set ablaze by a St Elmo's spark.

Several would-be witnesses went unheard, including one who surmised in the press that sharpshooters, concealed in the pine forest, could easily have fired at the airship and escaped unseen.

The German and American inquiries came to similar conclusions. The crash had been brought about by "natural" causes whose actual nature could only be guessed at.

But significantly most of the people who knew and flew zeppelins embraced the sabotage theory. In an interview with a German radio station the characteristically incautious Dr Hugo Eckener pointed out how safe zeppelins had been over the years. He tended to believe, he said, that the fire had been deliberately caused, probably by somebody opposed to the present government. To the image-obsessed Nazi regime this suggestion was intolerable. Hermann Goering called the troublesome zeppelin expert to the Air Ministry and warned that if he spoke further about sabotage he would suffer severe consequences. He ordered Eckener to appear on radio again – nationally this time – and recant what he had said.

After the inquiries into the airship's fate a deep official silence fell. But the rumors in the free world's press and in the tyranny's streets would not be stilled. A report considered particularly feasible had it that in their study of the cooling wreckage American investigators found a remnant of a timing device along with traces of an explosive. But nothing could be proved.

What really happened during the *Hindenburg*'s final flight? The truth will never be known.

Spy-Ship Secrets

In the wake of the *Hindenburg* tragedy the Nazis continued to fund the building of zeppelins. The most notable was a giant known as the LZ 130, designed to be held aloft by the "safe" gas helium, which could only be bought from the United States.

Hermann Goering sent Dr Hugo Eckener to Washington to persuade Congress to reverse its ban on helium exports. The mission was successful. American public opinion, stirred by newsreels showing the Hindenburg aflame, prompted Congress to amend the Helium Control Act, allowing the gas to be sold to Germany for non-military uses only.

But in 1938, when the Third Reich annexed Austria, the United States reconsidered again. At the urging of President Franklin D. Roosevelt Congress renewed its helium ban. It was a sensible move. After the dictatorship was defeated in 1945 historians learned that the LZ130 (flying on hydrogen) had had part of her passenger space converted to house a secret detection unit.

As the zeppelin flew over such countries as France, Czechoslovakia and Poland agents concealed aboard her took thousands of aerial photographs of military defenses: pictures which would substantially help Germany's invasion forces.

During these spy flights the LZ 130 suffered numerous unexplained engine failures and other technical problems. Was she, like the Hindenburg before her, the victim of sabotage?

The Toddler Who Identified Her Own Grave:
Riddle of Reincarnation

In 1985 members of Melbourne University's Mind Research Society gathered to watch a startlingly controversial videotape. It depicted a hypnotic regression during which an English schoolgirl described a previous existence as her sister, who had died aged two. While the audience hung, hushed on her words, the regression subject – speaking as her dead sibling – described how she had floated above the graveside watching her own burial. Since the 1950s psychologists in the Western world have recorded thousands such purported testimonies from vanished time and space. Many "regressees" display detailed knowledge of foreign languages, places and people unknown to them in everyday life. Are these patients psychically tapping into some unperceived realm of reality? Or do their narratives offer proof that we return to Earth again and again...?

IN 1972 AN ENGLISH CHILD named Mandy Seabrook died. Three years later her parents, still struggling with their grief, welcomed another daughter into the world. They christened her Mandy.

The second Mandy became the center of a case so extraordinary that the Sydney psychologist Peter Ramster, one of the world's leading specialists in reincarnation research, devoted considerable time to studying it.

The "rebirth" drama began when Mandy, then 2, was traveling with her parents on a freeway near Leeds. "Suddenly," Peter Ramster recalled, "she pointed to a distant cemetery and said, 'That's where I'm buried."

"The parents were shocked. They had never told Mandy about her sister, of the same name, who had died several years earlier. And they could not imagine how the second Mandy had correctly pinpointed the graveyard where her sibling lay. For a time the Seabrooks tried to ignore the incident. But Mandy kept referring to the funeral – asking one day why everyone had cried so much when she died. When her mother reassured her that she was not dead Mandy simply looked at her and said, 'No – when I died before.'" In the weeks that followed the little girl accurately described what her coffin had looked like – and the fact that on the rainswept day of the funeral her distraught mother had slipped and nearly fallen into the grave.

The toddler's parents drove Mandy to the cemetery – and asked her to show them the grave. Mandy ran straight to the site. And that was not the end of it. She further bemused her parents by describing objects that had been placed in the first Mandy's coffin – a favorite bracelet, from an aunt, and a white ball.

"Mrs Seabrook denied that the ball had been placed in the coffin," Peter Ramster recalled. "She had forbidden it. But the following week relatives admitted that they had put the ball in without her knowledge."

On the hypnosis videotape the second Mandy, now a schoolgirl, describes her sister's funeral. "I'm in a little white box," she says. "It's very pretty… I'm being put into the ground. My mother is crying… everybody's crying. But I don't cry. I wasn't sent down at the right time. I have to go back."

Peter Ramster told me, "It's possible to place various interpretations on such evidence. But cases like Mandy's seem to have one meaning: that the grave is an illusion, separating us from true knowledge of our eternal nature."

Like most of his academically trained colleagues Ramster initially regarded notions of reincarnation as far-fetched. But his attitude began gradually to change when certain patients undergoing hypnotherapy talked about events which did not sound as if they had occurred in modern Australia. "In my spare time – and to the greatest extent possible – I started checking out some of the stories," he said. "I discovered things that sent me in a new direction."

In 1982 Peter Ramster's extraordinary film *The Reincarnation Experiments* was screened by Australia's Seven Network. One of the documentary's hypnotized subjects was Cynthia Henderson, a Sydney woman who recalled having lived during the French Revolution. While in trance she communicated in fluent French: a language she had never learned in contemporary life. A Sydney academic who studied the tapes opined that she was speaking in an eighteenth century dialect.

In the film Cynthia described her life in an old chateau. Still hypnotized, she drew accomplished sketches of the building and its gardens. Accompanied by a network camera crew Ramster subsequently took her to France – a country she had not previously visited. She was able to direct the crew to the chateau, which was still standing. She based all her instructions on the names of streets which were discoverable only on antique maps. When the chateau was still more than a mile away she was able to describe the ornamentation that would be found in its rooms. And her drawings of the building and its interiors – filmed in Sydney before the expedition began – proved stunningly accurate.

The Artist and the Excavated Floor

Like Cynthia Henderson, Gwen MacDonald had not traveled outside Australia. She had no particular belief in reincarnation (if indeed she thought about it at all). And yet, under regression she not only remembered a life in Somerset between 1765–1782, but was able to draw pictures of what she had "seen" there. Gwen MacDonald's case was arguably the most dramatic and evidential in the Ramster film:

- On arrival in Somerset she was able immediately to point out in three directions the location of villages she had known.

- She directed the film crew to a waterfall she had described under hypnosis – and pointed to a place where, she claimed, stepping stones had been set. Locals confirmed that the stones had existed but were removed 40 years earlier.

- With equal accuracy she pinpointed another long-vanished landmark: a cider-house which had stood amid four other houses at what now was an intersection.

- Obscure people she claimed to have known were proved to have existed. One was an officer listed in a regiment's ancient records.

- She displayed detailed knowledge of old Somerset legends, some of which were in verbal form only.

But Gwen MacDonald's most astonishing flash of insight had come when she was in a trance – and under the cameras – in Sydney. She described a house she had known as a young woman in eighteenth century Somerset. It was close to a stream and about 1.5 miles from Glastonbury Abbey. On the stone floor of the house, she said, was an intricate design which always intrigued her. At Peter Ramster's prompting she drew the design as if she were looking at it now.

In Somerset Ramster asked her if she could find that house and its decorated floor again. Using her recollection of an inn – still standing – as a signpost she led the team directly to the cottage, which had been converted into a chicken shed. But the stone floor, with its intriguing swirl of pictures, was gone. Perhaps it had never existed.

Peter Ramster asked the cottage's owners for permission to excavate a small area in the corner. They agreed. The archeological dig produced a positive result.

Buried beneath accumulated centuries of dirt was the old stone floor Gwen MacDonald had described. It bore the design she had drawn for the cameras in Sydney, three months before.

Reflections on Reincarnation

- It is no more surprising to be born twice than once. *Voltaire*
- It is a strong proof of men knowing most things before birth, that

when mere children they grasp innumerable facts with such speed as to show that they are not taking them in for the first time, but are remembering them. *Cicero*

- As we live through thousands of dreams in our present life, so our present life is only one of many thousands of such lives which we enter from the other, more real life... and then return after death. Our life is but one of the dreams of that more real life, and so it is endlessly until the very last one, the very real, the life of God. *Tolstoy*

- As long as you are not aware of the continual law of Die and Be Again, you are merely a vague guest on a dark earth. *Goethe*

- The soul comes from without into the human body, as into a temporary abode, and it goes out of it anew. It passes into other habitations, for the soul is immortal. *Emerson*

- The tomb is not a blind alley. It is a thoroughfare. It closes on the twilight. It opens on the dawn. *Victor Hugo*

- I know I am deathless. No doubt I have died myself 10,000 times before. I laugh at what you call dissolution, and I know the amplitude of time. *Walt Whitman*

- I know that we live again. The souls of the dead are in existence, and the living spring from the dead. *Socrates*

Hidden Crypt "Validated" a Past-Life Memory

A second regression case in which an excavation would prove crucial was televised by the BBC in 1974. The Cardiff hypnotherapist Arnall Bloxham placed a housewife, Jane Evans, in a trance, during which she recalled her life as Rebecca, the daughter of a Jewish couple in the York of 1190. Emotionally she described how her family and other members of the Jewish community were attacked by a mob led by the nobleman Richard Malebisse.

After unsuccessfully seeking refuge in York Castle the family fled to a small church outside the city, where they hid in a crypt *"just under the copper gates."* For a time they imagined they had escaped their persecutors. But eventually a party of soldiers broke into the crypt. To the distress of the TV audience "Rebecca" tearfully described the appalling butchery that followed.

A group of dedicated debunkers went to work on the story. After a fortnight's hard work they announced to the media that Jane Evans's regression memories could not possibly be factual. Old maps and records showed without a shadow of doubt that no small church incorporating a crypt beneath copper gates had existed in twelfth century York – or at any other time, for that matter. It seemed plain, said the skeptics, that Jane Evans had heard about the pogroms of the era and had unconsciously woven her knowledge into a fantasy of a past life.

Professor Barrie Dobson of York University was not convinced. He was no reincarnationist, but his specialty was the Jewish history of tenth to fourteenth century England. To Dobson, Rebecca's story had an oddly authentic resonance. Intrigued, he asked the BBC for a transcript of the program and began to study the regression subject's statements line by line.

To Professor Dobson, Jane's description of the church in which the family had been murdered sounded very much like St Mary's Castlegate. But as this church had no crypt he finally accepted that the massacre in her narrative had been an unconscious invention after all.

For six months the controversy rested there. Then Dobson learned that workmen, restoring St Mary's Castlegate, had accidentally broken into a long-forgotten crypt below the chancel. The gates and the re-used Roman and Anglo-Saxon masonry, comprising round stone arches and vaults, pre-dated 1190.

Archeologists excavated the site, which had lain in darkness for at least seven centuries. The crypt's architecture significantly matched the description Jane Evans, speaking as the murdered Rebecca, had offered on television.

A Celebrated "Rebirth" in India

Shanti Devi, born in Delhi on December 11 1926, was uniquely responsible for making reincarnation a major topic of discussion in the Western world. Shanti behaved oddly from the age of 2, when she began pointing to herself and lisping that she was the wife of a man who owned a shop. As her linguistic skills developed she regaled her parents with stories about her life in Mathura with her spouse, who had a large wart on his left cheek and wore glasses. His shop, where he sold cloth, was located outside the Dwarkadhist temple.

Although reincarnation is accepted in India as a fact of life (or life-after-life) few people are happy to have it intrude into their own families. Shanti's parents tried determinedly to persuade themselves that their daughter's stories were mere childish imaginings. But when, at six, she gave an account of her death after childbirth, they sought help from their doctor.

The physician asked Shanti to repeat her story. He was astonished (as he later told investigators) by her detailed knowledge of complex surgical procedures.

As the girl grew she displayed an increasing obsession with Mathura and repeatedly begged her parents to take her "back" there. For the first time she revealed the name of the man whose wife she claimed to be. He was Pandit Kedarnath Chaube. An uncle made inquiries and ascertained that the man not only existed, but owned a cloth shop, had a large wart on his cheek and was a widower whose wife had died while giving birth.

Several of the shop-owner's relatives traveled to Delhi and questioned Shanti Devi about the life she claimed she had led with Chaube. She responded with detailed descriptions of the house and of a well in the courtyard in which she habitually took baths. She also said she had buried money several months before her death.

Chaube, who had since remarried, reluctantly agreed to visit Delhi and speak to the 9-year-old girl who insisted she had once been his spouse. He brought with him his new wife and his son Navneet who had survived when his mother died. Although no one introduced him, Shanti immediately shouted Navneet's name and hugged him passionately, tears welling in her eyes. Daube asked how she had known the boy was her son, when she had allegedly seen him only once, as a newborn infant, before she died. She replied, "My son is a part of my soul. My soul knows him eternally."

Shanti was able to tell Daube so much about their life together that he was convinced she was telling the truth. He was particularly impressed by her response to his question about how she had become pregnant.

In the final 18 months of her life Daube's wife had been confined to bed with arthritis. To make intercourse possible the couple had been obliged to adopt unusual positions which Shanti was able graphically to describe.

The story of "the Girl Who Lived Twice" reached the newspapers. Mahatma

Gandhi invited Shanti to meet him – and was impressed enough to appoint a 15-member committee comprising physicians, parliamentarians and academics to investigate her case. The group took her by train to Mathura. She was able to lead them directly from the railway station to the marital house, whose layout she predicted before she entered. Numerous people from her "past life" were brought to the house to meet her. Without exception she recognized them all and addressed them by name. When the committee's president asked her to show where she had hidden the money she went straight to what she said was the spot, but was bewildered to find nothing there. Chaube then admitted that he had discovered and taken the cash after his wife died.

The committee concluded that Shanti was in command of so much detail – right down to her knowledge of Mathura's narrowly specialized idioms – that fraud would have been impossible.

Professor Ian Stevenson of the University of Virginia spoke with Shanti Devi after she had grown to womanhood. Stevenson, who has conducted more analyses of past-life claims than any other scientific investigator, wrote: "I interviewed Shanti Devi, her father and other pertinent witnesses, including Kedarnath, the husband claimed in her previous life. My research indicates that she made at least 24 statements of her memories that matched the verified facts."

The Baby Born with Bullet-Marks

Ian Stevenson, son of a Scottish lawyer, was born in Montreal in 1918. He studied medicine in Scotland, then took a postgraduate degree in psychiatry. He published two standard texts on psychiatric diagnosis and was highly regarded in the medical world. But in 1964 he abandoned it all to devote himself fulltime to research into reincarnation.

Aided by graduate assistants he visited 11 countries where he interviewed 1,540 children whose statements and behavior suggested they were recalling previous lives. The prestigious *Journal of Nervous and Mental Diseases* recognized the work by publishing Stevenson's pioneering article about what he had discovered.

In most youngsters he observed, Stevenson noted familiar patterns. Like Shanti Devi "they'd start telling anyone who would listen that they had lived in another time and place. These statements would be backed by behavior foreign to the family's habits – but in harmony with the claims about reincarnation." Almost invariably the "reincarnated" child would beg to be taken to his or her previous home. The child's statements about place and family names "usually proved 90 per cent accurate."

Early in the research Stevenson made an intriguing discovery: a high proportion of the children he interviewed had memories of dying violently. And in many cases, birthmarks – consistent with police photographs of the wounds the previous personality had received – could be found on the child's skin.

Typical was the case of a Turkish boy who recalled being a criminal, close to being captured by police. He suicided by shooting himself with a rifle whose muzzle he placed under the right side of his chin. The child who had recalled this "past-life" incident had two birthmarks: one in the same place under the chin; the second on top of his head where the bullet would have exited.

Stevenson built a large library of birthmarks matched by police photographs, in "rebirth" cases from Lebanon, Burma, Turkey, India and North America. Fifteen cases in the collection were also matched with postmortem reports.

In 1988, when *Omni* magazine journalist Meryle Secrest asked Stevenson if his work had influenced his attitude toward life and death, he replied:

"I think so. I wouldn't claim to be free of the fear of death, but it is probably less in me than other people. These children sometimes provide reassurances to adults. We've had two or three incidents of children going to, say, a woman who has lost her husband and is inconsolable and saying, 'You shouldn't be crying. Death isn't the end. Look at me. I died and I'm here again.'"

Is there an even stranger explanation?

Meticulous researchers, of the caliber of Stevenson, Ramster and others are careful to classify their findings as "cases *suggestive* of reincarnation." These investigators are the first to concede that a previous life might not necessarily be the sole explanation for accurate and seemingly inexplicable memories of a distant past.

Often it's possible to find a pedestrian solution. In his book *Mind out of Time* Ian Wilson chronicles the case of a man who sincerely convinced himself and others that he had served as a sailor aboard one of Admiral Horatio Nelson's ships. His knowledge of eighteenth century warfare and of a gunner's duties were, in one observer's words, "accurate to a convincing degree." Under hypnotic regression, however, the purportedly reincarnated sailor recalled a fact that he had quite forgotten. As a small, bright boy he had read C.S. Forester's *Horatio Hornblower* novels.

Of course, as this chapter demonstrates, not all "past life" cases are so easily dismissed. Gwen MacDonald, who unerringly drew the pattern on a centuries-buried cottage floor ... Jane Evans, whose description of a hidden crypt was validated months later ... Shanti Devi, who predicted what her "former" marital home would look like are surely (say reincarnation proponents) living proof that we walk the earth more than once.

Not necessarily. Some parapsychologists surmise that what we call "reincarnation" may in fact be a demonstration of the human mind's unconscious ability to transcend time and space. Just as Jonathan Swift "saw" Mars' invisible moons, so some people may be capable of glimpsing the lives and contemporary habitats of the dead. It's an understandable temptation, say some theorists, to believe you have actually lived a past life when in fact you have been no more than a psychic spectator.

Amazing Airships –
Over Old America

The Wright Brothers did not make their first short flight until 1903. Dirigible designers took even longer to build engines capable of powering aircraft at high speeds through the heavens. And yet, in 1896–97 tens of thousands of Americans watched astonished as huge airships – shining brilliant spotlights – flew across cities from San Francisco to Chicago. Contemporary editorialists wondered whether these futuristic vessels might be the work of a gifted but secretive inventor. But the strange phenomena associated with the airships are prompting analysts in the twenty-first century to ask profounder questions...

"The object was huge and cigar-shaped
and had four wings attached."
Sacramento Bee, Nov. 1896

O N THE BLEAK DRIZZLY evening of November 17 1896 hundreds of residents of Sacramento California raised their eyes to the overcast sky to watch a gigantic "lantern" moving above the rooftops. One witness was George Scott, assistant to the Secretary of State. He urged friends to join him on the Capitol Dome's observation deck. There they were able to detect three lamps which seemed to be suspended from "a dark craft of some kind, cylindrical and at least 100 feet long."

The strange spectacle was the overture to an aerial display that would extend over 14 months and captivate the nation. Cylindrical vehicles, sometimes ringed by swiftly changing colored lights, would appear from west to east across North America, perplexing crowds from San Francisco to Chicago and across the border into Canada.

In an era when balloons were the only man-made vehicles known to be plying American skies the wind-defying airships sparked front-page headlines wherever they flew. So enormous was the coverage – in hundreds of metropolitan and rural newspapers – that historians a century later were still struggling to find and arrange all archived reports into a central database.

To the modern researcher the first Great Airship seems to have been an odd mixture of primitive engineering combined with technology bordering on magic. Some observers described the craft as gliding serenely at one moment, then taking off at immense speed, vanishing within seconds in a blaze of light. This technical prowess was severely at odds with the testimonies of such witnesses as railwayman R.L. Lowery, who in several newspapers was quoted thus:

"It was a body of some length, shaped just like a cigar. When I looked up I saw two men underneath seated on a frame like a bicycle-frame, pedaling. Then I heard one of them call out, 'Throw her up higher, she'll hit the steeple.' She also had wheels at the side, like the wheels on Fulton's old steamboat."

Many newspapers of the time habitually exaggerated. Their editors had no inhibitions about hoaxing readers if they thought it would increase circulation. Nevertheless historians generally agree that the sheer mass of published airship reports – along with the multitude of prominent people willing to swear they saw the intruders – are an indication that the phenomenon was genuine.

The November 17 airship (if indeed it was the same machine) reappeared over Sacramento on November 22. This time eager thousands watched as it crossed the city at a leisurely pace. Among people willing to put their names on the public record as witnesses were a district attorney and the city's deputy sheriff.

On the same night an airship also traversed San Francisco. It was observed by hundreds, including the mayor. On this occasion it shone a brilliant searchlight onto the roads and buildings below. As it moved out over the sea, its powerful beam spearing into the dark water, terrified seals plunged from the rocks.

Rumors spread that a wealthy inventor had launched one or more airships from a secret factory in Oroville, north of Sacramento. But journalists who descended on the town could find no factory and no sign of the extraordinary vessels.

Jewel in the sky. Contemporary newspaper illustration of an airship, glittering with colored lights, which reportedly appeared over several American cities. The vehicle appears to be shining a spotlight on the cityscape below.

Throughout February 1897 the airships were seen above dozens of locations throughout Nebraska. A farmer told one newspaper that while herding cattle he had discovered one of the craft on the ground, under repair by two young men of unremarkable appearance. He was too cautious to speak to them, but did get a good look at their conveyance, which was "cylindrical, about 200 feet long and 50 feet across at the widest point."

On 26 March 1897 an airship allegedly dropped an anchor while hovering near Sioux City, Iowa. As it scraped along the ground the primitive braking device struck a man named Robert Hibbard, painfully dragging him for 30 feet. Whether such tales were true, invented or apocryphal we are too distant from the events to know. But significantly some papers also carried reports of other aerial anomalies: objects shaped like boomerangs, eggs, pears and letter Vs. These, blended in among the airships, were phenomena we have learned to associate with a twenty-first century UFO wave.

By April ships were purportedly being sighted in Kansas, Texas, Iowa, Missouri and Michigan – and new witnesses were describing encounters with craft that had landed or crashed. Occupants of one ship were identified in three separate accounts as being a middle-aged man with a full beard, a young man (clean-shaven) and a young woman. They spoke English, allegedly telling one farmer that they subsisted principally on pigeons which they caught in nets from the airship's deck. Occasionally they landed to steal vegetables and replenish their water supply.

Skeptics of the period asserted that every airship report was either a tall tale or the invention of someone who had been reading Jules Verne's scientific romances. In many cases they were probably right. But analysts find it difficult to discount the considerable number of circumstantial articles in which newspapers known to be conservative in their editorial policies quoted seemingly solid witnesses.

- *The Gazette*, Kalamazoo Michigan. April 14 1897: The strange body that passed over the city Monday evening and that was taken by many for an airship was seen by the proprietor of *The Gazette* as well as many other citizens...

- *The Daily Palladium*, Benton Harbor Michigan. April 15 1897: Some of our citizens imagined that they saw the airship again Wednesday night. It appeared in the sky off west of the city [and] sailed southward until the lights disappeared. Dr Scott of St Joseph was among those willing to take oath that they saw it.

- *The Daily Journal*, Battle Creek Michigan. April 15 1897: Again last evening at about 8 o'clock, the airship, or what has been called such, was visible to Battle Creek residents, many of whom saw the aerial wonder as it traveled rapidly westward in plain sight... That the mysterious object was not of human origin is plainly evidenced by the speed at which it was moving, and that too being against the wind.

- *Cincinnati Enquirer*, April 25 1897: Mr J.W. Lansing of Brundage and Lansing, Commission Merchants has just returned from a trip through southern Iowa. While in Grinnell, Mr Lansing said, he saw the much talked about airship. Mr Lansing is noted for being strictly temperate and does not wear glasses. In speaking of it he said, "I saw it twice, but at Grinnell it was very plain. It was early in the evening and the ship could be seen distinctly. It was shaped like a cigar and it moved in various directions, some of the time against a strong wind. The general impression of those who saw it seemed to be that it was an airship worked by electricity. I couldn't say myself that it was, but it was some kind of a manufactured thing floating about overhead."

* * *

This was among the last of the airship reports. By early May the phenomenon had vanished from the sky – but its powerful images persisted. During the century and more that followed, arguments about who had built and flown the ships – or whether they had existed at all – continued unabated.

A tendentious theory dear to many analysts of UFO behavior is that the vessels were constructed by a superior civilization, but disguised as primitive steam or pedal-powered devices. As in the Father Gill "waving" incident (page 180) the visitors of 1896-97 were, according to the theorists, intent on making humankind aware of their presence in a simple and palatable way. Gliding across America they teased the groundlings with glimpses of a technology which initially seemed not only comprehensible but achievable. (The subsequent bursts of mega-speed were another matter.) The notion of first contact taking the form of an elementary lesson has long been popular – despite the absence of evidence.

Another vaunted explanation is that the airships were secret devices being tested by the defense-conscious American government. Proponents of this theory do not explain why such clandestine machines were allowed to advertise their existence over major population centers.

Were the airships flown by practical jokers? That's always possible: but only if they were jesters capable of improving vastly upon the engineering science of 1896 and of raising large sums of money to build the craft.

Did all the witnesses, and all the newspapers, lie? In a 14-month sighting period, involving 20 American states this, statistically, would be as unlikely as if everyone had told the truth. There can be no serious doubt that large numbers of people did watch something move through North America's skies.

"Aerial Impossibilities" Above Australia, NZ

THE INVADING AIRSHIPS of the late nineteenth century did not confine their activities to the United States. In the 1890s New Zealand, and to a lesser degree, Australian, newspapers reported similar sightings of undercarriage-equipped oval aircraft, which were not only capable of colossal speeds, but were maneuverable in ways which outclassed the known technology of the time. Melbourne's *Argus* even published a half-page line illustration showing a dirigible-shaped vehicle hovering over Port Phillip Bay.

In the first decade of the new century the phenomena (dubbed "aerial impossibilities" by a Wellington letter writer) returned. Between June and September 1909 an airship wave of unprecedented proportions swept New Zealand. As the countless contemporary press reports attest, fear and paranoia swept both islands of the emerging nation. Many New Zealanders were convinced that German spies were reconnoitring in preparation for an attack. Cooler-headed commentators asked what conceivable interest Kaiser Wilhelm might have in a few sleepy farms surrounded by sheep-stippled fields.

But the torrent of testimonies continued.

On July 29 1909 the *Clutha Leader* published an interview with three shaken men who said "a large boat-shaped object, dipping up and down in the air" had swept down toward them from the sky. The previous day, under the heading THE KELSO AIRSHIP, a "Special Reporter" had written, "A busy afternoon's investigation utterly dispels any supposition that the reports about the airship are entirely mythical. There is far too much evidence for the belief to be easily dispelled…"

The journalist went on to chronicle what we would describe today as a Close Encounter. The incident involved a teacher (Mrs Russell) and pupils at a local school. "All those scholars who saw the airship on Friday at noon," he wrote, "were asked to draw an impression of what they had seen. The drawings were done separately and with no reference from one person to another. The result was six drawings, the degree of resemblance and unanimity of which was nothing short of dumbfounding to all skeptics. One boy was able to draw a diagram of the vessel from beneath, as the airship passed over his head, and this showed two sails on each side. Another boy drew… a revolving propeller at the rear. Mrs Russell saw it, and her evidence confirms the schoolchildren's story.

"Thomas Jenkins gave a very clear account of the whole incident. He saw the vessel first as he was going home from school… When it was near the gorge, about seven miles away, it remained stationary for a few minutes, then turned and came back. As it passed over, he saw that it had supports on each side, but those sails did not move. There was a wheel at the rear, revolving very rapidly. There was a box beneath the body of the ship, but he could not see any man in it. The vessel was entirely black in color…"

Nobody, in New Zealand or anywhere else, was ever able to discover what the airships were – or what their pilots' purpose might have been. An L.J. Allen, writing in the *Evening Star* on July 31 1909, gave wry voice to the bewilderment of the people below:

There floated on high
In the month of July,
An airship of wondrous construction.
The folks got a fright
When they saw its bright light,
For they thought it was bent on destruction.

"Curious Craft" Electrified England, Europe

WITNESSES WERE reporting airships in English skies for at least 50 years before the machines appeared en masse above America and the Antipodes. One characteristic event, chronicled by the anomaly-collector Charles Fort occurred at Neston in 1857. A farm manager, Robert Clancy said that while rounding up stray sheep he and a female companion noticed a large silvery vehicle standing at the edge of a field. Beside the craft was a young woman in green clothing. She waved to the pair, then climbed back into the airship. It rose swiftly from the ground, then hurtled at high speed toward the north. For months afterward, grazing sheep shied away from the area where the ship had stood.

From 1892 onward, English witnesses sporadically reported immense cigar-shaped airships ringed with brightly-colored "lanterns" which shone dazzling beams of light on the towns and countryside below. British historians subsequently discovered that similar craft had appeared at roughly the same time over Russia, Poland and Germany. Unlike balloons the vehicles were reportedly able to accelerate against the wind.

In the early months of 1909 the trickle of such phenomena became a flood. What is believed to be the earliest in the new wave of British reports came from Peterborough in Cambridgeshire. In the dark early hours of 23 March two policemen saw an immense brilliantly lit cigar traveling south at what one called "hardly-believable speeds." As it passed, making an earsplitting noise, the object raked the ground below it with a spear of light.

During the weeks that followed, concerned citizens from Leeds to Hertford besieged newspapers and the authorities with reports of similarly colossal skyships. The *London Weekly Dispatch* listed 24 locations above which the vessels had been seen in the previous three weeks.

One of the oddest of these encounters occurred on the clear night of 20 May. The captain and crew of a fishing boat near Lowestoft said they had crowded onto the deck to establish the source of a "terrific noise" over the sea. Outlined against the stars was a torpedo-shaped craft of frightening size. The captain said the vessel had portholes, through which the figures of men were clearly visible. He dared to signal with a flare – whereupon one of the occupants lit a flare in reply.

The England of 1909 was riven by fears of impending war. Many citizens (the editorial writer of *The Times* included) were convinced that the airships could only be German zeppelins conducting surveillance in preparation for an attack. But the Secretary of State for War, Winston Churchill insisted that no German dirigible would be capable of the speed, maneuverability or range of which the intruders seemed capable.

Who, then, did build the gigantic searchlight-equipped sky vehicles that bewildered Britons between 1909 and 1913? No historian or aviation expert has found a satisfactory answer.

To paraphrase the words Churchill was to use in another time and circumstance, the provenance of the grand airships that flew over England will probably remain a mystery wrapped in an enigma.

Did a Murdered Woman
Name Her Killer?

It was one of Britain's most controversial homicide cases. The focus of public interest was a medium who alleged that a strangling victim's tortured ghost had told her the murderer's name. Also prominent was a retired police detective, so convinced the haunting had happened that he had privately kept the investigation alive for 18 years. The eerie affair culminated in an arrest and – in August 2001– a trial at the Old Bailey where the accused man was found guilty and sentenced to life imprisonment. The drama divided the nation. Skeptics insisted the conviction was the result of advanced DNA analysis and little more. But others, including some police closely involved, felt compelled to ask a tantalizing question: Had a murdered woman's spirit somehow returned from the grave, to seek justice?

Ruislip, West London.
February 14 1983. About 2 a.m.

CHRISTINE HOLOMAN WAS deeply asleep when – something – shocked her into wakefulness. As she tells it, she sat up in the cold winter darkness, becoming simultaneously aware of two alarming facts. Her bed was shaking violently – and an intruder was in the room. Standing near the door, in a pool of soft white light, was a young woman, blonde-haired, her face contorted with pain.

The woman spoke. Her name was Jackie, she said. She had been choked to death. According to Christine the young woman then proceeded to relive the entire horrific scene – not in words, but in a series of "freeze-frame pictures.' As the unwilling witness watched, immobilised by fear, the killer raped his victim, then strangled her with a bathroom light cord, savagely applying pressure until the life faded from her eyes.

After what seemed "an interminable period of time" the encounter ended. It left Christine Holoman shivering and exhausted. She was in no doubt she had seen a ghost – and that the apparition had visited her for a reason. Effortfully she rose, pulled on a dressing gown and hurried to the kitchen. She found a pen and paper, sat at the table and noted down every detail she could remember.

Next morning she visited friends, a retired policeman and his wife, and asked what she should do. After reading what Christine had written, the ex-detective urged her to go a police station immediately. He knew that on the previous Sunday a 25 year-old local woman had been found raped and strangled in the sittingroom of her flat. She was a barmaid, separated and alone after only 16 months of marriage.

Her name was Jackie. Mrs Jackie Poole.

Christine Holoman made her living as a clairvoyant and trance medium: a line of work which had accustomed her to unfriendly reactions from officialdom – the police not excepted. But she realized it was her duty, nevertheless, to tell them what she knew. Even if, in their estimation, her knowledge amounted to nothing. Following her friend's advice she rang the local police district and asked if she could speak to the officer in charge of the Jackie Poole murder investigation.

Detective Tony Batters had been first at the murder scene. He was less interested in Christine's "dream," as he thought of it at the time, as in the possibility she might know something concrete. With a fellow-detective he spoke to her in the interview room, thoroughly expecting that the conversation would last no more than 15 minutes or so. It continued, in fact, for hours.

Almost two decades later, in an article for the *Police Federation Magazine*, Batters would describe the extraordinary confrontation. Christine Holoman, he wrote, astonished him immediately with her minutely detailed knowledge of what had happened in Jackie's flat at the time of her death. "She was able to describe exactly what the victim was wearing, many of her injuries and the position in which the murderer left her," he said.

"Frankly her knowledge (knowledge shared only by the murderer, his victim and us) was stunning. She even knew that although the man had taken most of Mrs Poole's jewelry, he'd been forced to leave two rings behind ... simply because he was unable to get them off her fingers."

More in hope than expectation the detectives asked Christine if she knew anything about the killer himself. "She described him in considerable detail, mentioning that he had a criminal background," Batters recalled. "She even knew his height, hair color, age and month of birth – and was able to specify tattoos and where they were placed on his body."

Detective Batters asked Christine if she had a name for the killer. She shook her head slowly. It was one piece of information she had not received. But she offered to go into a trance, to try to make contact with Jackie Poole again. As the policemen watched she closed her eyes and began to breathe slowly and deeply. After a few moments she said, "Jackie's here. She knows the man, but for some reason she's only giving me his nickname." Without opening her eyes she reached for a pad and wrote: "Pokie."

* * *

"I was very impressed when I saw Christine write that name," Tony Batters recalled.

"We'd already interviewed our prime suspect, a mechanic named Anthony Ruark. And we knew that Pokie was his nickname. Most of what Christine told us seemed to validate what we'd already discovered – and convinced us we'd got our man."

But the detectives' optimism was premature. They were unable to retrieve the stolen jewelry, let alone link it to Ruark – and they could not find evidence enough of his guilt to satisfy a committal hearing. At Christine's behest they retrieved a soiled jumper which Ruark had dumped in a garbage bin, but this also failed as evidence.

The investigation continued for a further, fruitless 15 months – but the suspect remained free. However, Batters was loath to give up. So profoundly affected was he by his conversations with the medium that he continued unofficially to work on the case whenever time allowed. When he retired he took his personal dossier of notes and documents home with him. He told friends that he believed, on the profoundest level that Christine Holoman had "seen the truth of the matter."

In 2000, Tony Batters' belief was vindicated. Anthony Ruark was taken into custody for a relatively minor theft. Police, as the law decreed, ordered a DNA sample. It was placed on the national database. And it immediately matched a blood sample taken from beneath the fingernails of Jackie Poole. While scratching desperately at her attacker in self-defense, she had unwittingly collected the evidence that sealed his fate.

In court the prosecutor William Boyce QC told the jury: "This is proof that Mr Ruark's body samples were on the deceased. It brings him here to be tried by you for a crime committed 18 years ago." After the jurors found Ruark guilty, Judge Kenneth Makin remarked, "This was a brutal murder of a defenseless woman…But for the advances of science, the defendant would not have stood trial."

Christine, who long before had returned to her native Ireland to live, remarked, "I'm so relieved they finally got that man. I'm going to put some flowers on Jackie's grave. She'll have peace now, at last."

Judge Accepted a "Ghost's" Evidence

IN A MURDER TRIAL believed to be unique in the world, an American judge admitted the alleged testimony of a ghost.

The murderer's victim was 24 year-old Zona Shue of Greenbriar, West Virginia. After she suddenly died a local doctor, acting as coroner decreed that the cause was "complications arising during childbirth." Zona's mother, Mary, was outraged by what she described as a hasty and careless assessment. Neither she, the neighbors nor any of her daughter's friends believed that Zona had even been pregnant.

Initially the authorities took little interest in the case. Their attitude reflected the fact that Zona had been tainted by scandal. Two years earlier she had had a child out of wedlock: a shocking moral lapse in the pious Greenbriar of 1895. Zona, a deeply conventional young woman, was desperate to retrieve her respectability – and when Edward Shue, a tradesman recently arrived in Greenbriar proposed marriage she gratefully accepted. Ignoring her mother's warnings that Shue seemed a "frightening" man, she became his wife in October 1896.

In January the following year a delivery boy found Mrs Zona Shue's corpse spreadeagled on her kitchen floor. Dr George Knapp, a local physician who doubled as coroner, arrived at the house an hour later. He was surprised to find that the apparently griefstricken Edward Shue had carried his wife's body upstairs and dressed her in the expensive high-collared dress she wore to church. Dr Knapp did his best to examine Zona to determine the cause of death, but (as he subsequently testified) the weeping Edward refused to release his grip on her. Knapp, a mild man and easily intimidated, gave up and wrote a vague report which blamed childbirth for the young woman's demise.

At the funeral Zona's mother and other witnesses noticed that Shue was behaving strangely. Throughout the service he stood beside the open coffin cradling his dead wife's head in his arms. The neck was swathed in a thick ugly scarf which, he claimed, had been his wife's favorite. Mary found this difficult to believe. She had never before seen her daughter wearing the scarf – and she knew her tastes well enough to be sure she would have disliked it. Edward Shue was obviously hiding something. But what?

Several months after her daughter was buried, Mary visited the local prosecutor, John Preston, with a remarkable claim. Zona, she said, had appeared to her as a spirit on four occasions, to say she had been murdered. During a violent argument her husband had brutally attacked her and broken her neck. Preston was unconvinced by Mary's account. But her story reignited his own suspicions about the manner of the young woman's death. He ordered that her body be exhumed.

The autopsy on Zona Shue revealed that her neck had indeed been broken, crushing the windpipe. Her husband was arrested and charged with murder. During the trial it emerged that Shue, in his life before Greenbriar, had served time in jail and had been married twice. One of his wives had died from unexplained head injuries.

The judge allowed Mary's evidence regarding the dead Zona's visits to stand. Whether or not she really had seen a ghost, he said, she had accurately described the wounds the autopsy would find – several days before the body was exhumed. He directed the jury that although the evidence against Shue was no more than circumstantial, there was a strong likelihood that he had committed the crime.

The jurors found Shue guilty. The judge sentenced him to life imprisonment. He died in March 1900. Newspapers of the era dubbed him "the killer jailed by a ghost."

Insane Egotist
The Multi-Murderer
Who Adored Publicity

The killer was a cold psychopath who took lives for the love of it. Choosing victims at random, he despatched them in a gruesome variety of ways: shooting some, strangling or bludgeoning others. In fevered, boastful letters he claimed (perhaps exaggeratedly) to have added 37 scalps to his belt – and threatened to drive the death toll higher if newspaper editors refused to publish his self-preening logic puzzles. No one, including experts from the FBI, universities and the postal service, managed to unravel the madman's intricate codes. But then a humble high school history teacher sat down for several days and cracked the Zodiac Killer's cipher…

IT WAS FIVE DAYS BEFORE CHRISTMAS, 1968 – and pretty Betty Lou Jensen was out on her first date. Her parents had been reluctant to let her keep company with a boy when she was barely 16, but she had worn them down.

Betty's companion David Faraday was a year older than her, but (if adults' subsequent statements were to be believed) equally naive. However, he owned a station wagon, a badge of status in that era – and by 11 p.m. he and Betty Lou were sitting in a parking area near remote Lake Herman outside Vallejo, California.

Perhaps, sitting under the clear, brightly starred sky, the couple exchanged kisses. Possibly they simply talked, as teenagers do. Nobody knows, because they died that night.

A local resident, Stella Borges, was enjoying a late-night stroll when, under the parking bay's single bright light, she happened upon the scene of carnage. Police later reconstructed the events. Betty Lou, obviously in fear, had scrambled from the station wagon first, but had been shot five times in the back as she fled. She died instantly.

David endured a slower death. As he stepped from the vehicle, the maniac shot him point-blank in the back of the head. His heart, said a forensic pathologist, would have stopped several minutes later.

Detectives could find no evidence of robbery or of sexual attack. It looked either like a hate crime or a murder for murder's sake. The young couple's staid, conservative parents were devastated, insisting to police and the press that their daughter, and their son, had no enemies who would have perpetrated so vile a crime.

It was all a terrible mystery. And for seven months it remained that way.

On July 4 1969 the madman struck again. But this time he made a mistake. One victim survived and was able to offer police a description.

Several minutes before midnight 22-year-old waitress Darlene Ferrin and her 19-year-old boyfriend, Mike Mageau, a laborer, were sitting in Mike's car in Blue Rock Springs Park outside Vallejo. A second car, possibly a Ford Mustang, pulled up beside them. The driver emerged – and without speaking, shone a flashlight on the couple and began to shoot. Five bullets struck

Darlene, who died instantly. Mike was shot twice and began to scream with pain, whereupon the murderer returned and calmly emptied further bullets into him. Obviously thinking both of his targets must be dead he strolled back to his car and drove away.

Zodiac victim: waitress Darlene Ferrin, photographed 1966.

Neighbors heard the noise and alerted police, who found Mageau unconscious and still breathing. Next day, at the local hospital, he revealed that he had "got a good look" at the attacker. He was white, brown-haired, about five feet nine inches tall and of stocky build. And he looked to be in his late 20s. He couldn't describe the man's accent, because he had never uttered a word.

Mike Mageau: survived bullet wounds to give police a description of the Zodiac gunman.

By this time, however, Vallejo police were convinced *they* had heard the killer speak. Less than an hour after the shootings a man with a light youthful voice and displaying every sign of pride had telephoned to claim responsibility for what he imagined were the deaths (plural). He accurately identified the weapon he had used as a 9 mm automatic pistol – and offered other details from the crime scene that only the perpetrator or an accomplice could have known about. The detective who took the call, and colleagues who listened in, agreed that the caller had seemed positively anxious to prove his credentials. He said that he had been responsible for numerous unsolved murders in California and would disclose the details in due course. But he'd confine himself for now to one other case: the slaughter of Betty Lou Jensen and David Faraday. He glibly recited details of their murders that the police had never made public – confirming in the detectives' minds that he had been responsible.

Californian newspapers gave strong coverage to Darlene Ferrin's death. But after several days, with the investigation stalling, editors found other stories to interest their readers. Today, most criminal psychologists agree that this sudden silence must have piqued the limelight-loving butcher – and set him to thinking of ways to ensure his importance was more permanently recognized.

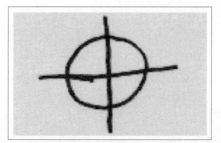

Tawdry trademark: the Zodiac killer's crudely-drawn logo.

He did not take long to find a way. He gave himself a name, the *Zodiac Killer,* and a *logo*: a simple cross inside a circle. But first he invented a series of *cryptic puzzles* which, he claimed, concealed his identity. At a stroke he differentiated himself from every other mean-spirited bludgeoning, bashing, shooting and strangling brute in American history – badging himself as a serial murderer deserving to become famous around the world (as he ultimately did). Had he paid a million dollars to an advertising agency he could not have achieved a more satisfactory result, for himself.

Lunatic's logic puzzle: one of the early cryptic problems
the mass-murderer sent to newspapers.

The Zodiac Killer's first letters, accompanied by his dauntingly difficult cryptic puzzles, arrived on July 31 1969 at Vallejo's *Times-Herald* and San Francisco's *Examiner* and *Chronicle*. The crazed correspondent demanded that his contributions be published immediately, and in full. If not, he would embark on a fresh series of murders that would shock the nation.

The letter to the *Times-Herald* read:

Dear Editor,

I am the killer of the two teenagers last Christmass at Lake Herman and the Girl last 4th of July. To prove this I shall state some facts which only I and the police know.

Christmass
1   Brand name of ammo Super X
2   10 shots fired
3   Boy was on back feet to car
4   Girl was lyeing on right side feet to west

4th of July
1   Girl was wearing patterned pants
2   Boy was also shot in knee
3   Brand name of ammo was Western

Here is a cypher or that is part of one. The other 2 parts have been mailed to the SF Examiner ' the SF Chronicle.

I want you to print this cypher on your frunt page by Fry afternoon Aug 1, 69. If you do not do this I will go on a kill rampage Fry night that will last the whole week end. I will cruse around and pick off all stray people or coupples that are alone then move on to kill some more until I have killed over a dozen people.

The cryptogram was in three different parts. Each, the unhinged compiler claimed, had to be solved and matched with the other two to reveal his identity.

Editors (none of whom wanted a bloodbath on his hands) complied with the killer's demands. Police studied the crypto puzzles and the covering letters, but could find no fingerprints. And the triple cryptogram itself seemed unsolvable – baffling not only the FBI and the US Postal Service, but code experts and mathematicians at several American universities.

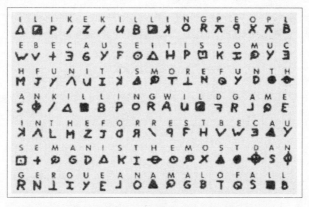

The crazed killer's cryptograms baffled the FBI, but were
solved in days by a scholarly amateur.

Happily, however, Don Harden, a reserved and modest history teacher, managed to break the cipher. An aficionado of cryptic crosswords and math puzzles, he streaked past the PhDs and specialists by worrying at the code for five exhausting days – finding a solution at five minutes past midnight on August 8. In an interview that he reluctantly granted to the San Francisco *Chronicle,* Harden said he had started with the assumption that the killer's ego might prompt him to begin his message with the word "I". And he would probably use the words "kill" and "killing" – both of which contain a double-

L. Don Harden proved right on both counts, and was soon able to transcribe a message that read, in "clear":

> *I like killing people because it is so much fun it is more fun than killing wild game in the forrest because man is the most dangeroue animal of all to kill something gives me the most thrilling experience the best part of it is that when I die I will be reborn in paradice and all I have killed will become my slaves I will not give you my name because you will try to slow down or stop my collecting of slaves for my afterlife*

> *EBEORIETEMETHHPITI*

The newspaper's readers were intrigued by the postscript comprising 18 apparently random letters. Some wrote in to suggest that, contrary to the killer's statement, they might be a crude anagram of his name. If they were, it was the closest the murderer came to keeping his promise and revealing his identity.

For five years the Zodiac Killer (and imitators) continued to pester editors, journalists and police with phone calls, strident letters and increasingly insoluble puzzles. Police found several finger- and palmprints on these documents, together with other clues they kept secret – but they never made a breakthrough. Amid the growing tally of murders (claimed by the killer, but not all of them his) detectives continued to flounder in speculation.

- Was Zodiac genuinely a sub-literate oaf? Or was he – as Jack the Ripper almost certainly had been – an educated man who tried to muddy the trail with misspellings and poor grammar?

- Was he simply lucky? Or the possessor of a powerful, albeit twisted, intellect which left law-enforcers far behind? In one letter he quietly expressed the conviction that he was invincible: *"The police shall never catch me because I have been too clever for them."* Perhaps an unconscious slip, but no misspellings there.

- Was there anyone out in the killing fields (a mother, perhaps) who suspected or was aware of his activities, but remained silent? Police made many appeals for such a witness, but without result.

- And was he a Satanist? His behavior suggested it – and some police worked tirelessly on this line of investigation, hoping to find associates who might lead them to the will-o'-the-wisp himself.

Desperate Search

The Zodiac Killer had an odious post-murder habit of writing to victims' relatives to gloat about the grief they must be feeling – and assuring them there was more suffering in store for the families' loved ones when they joined him as his slaves in "paradice."

These outrageous contacts often resulted in police hauling men in for questioning on the flimsiest of evidence. It was imperative, they knew, that they be seen doing something. One of these "suspects" was a former sailor who had boasted in a bar that he had read Zodiac's letters so often he knew them by heart. He also had an interest in abnormal psychology, having worked in a mental asylum shortly before he became an inmate.

This letter, believed genuine, was published by the
San Francisco Chronicle, 26 June 1970.

To the detectives he seemed a perfect theoretical fit. A small problem, however, was that his finger- and palmprints did not match those detected on the Zodiac documents. The murderer's hands were considerably larger.

Another drawback: a minute search of the man's Santa Rosa property yielded nothing. But the investigators remained convinced that this person – dishonorably discharged from the navy – was their best lead so far. A particularly significant clue was that he was wearing a Sea Wolf watch, from the Swiss manufacturer Zodiac. He insisted that his mother had given it to him as a present, and she confirmed that she had – but police suspicions were not assuaged.

Detectives submitted the shamed sailor to a gruelling 10-hour polygraph test. He passed it. The man's recently hired lawyer demanded that he be released. Police had no other option – but some continued to confide to journalists that they believed this man was the mass-murderer. In 1992, still traduced by the media, but insisting he was innocent, the man died, legally blind and stricken with diabetes.

Murders of the Zodiac kind are still being committed in California. But they are deemed either to be imitations or inheritors of a bleak tradition. In 2004 Californian police and the FBI decided they had enough negative evidence to close the case. Zodiac, they announced, no longer seemed to be active.

Possibly today he lives in open hiding somewhere, relishing the memory of his past obscenities. Conceivably too silent for so rabid a publicity seeker, he might have pined away and died of natural causes. Or perhaps he took out one of his treasured guns and ended his essentially pointless existence.

Roll-call of the Dead

Zodiac's black boasts varied. On some occasions he alleged he had killed 15 people; on others, 37.

Police compiled a list of seven "definite" victims, followed by four who "almost certainly" had suffered or died at the maniac's hands. During the era in which he created fear on the streets, many more murders, not listed here, were deemed to be the "possible" work of Zodiac.

Betty Lou Jensen Shot dead December 20 1968 near Lake Herman outside Vallejo.

David Faraday Fellow victim. Shot dead.

Darlene Ferrin Shot dead July 4 1969 at Blue Springs outside Vallejo.

Mike Mageau Fellow victim. Shot, seriously injured.

Cecelia Shepard Stabbed to death September 27 1969 at Lake Berryessa, Napa County.

Bryan Hartnell Fellow victim. Stabbed, seriously injured.

Paul Stine Shot dead October 11 1969 in San Francisco.

Cheri Jo Bates Strangled and stabbed to death October 31 1966 in Riverside, California. Her connection with the Zodiac was demonstrated in 1970 when *San Francisco Chronicle* columnist Paul Avery listed similarities between her death and the 1968-69 killings.

Kathleen Jones Kidnapped with her baby 22 March 1970 near Modesto, California. Before escaping she spent several terrifying hours in a car with a man who promised he would kill her and the child. He said enough to convince her he was the Zodiac.

Linda Edwards Shot dead June 4 1963 at a beach near Lompoc, California.

Robert Domingos Fellow victim, also shot dead. These two homicides were subsequently linked with Zodiac because of their similarities to the 1968-69 murders.

• • •

Donna Lass Vanished from South Lake, Tahoe, Nevada, September 6 1970. Body never found. On 22 March 1971 the *San Francisco Chronicle* received a postcard that could be interpreted as the Zodiac claiming a victim.

"Don't Disturb the Dead"
Enigma of the Iceman's Curse

Nobody could say with certainty why the American molecular biologist Dr Tom Loy died. At the inquest, conducted in Brisbane in 2005, a coroner could find only that the renowned scientist had expired of natural causes, an accident, or both. But while the tragic affair remained shrouded in doubt, one stark assertion was being repeated around the planet: Tom Loy was the latest victim of the Iceman – the ninth person to perish after contact with Oetzi, a 5300-year-old corpse found frozen in the Italian Alps. Whether these deaths were attributable to coincidence or to curse, the grim list was growing longer...

THE ANCIENT HUNTSMAN'S CADAVER had rested deeply entombed in the alpine glacier for 53 centuries. Bearskin-hatted, attired in a woven-grass cloak, armed with a copper-headed ax, the perfectly preserved Stone Age warrior inhabited this place long before Stonehenge or the Great Pyramid of Cheops were dreamed of.

But now that long span of silence and primal darkness was drawing to a close.

The searing northern summer of 1991 had melted the permafrost in the Otztal mountains to its lowest level in 2000 years, casting up the forgotten artifacts of countless generations; revealing stores and weaponry from World War I and conflicts long before.

The unfortunate discoverers of the Iceman were two German tourists, Helmut and Erika Simon, who were hiking near the border of Austria and Italy. Glimpsing a head and shoulder protruding grotesquely from the ice sheet, they assumed they had stumbled upon evidence of a murder – a modern murder – and hastened to a nearby mountain refuge where they alerted the landlord.

On September 19 1991 an Austrian rescue group arrived and tried, unsuccessfully at first, to chip and power-drill the corpse from its glacial grave. Next day a reinforcement team flew in. Applying greater muscle, but rather less skill, the workers managed to work the Iceman free, breaking his longbow in the process.

Rainer Henn, a forensic pathologist, picked up the corpse with his bare hands and placed it in a bodybag. Dangling from beneath a helicopter the Iceman's disinterred remains were flown to Innsbruck, in Austria. Aboard the aircraft, in a plastic bag, were the huntsman's last pathetic possessions: among them the ax, a flint dagger in a woven sheath, and the broken bow.

Local police, imagining a bullet might have created a hole they found in the skull, immediately opened a murder inquiry. But before long a forensic pathologist had advised that the cranial fissure was probably the result of sun-damage, inflicted long ago. And a mountaineer, after unofficially studying the body, opined that it might be the century's greatest archeological discovery. He was right. Within days the Iceman had been named Oetzi, after the mountain range in which he was found, and was wrapped in a sterile operating gown. He was then subjected to carbon dating, which placed him circa 3300 BC. Next came examinations of his whipworm-infested gut, the contents of his stomach and intestines, the remains of his brain – and even his penis.

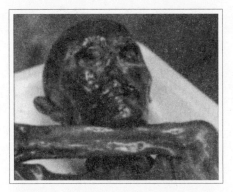

Older than the Pyramids: grim remains of Oetzi the Iceman.

After 5300 years of frozen silence, the corpse of Oetzi the Iceman was suddenly at the heart of chaos. While biologists scraped antique scraps of venison and edible grasses from his stomach, film cameras whirred and specialists minutely photographed the 60 tattoos that ornamented his body. Astonishingly, the pictures' positions coincided with the pressure points used in acupuncture, thought until then to have originated in Asia 2000 years after Oetzi's death.

Throughout the busy days and nights, the stir of activity around the antique corpse was constant and loud – as were the disputations of a procession of visiting academics. Everyone had an opinion on how and why the Iceman had perished. Some pointed to the deep cuts on his right hand and forearm and the flint arrowhead lodged in his body and pronounced that an enemy must have ambushed him, fatally. Others suggested that the ridges on his fingernails, which might have been deemed unlucky, had led to him being ritually murdered.

But the most intense argument of all centered on who owned the cadaver. Austria, whose rescue teams had retrieved Oetzi in the first place, insisted that he was state property and defiantly held him in a government laboratory. But Italy was adamant that it owned the Iceman, whose remains, it asserted, had been retrieved from its sovereign territory. Eventually an international boundary commission agreed – and in 1998 the Iceman was uprooted again and transported in a refrigerated truck over the Brenner Pass to Italy. His new home became the South Tyrol museum in Bolzano where scientists of every persuasion have since studied him. Not even the mummies of ancient Egypt have been subjected to scrutiny so intense. Oetzi is possibly the most-watched corpse in history.

He is also an invaluable tourist attraction. Vacationers pay millions of dollars annually for the right to peer through a small window beyond which he lies on a glass slab, an arm across his chest, staring up at the ceiling of his high-tech tomb. To heighten the effect a recording of a whistling alpine wind is piped through to the visitors.

In the museum's specialist shops, tourists can buy everything from Oetzi T-shirts, plates and cups to bottles of Iceman soda-pop, pizza triangles and bars of chocolate decorated with a crude reproduction of the cadaver's elegantly dressed remains.

"Stop the Curse – Bury Him, Now."

Unsurprisingly many people (clergy in particular) are distressed by this exploitation of a dead man, regardless of whether the reasons are commercial or scholarly. They believe that Oetzi deserves a funeral and the right to lie again in his grave, free of gawkers and experimenters.

One tireless campaigner for the Iceman's right to peace is the Italian archeologist Professor Domenico Nisi: "Proverbs along the lines 'Do not disturb the dead' can be found in every culture and every age," he wrote. "This is an ancient person, but he is also, simply, a dead person and should not be endlessly tweaked and measured and harvested and subjected to indignities, and neither should he be used to make money. He should be respectfully buried again, in the place where he was found. Put him back and leave him alone. And then perhaps the curse will end."

Few of Nisi's fellow academics are incautious enough to use the word "curse" when discussing the nine circumstantially linked deaths that have followed the Iceman's exhumation. The scholars prefer to talk about chance, coincidence, or a series of unrelated events. But other observers are less sure. They believe it's at least possible that the deaths form an unsettling pattern, generated by forces beyond our understanding.

- The "curse" – confined entirely to people who had had close contact with the mummy – began to operate in 1992, the year after Oetzi was removed from his ice tomb. First to die was forensic pathologist **Dr Rainer Henn**, 64, who headed the team that first examined the body. He perished when an oncoming vehicle crashed into his car head-on. Dr Henn was the man who had lifted the cadaver with his bare hands and placed it in the bodybag that swung beneath the helicopter en route to Innsbruck. When Henn was killed he had been on the way to a conference at which he planned to describe new findings regarding Oetzi's remains.

• Several weeks later **Kurt Fritz,** the mountaineer who had guided Dr Henn to the Iceman's body, died in an avalanche. Fritz, an experienced climber who had known the region all his life, was the only member of his party to be struck by the flying rocks. He had been the first person to lift Oetzi's head and to see the soon-to-be-famous grimace. He had later given tours to the site.

• Next purported victim was **Rainer Holz**, 47, the Austrian journalist who exclusively filmed the cadaver's removal from the ice-cocoon. Holz wove the footage into an hour-long documentary shown around the world. Several months later he died of a brain tumor.

• **Helmut Simon**, the retired Nuremberg caretaker who, with his wife Erika, had found the Iceman, subsequently ventured alone on a second hiking trip, 93 miles from Oetzi's tomb. When he did not return, an Austrian rescue team went out and found him lying dead at the bottom of a 294 foot crevasse. His body (like Oetzi's before him) was frozen in the ice and had to be removed with picks and a drill. The rescuers assumed Simon had lost his way during a freak blizzard that struck the area days earlier.

Erika Simon subsequently revealed that her husband had returned to the area to celebrate winning a court case, entitling them to a $140,000 Italian government "finder's fee" for discovering Oetzi's body. But because Helmut had not signed the court papers, his widow received no money. The judge had earlier dismissed a Slovenian woman's claim that she saw the Iceman first. She said she had spat on the corpse to mark the discovery with her DNA.

• **Dieter Warnecke** led the mountain rescue team which found Helmut Simon's body. Less than one hour after Simon was buried, Warnecke died of a heart attack. He was not known to have cardiac problems.

- **Professor Bernardino Bagolini**, an Italian archeologist who had specialized in studying the Iceman, visited his mother's grave on the first anniversary of her death. The following morning he suffered a fatal cardiac arrest.

- **Professor Friedrich Tiefenbrunner** of Innsbruck worked at close quarters with the mummy for several years, perfecting a way of protecting it from fungal and bacterial attack. He died during open-heart surgery in January 2005.

- Head of the team to which Tiefenbrunner belonged was a fellow-Austrian, archeologist **Konrad Spindler**, who was regarded as the leading expert on the 5300-year-old cadaver. He had often dismissed journalists' questions about a continuing jinx as sensationalism, declaring on one occasion, "It's all media hype. The next thing you'll be saying is I'll be next." Spindler died in April 2005 of complications arising from multiple sclerosis.

- "Victim" Number Nine, Californian-born **Dr Tom Loy,** gained his PhD from the Australian National University before joining the University of Queensland in 1995. He headed a team of molecular biologists which minutely studied the Iceman's body, his clothing and weapons, and his ancient DNA. Dr Loy won regard as an international expert on Oetzi after he and his colleagues identified four different types of blood on the hunter's clothes – and were able to formulate a persuasive theory explaining how he perished. In 2004 Tom Loy told the ABC's *Science Show,* "He shot somebody or two somebodies at different times. He retrieved his arrow and then, the last time he shot it he missed. He might have had a partner who was wounded and was helping him away."

When he died of unknown causes, Dr Loy had almost completed a book on the Iceman. The manuscript answered many questions about the long-dead hunter's bitter and perilous life.

But there was one question it did not address.

Could it be that that when Oetzi's ice crypt was destroyed, *some dark form of consciousness* stirred in its immemorial inhabitant? And might that consciousness somehow have reached out to create a trail of vengeance and death?

Did a Furious Pharaoh Sabotage BBC Film?

ICEMAN OETZI was not, of course, the first mummy to be accused of wreaking havoc from beyond the grave.

Early last century, 24 deaths occurred among the archeologists and other workers who had helped open the tomb of boy-Pharaoh Tutankhamun. The eerie and often fatal "coincidences" continued to resonate across subsequent decades.

One sinister example of what a newspaper called "Tut's troublemaking" occurred in 1992 when Professor Christopher Frayling made a BBC documentary, *The Face of Tutankhamun.* After days spent filming in the pharaoh's desecrated burial vault, Frayling and producer David Wallace almost died when the cable of their hotel lift snapped – sending them plunging 21 floors to the basement.

Later the lights fused inside the tomb, leaving two crew members stranded on a platform in pitch-darkness. In an attempt to rebuild morale a well-meaning associate director persuaded the unit workers to re-enact a play intended to raise friendly departed spirits. Instead most of the crew were blinded by a sudden violent sandstorm which left them with severe conjunctivitis. After the film unit returned to Britain a sealed canister containing the print arrived at the BBC from an Egyptian laboratory. Mysteriously the canister was covered in fresh earth.

Frayling, Professor of Cultural History at the Royal College of Art, was interviewed by the TV program *Today* (November 17 1992). "I was extremely skeptical when I went out to Egypt," he said. "But now I'm not so sure. I know this sounds like hype, but I promise you that I don't come from the sort of academic background where we get involved in hysteria."

• • •

Pharaoh Tutankhamun was born around 1367 BC and ascended the throne at age nine. He died – possibly from infection in a broken leg – eight years later and was mummified and entombed in secret splendor in the Valley of the Kings.

Enclosed within the mummy's wrappings were 143 charms and amulets to ward off evil spirits and repel sacrilegious tomb-raiders.

Tutankhamun's concealed remains lay in silent, impenetrable darkness for more than 3000 years. Then, on a distant island which had been home to primitive tribes in Tut's lifetime, Lord Carnarvon, a rich Egyptologist, decided to mount a search for the burial chamber. Convinced he would find it in Luxor he spent five years studying old records and digging, but without success. Finally he entrusted the task to the British archaeologist Howard Carter, who, toward the end of 1922, enjoyed a stroke of what he modestly called "unbelievable luck." A member of Carter's digging team literally stumbled upon a step carved into rock beneath the debris of an ancient structure.

Pharaoh Tutankhamun: torn from stygian darkness
after 30 centuries.

Carter's men excavated the site and found a flight of stairs leading to a doorway. On it, hieroglyphically carved, was the name TUTANKHAMUN. Overwhelmed, Carter immediately conveyed the news to his patron, who immediately canceled all commitments and traveled post-haste to Luxor.

On November 26 1922 Lord Carnarvon and Howard Carter knelt peering through a hole their men had made in the sealed doorway. Before them, in the powerful light of their lanterns, lay a breathtaking display of antique riches: a golden throne inlaid with precious stones, gilded chariots, ornamental caskets and alabaster vases. And when they managed to enter this mere anteroom they discovered beyond it a chamber in which stood a stone sarcophagus containing three nesting golden coffins, the inner one housing the mummy of Tutankhamun.

In his diary Carter wrote, "It was a sight surpassing all precedent."

Sacred beasts, birds and reptiles guarded the
pharaoh's lavish tomb.

According to contemporary newspaper reports (possibly embellished), Howard Carter returned to his hotel that night to hear that a cobra had swallowed his pet canary. The terrified manservant warned that by interrupting the pharaoh's long sleep, Carter had unleashed a deadly curse and should leave Egypt without delay. A cobra and a vulture were the pharaoh's magical guardians, the servant correctly asserted. (Both, in fact, can be found on Tut's ceremonial headgear.)

Carter was saddened by his bird's demise, but had no time for superstition. He grew even more impatient the following day when he returned to the dig to find that many of the native workmen had fled. They had learned, a trusted associate told him, that the tomb's exterior was inscribed with a terrible curse:

> DEATH SHALL COME ON SWIFT WINGS
> TO HE WHO DISTURBS
> THE PEACE OF THE KING.

Pharaoh Tut's alleged threat swiftly found its way into international headlines – and can still be found today in numerous histories of the excavation. But, in fact, no such inscription was ever discovered. The only "warning" remotely close to it can be found on the *Anubis* shrine: a carved jackal on a pedestal, whose hieroglyph reads:

> IT IS I WHO HINDER THE SAND FROM
> CHOKING THE SECRET CHAMBER.
> I AM FOR THE PROTECTION OF THE DECEASED.

But there are many unsettling facts in the Tutankhamun case on which skeptics and "curse"-believers agree:

- Of the original tomb-raiders only the discoverer, Howard Carter, and a minor member of the party, Richard Adamson, survived into old age. Carter died in 1939 of natural causes.

- Two weeks after the tomb's official opening, Lord Carnarvon was bitten by a mosquito at his hotel. Next morning he cut the bite while shaving, and it became infected. His resistance lowered, he succumbed to pneumonia and died. *Official records show that at the moment of his demise the lights went out in Cairo.* And there was a second matching of events. Relatives in distant London testified that they were perplexed when Carnarvon's pet dog Susie suddenly began to howl pitifully, in an unprecedented way. Not until the news, and hour, of Carnarvon's end reached them did they realize that the dog had keened at the time of her master's passing. Susie herself died several hours later.

- Shortly after Lord Carnarvon's funeral a blemish was found on the Tut mummy's cheek. It mirrored the position of the mosquito bite on Carnarvon's face.

- In the fortnight following Lord Carnarvon's death, expedition member Arthur Mace fell into a coma and died, puzzling his doctors.

- Antiquarian George Gould traveled to Egypt after learning of his friend Carnarvon's fate. Before leaving he visited the pharaoh's tomb. Next day he collapsed with a high fever – and 12 hours later was dead.

- Archibald Reid, the radiologist who used X-rays to determine Tutankhamun's possible cause of death, was struck down by a condition doctors could not diagnose. He sailed back to England and died soon after disembarking.

- Richard Bethell, who had been Carnarvon's secretary, died of heart failure four months after the tomb was opened.

- British industrialist Joel Wood visited the tomb and was dead weeks later, following an unidentifiable illness.

Theorists produced elaborate scenarios to explain these events. Perhaps, they surmised, the unsealing of the tomb had released lethal spores which entered the lungs of certain excavators and visitors. Or possibly, later speculation suggested, the burial chamber's floors were covered with a radioactive substance... But no evidence of spores, tomb viruses or uranium has ever been discovered.

As decades passed, Pharaoh Tut remained fresh in the public's memory – largely because people associated with him kept dying or suffering inexplicable injuries.

- In 1966 Mohammad Ibrahim, Egypt's Director of Antiquities, warned his government not to allow Tut and his tomb's treasures to tour abroad. "I have experienced terrible nightmares about what will happen if they leave our country," he said. On a bright, cloudless day Ibrahim left a final meeting and stepped out onto a quiet road. A car struck and killed him.

- Ibrahim's successor Dr Gamal Mehrez told a press conference that it was "ridiculous" to blame a pharaoh's curse for a road accident. "I've spent my entire life in Egyptology – and I can assure you that all the deaths and misfortunes over the years have been pure coincidence," he said. "Tutankhamun has been deceased for a long time and he has no ability to influence the course of our 20th century lives." In 1972 Mehrez signed papers authorizing the removal of Tut's golden mask from Cairo Museum so that it could be sent to London to appear in a Pharaoh's Treasures exhibition. "I'm in charge and I don't have the slightest fear," Mehrez told a media conference. On February 3, the day the golden mask was flown out of Egypt, Mehrez died.

- An RAF transport command plane flew the pharaoh's mask to London. Over the next five years six members of the plane's crew died or experienced severe misfortune. The trouble began on the initial flight when technical officer Ian Landsdowne playfully kicked the crate containing the mask. Shortly after arriving back in England he broke the "offending" leg. The transport aircraft's navigator Jim Webb lost all his possessions in a fire. Sergeant Brian Rounsfall suffered two heart attacks. Chief pilot Rick Laurie and engineer Ken Parkinson had passed many stringent fitness tests for the RAF. But in the wake of the Tutankhamun trip they were assigned to ground duties. The reason: they began having regular cardiac arrests – *always on the anniversary of the golden mask flight.*

- Richard Adamson, sole survivor of the British expedition that found the boy-pharaoh, had long been strident in his belief that there was no curse. In March 1970 he appeared on BBC TV to explode the myth yet again. He did admit to the interviewer that, within 48 hours of his previous debunking of the jinx, several "unpleasant coincidences" had occurred – one being his wife's death, which was followed by a car accident in which his son broke his back. In this latest interview Adamson stuck to his skeptical guns. But soon after he climbed into a cab outside the TV studios it crashed. A week later, recovering in hospital from head injuries, Adamson conceded to reporters that he was "now having second thoughts."

More than 85 years have passed since Tutankhamun was torn from the tranquillity and darkness in which he lay for millennia. Since then, like Oetzi the Iceman, he has seldom been left alone. On January 6 2005 the noise, chatter and harsh lights surrounded him yet again. An officially sanctioned team of specialists had brought the mummy to Luxor for a high-tech CAT (computer tomography) scan, intended to produce three-dimensional images of the pharaoh's much-studied remains.

At the end of a disturbing day the scan's supervisor, Egyptologist Zawi Hawass, remarked to journalists, "After the incidents of the past few hours I think we should still believe in the legendary curse of the pharaohs."

En route to the site one researcher's car had run out of control, narrowly missing a child. Then a gigantic windstorm blew up in the Valley of the Kings, delaying the expedition. When the party eventually reached Luxor, the usually reliable CAT scanner malfunctioned for two hours. And as soon as computer specialists had it taking pictures of the pharaoh again, one Egyptologist developed a coughing fit so violent that he had to leave.

Zawi Hawass commented, "It's easy, if you're not in this specialist field, to dismiss such occurrences as random and meaningless incidents. But when, as I have, you have excavated numerous tombs and removed many mummies from sarcophagi, you learn that strange events will reliably happen in those places... events sometimes beyond rational explanation."

A Jinxed Ship's Gruesome Secret

THE BRITISH IRON STEAMER *Leviathan,* later renamed the *Great Eastern,* was publicized as the biggest ship ever built. She was also the unluckiest.

As her tally of deaths and hideous injuries multiplied the owners were obliged to offer ever-steeper wages to tempt sailors aboard. But for many, a single voyage was enough. Not only was there the "curse" to cope with, involving at least one major mishap every time she went to sea, there were also the ghosts.

Great Eastern, as she was known for most of her disaster-ridden life, was designed by the renowned English engineer Isambard Kingdom Brunel. Standing five feet six inches in raised boots, he was known for the grandiose nature of his creations – but his investors were excited by the rewards he had promised them this time. His towering sail, steam and paddle vessel – five times the size of any ship afloat – was to be used as a lucrative passenger and mail service linking Britain with India, China, and Australia. It would carry such enormous stockpiles of fuel that there would be no need for coaling stops en route. Everyone associated with the ship and her yet-to-be-built mega-sisters would become rich.

The newly popular travel agents were not exaggerating when they called *Great Eastern* "the wonder of the sea." But she wasn't at sea yet.

Brunel announced that he would launch his vessel on November 3 1857. More than 150,000 Londoners converged on the Isle of Dogs to enjoy the spectacle. Equipped with picnic hampers they were prepared to wait patiently. The *Times* that morning had predicted that pushing the massive craft down into the river would "probably occupy eight to 10 hours." It was an underestimate.

An early painting of the *Great Eastern* under sail.

Standing in his supervising tower the top-hatted and nervous Brunel signaled with a white flag for the securing lines to be released. The crowd fell breathlessly silent – a hush that was broken by cacophony as the vast hull began slowly to move down the slipways toward the water. After less than six inches she stopped. But the tiny movement had been enough to place intolerable pressure on the chains.

The windlass collapsed under the strain, its massive handles spinning out of control. To the crowd's horror four laborers were hurled aside and slammed into the wheelhouse, their bones exploding from the skin of shattered legs and arms. A fifth man was catapulted into the air and fell back into the machinery, which tore his head from his body.

Brunel, cheeks glistening with tears, called off the launching.

Over the following weeks (with gawking spectators kept clear) he tried six times more to launch the vessel he regarded as his masterpiece. But each time the giantess mulishly resisted all attempts to move her forward.

Not until January 31 the following year did *Great Eastern,* prodded by rams and dragged by tugs, reach the water at last. The multiple launches had cost the company more than £200,000 – a sum which distressed the backers, who had been promised early and easy profits. But the spending couldn't stop now. As the mighty vessel rested in the Thames Estuary the final opulent touches had to be added to her lavish interiors: marble pillars and surfaces for the vast Grand Salon; the world's biggest hot water system to supply the baths installed in every cabin; ornate wrought-iron ornamentation everywhere. And at Brunel's insistence, a horde of wooden rocking-chairs. Americans adored them, and Brunel was determined that the US tourist trade would become the backbone of his bold enterprise.

But fear nagged at him. Already he had begun to hear the first reports of frightening phenomena aboard his ship. He speculated – accurately as it later transpired – about a possible reason for the disturbances, but dared not share his theories with more than a few trusted colleagues. He dreaded the slightest gossip about the ugly matter. If the wider public became aware that there were ghosts – terrible ghosts – aboard *Great Eastern* it would almost certainly be the end of her.

Isambard Kingdom Brunel did nothing and hoped the problem would go away.

Horror on the Trial Voyage

In the pre-dawn darkness of September 9 the *Great Eastern* set out on her first proving trial around England's southern coast. Aboard were the full crew and a dozen guest passengers. Brunel had objected to a public presence at this early stage in the testing regime, but the owners overruled him. He had still considered it his professional duty to go on the voyage, but when the day came was too ill and pessimistic to leave his bed.

As the ship approached Hastings at about 7 a.m. "a powerful tremor" ran through her, jolting some passengers from their sleep. A massive explosion followed, blowing the forward funnel from its moorings and hurling hot chunks of metal across the decks. [A board of inquiry later found that an engineer had forgotten to open the stopcocks when the vessel left port. With nowhere to go the steam had swelled up in the funnel casing until it blasted its way free.]

Four men in the boiler room were immediately swamped by blistering steam. It scalded their lungs, killing them in seconds. A fifth died less mercifully, scrambling, screaming, up the ladder to the deck from which he jumped overboard, seeking the balm of the cold sea. But he was denied even that relief – falling instead into a gigantic spinning paddlewheel which shredded him alive.

Within hours of hearing the appalling news the ailing Brunel suffered a stroke. He died six days later.

However, the "curse" bubbled on without him.

Following the replacement of the funnel and other vital repairs, the *Great Eastern* steamed to the Welsh coast for a further trial. The captain, William Harris, decided to go ashore at Holyhead. With him in the ship's main boat were a coxswain and the purser's nine-year-old son. During the short journey to land, a powerful squall overturned the boat. The captain, the coxswain and the boy were drowned.

The *Great Eastern* on a trial voyage. Already 10 people connected with her had died.

In the face of all these catastrophes the *Great Eastern*'s owners had no choice but to remain publicly optimistic. Dismissing dark newspaper interpretations of the run of ill-luck that already had swallowed 10 lives, they spoke only of the pleasures and luxuries their revolutionary vessel offered. In a public relations effort that would be admired even by today's spin-practitioners, the company managed to sell tickets to more than 1000 people for the vessel's first voyage to New York. It was not generally known at the time, but many of these tickets were heavily discounted. Meanwhile the firm was obliged to tempt superstitious sailors with abnormally high wages – sometimes double the prevailing rate.

Under its new captain John Vine Hall the *Great Eastern* set sail (and steam) for New York. There were few accidents and no deaths – but the voyage was a disaster nonetheless. Because London's chefs and waiters were proving even less willing than seamen to come aboard, the company had been forced to recruit virtual amateurs – and their unsuitability showed in the form of repulsive meals, sloppily served. An equally unpleasant problem was the soot the funnels had begun to spew onto the decks, smudging the clothes and faces of everyone aboard. The gritty material also worked its way into water and food, prompting some passengers to fast until they disembarked.

Far worse were the reported ghosts. Passengers disembarking in London and New York swore to eagerly awaiting newspapermen that they would never set foot on the troubled ship again. Usually the story was the same: of being startled awake in the night by bloodcurdling bangings and frantic screams for help. As one American paper put it, "The cries were of a most terrible nature, seeming to emerge from Satan's deepest realms." The shipping line's managers denied these tales, once calling them "the fruits of fantasy and spite." But on both sides of the Atlantic Brunel's dream-liner was now principally known for its soot, phantoms and foul food.

Although few spoke well of the *Great Eastern* any more, she defiantly persisted with her transatlantic voyages, losing increasing amounts of money on every trip. But the trend became terminal in 1862 when she scraped across an uncharted rock outside New York. The accident tore a gash 82 feet long and 10 feet wide into the hull, necessitating $300,000 in repairs. Port authorities gave the hazard a name: "The Great Eastern Rock."

The proprietors had had enough. Abandoning all hope of creating a successful passenger and mail line they sold their jinxed giantess for a fraction of what she had cost to build. The new owners immediately put the *Great Eastern* to work on a project guaranteed to turn a profit – laying part of the new transatlantic telegraph cable.

The Curse's Cause "Revealed"

The work of cabling the ocean floor between Ireland and Newfoundland began in July 1865. After nine hours of sailing and laying, the galvanometer revealed that a fault had occurred somewhere back along the line. The ship reversed and drew the cable back on board while technicians minutely inspected it.

After retrieving more than 10 miles of the metallic snake, the inspectors identified the problem: a saboteur had driven a spike of wire into the cable, earthing the current. Despite encountering, and repairing, an identical flaw further along the line, the *Great Eastern's* crew managed to lay 1180 miles of cable – roughly half the total distance.

But then the ocean grew violent. The cable aboard the rolling ship snapped, its end slithering over the stern and sinking three miles to the sea floor. For days, the master tried with a grapnel to retrieve the immensely costly line from the bottom – but was forced in the end to leave the cable – all 1180 miles of it – deep in the ocean.

The following year the *Great Eastern* laid a fresh length of cable – successfully. But she was now so enmired in debt that her owners decided to junk her anyway. In 1889, she was broken up and her iron plates and four million rivets sold for $1.5 million – a better profit than she had ever made at sea.

Toward the end of the demolition, workers were confronted by a chilling sight. Between the casings, bearing the bloody smears of their desperate scrapings and bangings, lay the contorted skeletons of two laborers. The original builders insisted that the men's absence had not been noticed at the time, but it was plain that they had somehow become trapped in their narrow tomb during construction of the *Great Eastern*. The skeletons had sailed on every voyage the gigantic ship had made.

- Largely forgotten today is the unhappy history of the liner *Hinemoa*, launched in 1861, three years after the *Great Eastern*. From the beginning, superstitious sailors deplored the fact that the dirt constituting the ship's ballast had been bought on the cheap from a London graveyard. The vessel was dogged by a long series of accidents and mishaps, culminating, on her sixth voyage, in a storm which drowned all aboard. A court of inquiry heard that the *Hinemoa* had had six captains, one for each journey. The first died after days of drinking; the second was imprisoned for theft; the third was committed to a mental asylum; the fourth and fifth were found dead in their cabins (the latter a suicide) – and the sixth went down with his men when the ship sank.

Rocked by Ill-Luck

In 1983, frightened tourists rushed to rid themselves of reputedly cursed rocks they had souvenired from Hawaii's Mauna Lau volcano. At the time, Jan Erickson, a naturalist at the Volcanoes National Park, told me, "Sometimes we're receiving 30 to 40 parcels in a single day's mail. In most cases nothing has happened to these people. Rationally or not, they just fear what *might* hit them."

The great rock rebound began when newspapers reported a chain of deaths and mishaps linked to the stones. One victim was Ralph Loffert, an airline executive who vacationed near the volcano with his wife and four children in 1981. Ignoring warnings from local guides that the mountain's goddess Pele punished people who stole her rocks, Loffert took a bagful home to Buffalo, USA.

A black chain of coincidences followed. Son Todd suffered an appendicitis attack – then shortly after release from hospital, injured his knee so badly it needed an operation. On the day he left hospital the second time he broke his wrist. Meanwhile brother Mark sprained an ankle and broke an arm, and a third son, Dan, acquired a mysteriously lingering eye infection. This was not the pattern of daily life to which the family was accustomed.

When the Lofferts' daughter Rebecca lost two front teeth in a fall they decided it was time to get rid of the sinister stones – returning them to Hawaii by priority mail. "But the bad things kept right on happening," Ralph Loffert recalled. "Rebecca broke three more of her teeth, Dan broke a bone in his hand and Todd dislocated his elbow and broke his other wrist. We'd never known a pattern of such bad luck.

"It was only then I found Mark had held back three of the rocks. We mailed them back right away and the trouble stopped."

Allegedly the jinxed stones destroyed the life of Alison Raymond of Washington, a nursing sister:

A week after I took home a collection of the rocks from Mauna Lau my mother died of cancer, and soon after, my husband was killed in a head-on collision. While we were making the funeral arrangements my son broke his leg, then became gravely ill with a pancreas condition.

I'd been warned about the rocks, but I didn't believe it – and I don't entirely know if I believe it now. But for safety's sake I sent them back, with the bleak feeling that what I'd done was too late anyway. I've spent a long time regretting that I didn't leave the rocks on the slope of that mountain.

Whatever might be causing it, the sinister stones syndrome is not confined to Hawaii.

Visitors who souvenired stones from the ancient Australian monolith Uluru have contritely returned them to its Aboriginal guardians, sometimes describing similar patterns of ill-luck.

But the heaviest paranormal punishments – in Australia at least – have been suffered by tourists who appropriated samples of the sacred (and celebrated) bouncing stones from a beach near Cape Tribulation, Queensland. When thrown, these small black rocks rebound like tennis balls – and despite warning signs and guides' requests, visitors were pocketing them so often that the beach had to be closed.

However, if their letters can be believed, some thieves paid heavily for the desecration. "We've received many parcels of pebbles with apologetic letters inside," Hazel Douglas, the Guyalanji tribe's custodian of the bouncing stones, told me.

The tribespeople allowed me to read some of the letters. The writers revealed that since taking stones from the beach their families had been plagued by bad luck, illness – and even death.

"We're receiving a steady stream of our bouncing stones from all over the world," Marcia Tudor of the Far North Queensland Promotion Bureau said. "People are incredibly anxious to return them to us – hoping that by doing so they'll end their run of bad fortune. Some say they'd never realized the stones were sacred. A lot seem to be looking for forgiveness from the tribe."

Hitler's Hexed Battleship "Killed 2000 Men"

ILL-LUCK, INJURY AND DEATH plagued the German battleship *Scharnhorst* during her seven years at sea.

The jinx was reportedly at work long before the vessel set out on its maiden voyage.

During construction the *Scharnhorst's* shell rolled over, crushing 60 workers. Ignoring the crew's fears Nazi leaders gathered in September 1936 to see the ship launched. But it fell off its cradle and slid into the ocean. Mere days after the ship set out onto the still-peaceful seas her sailors began to die.

- Nine men perished when a gun exploded.
- Twelve suffocated when the air-supply to their gun-turret failed.
- While steaming up the River Elbe the destroyer collided with the passenger liner *Bremen,* damaging it beyond repair. And finally...
- By sheer luck four British cruisers fatally crippled the *Scharnhorst* in December 1943, firing at random from the "impossible" distance of 9 miles. The battleship sank into the North Atlantic ocean, drowning all but 32 of the 1968 sailors aboard.

Odyssey of the "Unlucky" Ax-Head

LES KOHRING of Molendinar on Queensland's Gold Coast has seen several examples of little-understood forces at work, both between individuals and via inanimate objects. He is even convinced that one artifact – an ancient ax-head – malignly threatened his own wellbeing. Les told me his story in October 2006:

I've had many friendships and contacts with Aboriginal people over the years, beginning with the time I was a 16-year-old boxer in the Western District of Victoria. Murri lads often took part in local fight nights and I was in quite a few of them, both as an amateur and a pro.

Later in life, working as a concrete contractor on the Gold Coast, I came into close contact with what I knew deep inside me to be raw Aboriginal power. I was preparing a small job at a place called Gaven when I picked up an old Aboriginal ax-head shaped out of stone. I immediately recognized what it was because we used to find them while we were cutting sugarcane. We learned back then that they were quite a few hundred years old – and this one certainly looked it.

I foolishly decided to keep the thing as a souvenir, so I took it home and cleaned it up and put it on a bookshelf as an ornament – something I was going to regret. From that time on I had a run of really evil luck. First I injured my arm and ended with an elbow so swollen I could barely work. Then the part-Aboriginal bloke who worked for me got a bad heart. I kept going, but with illnesses, mechanical breakdowns and every kind of misfortune you could name, I began to wonder whether someone had it in for me.

The final crunch came when the concrete cracked in a couple of house slabs I'd laid. That just shouldn't have happened. I knew a fair bit of Aboriginal lore and I didn't need to be told that that ax-head probably had something – a lot – to do with it. So I kept an eye on the local classifieds – and when I saw an ad from someone with an Aboriginal name wanting to buy old artifacts, I packed the ax-head up and sent it to him free. I didn't want a price, I just wanted someone who could handle the problem. After I'd posted it off, things soon returned to normal.

Aboriginal magic can be very powerful at times. Once, at Cooktown Hospital, I talked to a woman who was in bed very ill, but from no cause the doctors could find. She said she'd been walking in the bush when she stumbled by accident into a sacred spot where women were forbidden to go. She hadn't gone in deliberately – it was just a slip-up. But she was being punished all the same – and she didn't expect to live. I was pleased to hear that after a long illness she did survive, but I've seen others not so lucky.

In North Queensland hospitals, like Cairns, you can find people, very sick, who've unwittingly broken some old taboo and are dying because of that. Strangely enough, they don't even have to know about their transgression to experience its deadly effects. In some cases they seem to lose the will to live, and just fade away and die.

These curses seem to work in a frighteningly efficient way. Christian clergy are usually quite ineffectual in trying to remove them.

In 1956 the world's newspapers described how an Australian witchdoctor's apparently powerful hex almost killed a young Aboriginal mechanic. Daniel C. collapsed at a general store and was taken by ambulance to Darwin General Hospital. Pupils dilated and breathing raggedly, he told emergency department doctors that the "snake spirit" was stinging him to death. He gaspingly explained that he had been walking alone through the bush when he quite accidentally caught sight of an elderly witchdoctor from another tribe squatting in the earth preparing a spell.

Furious at this taboo-breaking breach of privacy the old man immediately pointed a ceremonial bone and chanted a song designed to admit a snake into the interloper's body, where it would slowly crush him to death. Over the following week Daniel's muscles tensed to such a degree that he was unable to eat and could scarcely breathe. Convinced that the snake was indeed crushing his lungs he resigned himself to inevitable death.

But the hospital's medical staff refused to give in. Assuring the young man that his problems were not physical but psychological, they placed him in an oxygen tent and fed him through a drip. Meanwhile the counseling continued. There was no magical snake. The death curse was an empty threat. What was real was Daniel and his wish to live. The 20th century healers prevailed. Several days later their patient, convinced that his medical team had defeated the bone-pointer, left the hospital cured.

Other victims of the snake curse have been less fortunate.

Horror of the Plasticine Doll

SIR ALEC GUINNESS learned in a frightening way that it can be dangerous to trifle – even playfully – with the occult. Guinness describes his unnerving experience in the autobiography *A Positively Final Appearance* (Penguin), published the year before his death in 2000.

As a young actor he was rehearsing for a season of *Romeo and Juliet* – and for his title role was expected to appear in a simple red velvet doublet formerly worn by Lawrence Olivier.

To his extreme annoyance he discovered that the wardrobe mistress, a Mrs Lewis, had tried to improve this simple costume by covering it with sequins.

"I blew my top," Guinness reveals – "(and) said they must all be ripped off or I wouldn't wear it."

Still seething, he went home to his theatrical digs, where wife Merula was in the kitchen preparing a haddock dinner. Through the open door to the sitting room he was continuing to rant indignantly about the wardrobe department's tastelessness when he noticed, on the mantelpiece, a gray lump of plasticine, presumably left there by a previous tenant's child.

He picked up the plasticine and began to model it into a crude figurine, while telling Merula, half-laughingly, what he was doing. *"You are Mrs Lewis,"* he said, *"and I've found a needle and I'm going to stick it into you."*

From the kitchen Merula immediately screamed that he must not do such a thing – it was very wicked. Guinness called back that he was only joking, and would not stick the needle into the figurine's middle, but merely into its left foot. He added a foot, plunged the needle into it, then forgot the entire silly business and enjoyed his dinner.

An hour later he was back at the theater, where he was greeted by ashen faces. Mrs Lewis had just been taken away by ambulance. *She had dropped a hot iron on her foot.*

Guinness asked which foot it was and was told – the left foot. "She was in terrible agony. I hope they don't have to amputate it."

Alec Guinness reports, "They didn't. I have remained conscience-stricken and chastened ever since."

The Deaths that Dogged a Famous Family

SOMETIMES AN ENTIRE FAMILY can fall under the influence of events so malign, and so persistently similar, that they seem to defy coincidence. In that respect, members of Britain's Guinness family have had much in common with the American Kennedys.

Both dynasties are respected, rich, and (at least in popular belief) jinxed. The "curse" that cut a black swathe of suicide, assassination and illness through the golden Kennedy clan has been endlessly documented. The hoodoo which seemingly has hung over Britain's leading brewers created a comparably pernicious pattern. The baneful roll-call included:

- Olivia Guinness, who choked to death on her own vomit in an Oxford University common room.

- Guinness heir Tara Browne, who died in a Chelsea car smash.

- Lady Henrietta Guinness, who drowned after falling from an aqueduct in Spoleto, Italy.

- Guinness heiress Janet Moore, who drowned in her bath the following month.

- Major Dennys Guinness, who was found dead on his Hampshire estate – an empty pill bottle beside him.

- Former prime ministerial adviser John Guinness, who survived a head-on collision in Norfolk, only to find that his four-year-old son had been killed and another son seriously hurt.

The author Arthur Koestler speculated that "jinxes" of this kind might be "a form of psychic disease" infecting a family for a century or more before petering out.

The "Unlucky" Play that Actors Avoid

MACBETH IS THE ONLY PLAY by Shakespeare in which evil incantations and witchcraft play a prominent part. From its first performance in 1606 the doom-laden drama has been beset by misfortunes – becoming known as the unluckiest play in world theater.

In his book *The Curse of Macbeth* (1983) the veteran British actor Richard Huggett opined that Shakespeare "went a little too far" when in Scene Three he introduced the witches' potion which begins with the words "Fillet of a fenny's snake..." Out of those verses, Huggett believed, was born a curse spanning four centuries of "death, doom and disaster." The superstitious lawmakers of the Bard's time were ahead of Huggett. After seeing early performances of the play they banned it for five years.

By 1611, however, opinions had changed – and *Macbeth* was allowed to reopen at the Globe Theatre. The building burned down soon afterward. The mishap shocked the people of Elizabethan England – and the authorities demanded that all references to black magic be removed from the text. Even in its rewritten form, the increasingly notorious drama did not reappear until 1667.

In 1794, when rationalism, scientific inquiry and abhorrence of credulity were flourishing, a London theater's enlightened management decided to restore the original text. With it, the malediction returned. Across England, theatrical companies were plagued by mysterious fires, collapsing sets, genuine injuries inflicted in the fight scenes, and technical failures of many kinds. Particularly disturbing were the numerous "freezes" in which actors forgot their lines at crucial moments.

By the dawn of the 19th century numerous performers were refusing to appear in *Macbeth,* even if (as most did) they needed the money. And it had become traditional among nervous thespians never to utter the drama's name – describing it instead as *That Play... The Unmentionable... The Comedy of Glamis... The Scottish Play... The Caledonian Tragedy...* or even *Harry Lauder.*

Lowlights of the chronicle of calamities associated with *Macbeth* include:

- Amsterdam, 1672. In a scene involving a dagger, actor Jan de Hoffmeyr used a real knife to kill his rival for the attentions of an actress in the cast. He did not win the lady's heart.

- Moscow, 1907. During a Russian-language performance, the prompter failed to prompt and was found dead in his box.

- Leeds, 1952. During the potion scene, one of the witches dancing around the caldron collapsed and died.

- Portugal, 1964. On the third night of a performance the theater burned down. It had stood for more than 300 years.

- New York, 1965. A young actor appearing in an off-Broadway production was knifed to death near the theater. Several days later the company manager was murdered with a knife in his apartment – and another actor suffered a fatal cardiac arrest on stage.

Samuel Beckett and His Death-bringing Dramas

WILLIAM SHAKESPEARE was not alone in writing dramatic material which *seemed* to trigger deaths.

Playwright Samuel Beckett: "suspended lifelong in a sticky web of ill-luck."

The Nobel Prize-winning playwright Samuel Beckett (creator of *Waiting for Godot*) often gloomily remarked that he had been suspended lifelong in a web of ill-luck and black coincidence. Beckett liked to remind interviewers that he was born on Friday, April 13. And he was openly distressed by the number of actors who had appeared in his plays and died soon afterward.

Other members of his performance teams were involved too. Alan Schneider, who had directed all of Beckett's productions in the United States, was killed on a London zebra crossing in 1984, moments after posting a letter to the playwright. By an odd coincidence the doctor who attended the dying man was also called Beckett.

The Controversial "Curse of Superman"

THE ANCIENT GREEKS believed their gods would destroy anyone who displayed hubris: arrogance and pride that sacrilegiously trespassed on the deities' hallowed territory. For much of the 20th century, actors associated with the *Superman* franchise had reason to ponder on that old superstition. It wasn't that these performers had been arrogant

– well, not unduly anyway. Their error (in the view of those who held such beliefs) was that they'd played the role of a god – a sure recipe for attracting a violent reminder of one's own mortality.

The Man of Steel movies and TV series brought so much misery to people who prominently appeared in or were associated with them that the media found shorthand to describe the syndrome: The Curse of Superman. Many commentators have disputed that there is any jinx at all, but the victim list makes thought-provoking reading nonetheless.

First to suffer – lifelong – were the two 17-year-old artists who created the interplanetary hero. In 1938, too impatient to see a lawyer, **Jerry Siegel** and **Joe Schuster** sold *Superman* to the company that would become DC Comics. They received a contract, of sorts. The corporation went on to coin countless millions from *Superman* comic books, paperback novels, toys, clothes, sponsorships, radio serials, cartoon shorts, and movies while Siegel and Schuster remained freelance artists struggling to make a living. As they grew older the jobs dried up. At one stage of his shattered career the financially strapped Jerry Siegel was forced to take a job with the US post office, processing parcels.

In the late 1970s America's National Cartoonists' Society, backed by the Writers' Guild and such prominent authors as Kurt Vonnegut and Norman Mailer, managed to pressure the corporate rights-holders to pay the two moral owners of *Superman* $20,000 a year each, for life. Jerry Siegel and Joe Schuster welcomed the handout, but it was a bitterly small reward for the creators of what Mailer called "America's great mythic icon."

The bitterness continued after Siegel's and Schuster's deaths, with their heirs continuing to fight the corporations in court. In 2002 *Superman* comic book No. 1 sold at auction for $US110,000. By 2006 its estimated worth was $250,000.

Actors were next to feel the cold breath of the purported jinx. **Kirk Alyn** had made 40 Hollywood movies before he was contracted to star in *Superman* (1948), followed in 1950 by *Atom Man vs Superman*. Both films were highly successful – but after they appeared Alyn seldom worked again. He later told the *Los Angeles Times,* "After *Superman* I could never get another job in Hollywood. Playing that part ruined my career. I'm bitter about the whole thing." Alyn, who had seemed to embody the glamorous Los Angeles lifestyle, retired to Arizona, where he died.

The second major performer to don the bright red boots and cape was **George Reeves**, a rising actor who had been one of Scarlett O'Hara's suitors in *Gone With the Wind.* Reeves was flattered when asked to play the demigod from Krypton in the 1950s TV series. But when the show ended, he too found it almost impossible to get other work. He believed his breakthrough had come when he was cast in the classic film *From Here to Eternity* – but his scenes were deleted after members of a test audience laughed and burst into ironic applause when they recognized Superman. Following years of unemployment and alcoholism Reeves shot himself – or was murdered.

Next to play Clark Kent and Lois Lane were **Christopher Reeve** (no relation to George Reeves) and **Margot Kidder**. In publicity interviews for 1978's *Superman: The Movie,* both performers denied that they either feared or believed in a curse. But jinx or not, they were to suffer cruel misfortune. Reeve starred successfully in the original film and three sequels. Then, on May 27 1995, he was thrown from his horse during a cross-country riding event. Paralyzed from the neck down he courageously continued his acting career to the greatest extent he could – campaigning also for increased research into spinal injuries. He died of heart failure on October 10 2004.

The following year Christopher Reeve's widow **Dana Reeve** publicly revealed that she had been diagnosed with lung cancer. She had never smoked. She died of the cancer on March 6 2006, aged 45.

In 1990 Reeve's co-star **Margot Kidder** was involved in a car accident that forced her temporarily into a wheelchair. In 1996 she declared bankruptcy with debts of more than $3 million. She then suffered a mental breakdown, hacking off her hair with a razorblade and accusing strangers of plotting to kill her. Police rescued her from a ditch in Los Angeles in which she was hiding. In 2002 she broke her pelvis in a second road smash. Happily she recovered from her mental and physical problems and has worked steadily, mainly on TV, ever since.

Les Quigley, who appeared as the baby Kal-El in *Superman: The Movie* died in March 1991 after inhaling solvents. He was 14.

Marlon Brando, who played Superman's biological father Jor-El, was beset by personal tragedies. In 1990 Brando's son Christian was tried for shooting Dag Drollet, the lover of his half-sister Cheyenne. Found guilty of voluntary manslaughter he was sentenced to 10 years' jail. Five years later, 25-year-old Cheyenne, still distraught over Drollet's death, hanged herself. On July 1 2004 Brando, despairing and ill, died aged 80. The cause of death was lung failure. Chronically obese, he had also suffered from congestive heart disease, diabetes and liver cancer.

• • •

Producers had hoped to begin production of the new film in the franchise, *Superman Returns,* as early as 2003. Their problem was that they could find nobody to play the leading role. **Nicolas Cage** said no – as did **Brendan Fraser**, **Josh Hartnett** and **Keanu Reeves** (again, no relation).

But finally, in another of those peculiar name-echoes that resound around *Superman,* the studio – denied a Brendan – found a Brandon: 25-year-old **Brandon Routh**. Working as a waiter when the call came, Routh was ecstatically happy to sign up for "the riskiest job in Hollywood." Like Christopher Reeve in 1978, he was virtually unknown, with only a few tiny TV roles to his credit. But critics and public admired his swashbuckling style and *Superman Returns* made respectable profits.

In February 2006 *Tribune Media* journalist Daniel Feinberg asked Routh whether he was worried by the *Superman* curse. Routh replied, "I'm nodding my head, but I'm thinking 'What curse?' To me it means nothing. There are a lot of things that happened to people, but I don't think of it as a curse."

In July 2006 Routh fell off his motorbike, catapulting over the handlebars. Two women helped him off the road and an ambulance took him to hospital. Disbelievers in the jinx theory would be completely justified in dismissing this minor accident as merely the latest in a decades-long chain of coincidences.

In the dark history of *Superman* there is more:

- In the late 1930s brothers **Max and Dave Fleischer** founded Fleischer Studios, which produced the feature-length *Gulliver's Travels* and later the cartoon shorts *Popeye* and *Betty Boop*. In 1940 the studio secured the rights to make a series of 10-minute *Superman* cartoons. Staff artists animated and backdropped these beautiful shorts so brilliantly that they still sell on DVD today, 66 years later. Shortly after work on *Superman* began, the Fleischer brothers fell out. Their quarrel bankrupted the studio, which was then swallowed by Paramount. Dave, his fortune gone, found work as a special effects adviser. Max died in poverty in a film industry charity hospital.
- In 1963 DC Comics asked **President John F. Kennedy** for permission to use him as a character in a planned *Superman* comic book. The story would support the president's plans for improving young people's health. Kennedy and his advisers approved the request. But on November 22 1963 the storyboard was hastily scrapped. President Kennedy had been assassinated in Dallas.
- Years later, an eerie fact came to light. A collector noticed that a *Superman* comic book had "predicted" **President Kennedy**'s murder – 24 years before it happened. The picture story, created by Jerry Siegel and Joe Schuster, was published by DC Comics in October 1939. It contains names and places hauntingly similar to the events that would occur in Dallas. In the antique comic, reporter Clark Kent's editor sends him out to cover the killing of a "**Jack Kennedy**". A suspect asserts, "I didn't do it" – a statement similar to that of Lee Harvey Oswald who, in his Dallas jail cell a quarter-century later, would tell reporters, "I didn't shoot anybody."
- In the comic, the Man of Steel (alias Kent) traces the real Kennedy-killing culprit to the *Hilow Club*, where he questions two performers, **Evelyn Curry** and **Bea Carroll**. This scene also contains glimpses of future events. In real-life Dallas, Jack Ruby – who later shot Oswald – owned the *Carousel Club*. Two of the performers who worked there

gave long statements to police. Their names were **Rose Cherami** (a surname with the same initial and e-sound ending as the comic book's "Curry") and **Karen Bennett Carlin** (whose middle name and surname bear the same initials as the comic's "Bea Carroll").

- Most intriguing of all are the names of the fictional and real-life nightclubs, *Hilow* and *Carousel.* A student of precognition would be entitled to speculate that when *Superman's* creators named their club the *Hilow*, they might unconsciously have been thinking of the up-and-down (high-low) motion of the horses on a carousel.

Superman was always more than a pulp comic. From the start it seemed infused with a mythic grandeur, most cogently expressed in the opening scenes of the 1978 film. *Superman*'s legend-and-religion-inspired theme of a godlike figure descended to earth inspired many imitations, but none captured its soul. Quite possibly the teenagers who wrote and drew the original episodes did not fully understand what they were creating. Nor might they have foreseen the power (and arguably the phenomena) their innocent storytelling would unleash.

The Book that Foretold
Diana's Doom
Premonitions in Print and Film

On August 31 1997 Diana, Princess of Wales, died in a high-speed car crash in a Paris tunnel. Ever since, persistent speculation has suggested that her death was not an accident but the result of conspiracy. Less widely known is the uncanny fact that Diana's miserable marriage and ultimate fate in the auto disaster had been described 17 years in advance in a remarkable novel. When young journalist Tim Heald's book was published in 1980 he was unaware that Diana Spencer even existed. But his prophetic narrative has admitted him into that pantheon of authors who – unconsciously – have created stunningly accurate visions of future events...

IN 1978, YOUNG NEWSPAPERMAN TIM HEALD was working in London as a specialist royal reporter. The press at that time was filled with conjecture about Prince Charles who, many Britons believed, was unlikely ever to break the comfortable bonds of bachelorhood. Heald sensed that there might be a book in the subject – a novel perhaps.

In his spare time he sat down and, lightheartedly at first, planned and wrote. But the nature of his story gradually changed, to something darker and more sinister than he had originally intended.

What if Charles failed to find a "true love?" What if he married the wrong girl? What if he became king, but was locked into an unhappy union? What if...?

Heald, always a fast writer, finished the novel in 1979 – a year whose final two digits, reversed, coincidentally form the year of Princess Diana's death. Although the plot (as he imagined) was sheer fiction he decided to use a nom-de-plume.

Caroline R, by "David Lancaster", was published by Hutchinson in 1980. It sold well and was re-released in March 1981 as an Arrow paperback. Even at that time, real events had begun to jostle on the novel's heels. Shortly before the soft-cover appeared, the Palace announced Prince Charles's engagement to an obscure 19-year-old kindergarten teacher, Lady Diana Frances Spencer. The wedding date was set for July 1981. "David Lancaster" (aka Tim Heald) felt obliged to write a "Foreword to the Paperback Edition" which read, in part:

> When I wrote this book I had never even heard of Lady Diana Spencer – indeed as far as I can make out Prince Charles had scarcely heard of her either. There was still talk of him marrying a foreign princess; there was still talk – loose talk – about his liking for vivacious blondes; and there was even some apprehension. He had said he would like to marry when he was around 30 but 30 had been and gone and he seemed as far from the altar as ever. Maybe he would never marry.
>
> That period of nervous speculation is now firmly in the past. The Prince has chosen a sensible, attractive English girl from an aristocratic family which has a long connection with the monarchy. They are a happy young

couple who one day, God willing, will make a popular and successful King and Queen. It has all turned out for the best.

But… just suppose that royal judgment lapsed… that he fell in love with a girl who was unfamiliar with royalty. What then?

Diplomatically Tim Heald continued:

That was the starting point of this novel. It *is* a novel and it is set in a future which is now impossible, where it was once only implausible…

The author little knew in 1981 that 16 years later his story would be proved neither "impossible" nor "implausible." The novel would be seen to contain numerous scenes that darkly mirrored Princess Diana's marriage, right through to her violent death in a car.

In 2006 Tim Heald conceded that his book had been "horribly prescient."

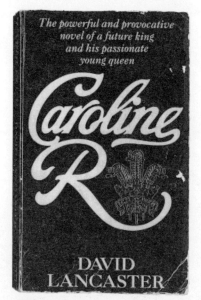

In a novel he imagined to be fiction, journalist Tim Heald
created stunningly accurate visions of future events.

Snapshots from the Future

The author describes Caroline, his novel's heroine, as "tall and leggy and slim and blonde" – *a description equally applicable to Diana.* The daughter of an old, rich American family, she dutifully bears her husband, the king, two children, but despite her love for them, recognizes that marrying into British royalty was not her wisest decision. The king seems distracted and is continually absent, leaving Caroline *(like Diana)* to sit, idle and unhappy, in the cold drafty royal quarters. A friend describes her as "a prisoner in a mausoleum."

Caroline tells her husband she wants to do useful work, rather than be a mere figurehead – and when at last he allows this, her life changes. She finds *(as will Diana)* that people love her and want to touch her. The prime minister's wife expresses the general sentiment, saying, "You've cheered me up no end… it's good to know there's some warmth and generosity left in the world."

"My book proved to be horribly prescient": journalist Tim Heald.

Increasingly the Palace mandarins regard Caroline as a major security problem. British intelligence operatives award her a codename, Apple Pie *(which rhymes with Di)*. They are particularly disturbed by her insistence on giving spontaneous, unscripted speeches – and are alarmed by her expressed desire to speak out on such issues as seal-hunting and nuclear armaments. *(Diana would subsequently outrage Western arms manufacturers by campaigning against landmines. She also had strong empathy toward animals – and detested the bloodsports the Royal Family enjoyed.)*

The fictional Caroline's sins seem venial enough – but now, writes Heald, she lives in an atmosphere of "distrust and threat." She is warned that if the monarchy crumbles, due to her misbehavior, Britain will no longer be central, through NATO, to Western Europe's defense. "The monarchy," she is warned, "is the one institution that guarantees British stability. And you're part of that stability."

Scandal begins to surround Caroline – especially when, in her loneliness, she engages in an affair with Julian, a political extremist on MI5's watchlist. When a paparazzo takes compromising photographs of the pair, intelligence operatives decide to "examine" their "options."

By now Caroline *(like Di)* is in a state of nervous exhaustion. To friends *(as will Di, in future reality)* she writes increasingly desperate and revealing letters. She feels that she has only one real friend in the Palace: a press secretary, Maurice Henderson. *(Diana's sole friend within the "royal mausoleum" was butler Paul Burrell, whom she described as "my rock.")*

The first hint that Caroline's life might be at risk emerges when two shadowy official plotters discuss the possibility of killing her in a "convenient car crash."

Caroline knows nothing of this conversation – but *(like Diana)* she begins nevertheless to have a chilling presentiment that her life is at risk. To a diary she has secretly been keeping she confides her fears – then tells press secretary Henderson that if she suddenly dies, he must retrieve the diary and give it to her best friend who lives in the United States. Tim Heald's novel had, again, been eerily prophetic...

In late 1996, two months after her divorce from Charles was finalized, Diana wrote a letter expressing fears that someone was plotting to kill her. According to butler Paul Burrell in his book *A Royal Duty* (2003) the Princess gave him the letter, saying, "I'm going to date this and I want you to keep it... just in case." According to Burrell, Diana attached a note which included the words, "This particular phase in my life is the most dangerous."

Eight months later she was dead.

In the letter, first quoted and photographed in Britain's *Daily Mirror* (October 2003), Diana named someone who was "planning an accident in my car, brake failure and serious head injury." On legal advice the newspaper blacked out the alleged plotter's name.

Millionaire retailer Mahommad al Fayed, whose son Dodi had died with Diana in the crash, immediately demanded an inquest. [Until then only French authorities had investigated the deaths.] *Mirror* editor Piers

Morgan shared Fayed's concern, telling BBC News, "There has been, to date, incredibly, no inquest into the death of Princess Diana and there has been no public inquiry in this country. Paul Burrell has watched and waited and nothing has occurred. He feels this is the time to come forward and demand these two things happen."

Publication of Diana's explosive letter prompted British authorities to mount an inquest in 2004. It was adjourned while police investigated the crash. In May 2006 British police said they had found new witnesses and forensic evidence.

In the 1980 novel the fictional Caroline's fears for her life are grimly validated when she dies in a car in which a time-bomb has been planted. The novel even describes rumors that a mysterious "second car' was involved in the plot – but was never traced. *(Following Diana's death 17 years in the future, witnesses claimed they had seen a "second car", white in color, tailgating the Mercedes through the Pont d'Alma tunnel in Paris. This "second car" was never traced.)*

Tim Heald's book further describes how the RAF flies Caroline R's shocked and guilt-wracked husband to London from a fishing trip in Iceland. *(In real life the RAF flew a grieving Charles to Paris to collect his ex-wife's body.)*

Within an hour of the fictional Caroline's death large quantities of flowers from grief-stricken Britons begin arriving at the Palace. Millions worldwide watch the televised funeral. *(London in September 1997 became a city of flowers. More than a million mourners stood in the streets to pay a last tribute to their beloved Diana. Hundreds of millions more, across the planet, watched the funeral on television.)*

The final chapter of *Caroline R* contains a second – quite shocking – twist. For the sake of readers who might manage to look out a dog-eared copy of this venerable book, I'll refrain from publishing the details here.

My thanks to Sandy Coghlan of Book Orphanage, who alerted me to the existence of this extraordinary and most mysterious novel.

Tim Heald was not the only journalist to experience unwitting premonitions of the tragedy.

BBC Film "Predicted" Royal Car Crash

A FORTNIGHT AFTER Diana's death Britain's *Radio Times* (September 13

1997) published an interview with John Morrison, editor of BBC-TV news programs:

> "Our business is to satisfy the public hunger for information, working to a strict protocol laid down in a BBC manual. We routinely rehearse possible future news stories. In one of those rehearsals recently we decided to work to a fictional scenario involving the death of a leading royal in a car crash in a foreign country.
>
> "That rehearsal proved amazingly prescient. When the real news came through from Paris on August 31, I felt as if I was dreaming."

Two Magazines Foreglimpsed Death Smash

ON NOVEMBER 14 1996 – nine months before Princess Diana died while fleeing from pursuing photographers – the British magazine *Big Issue* published a prophetic interview. A reporter interrogated royals-chasing paparazzi Glen Harvey and Mark Saunders. When the interviewer asked if there were any situation in which he would *not* take a picture of Diana, Harvey replied: "If she was driving along in front of us and she had an accident and it was a life-and-death situation, we'd save her life – (but) if there was a chance of a picture after that…"

In my book *Unexplained* I describe how an article in the British weekly *The Spectator* presaged Princess Diana's death, and the air of mystery surrounding it, just three weeks before the tragedy occurred. Author of the innocently predictive opinion-piece was Alan Clark, Conservative MP for Kensington and Chelsea.

The magazine advertised the controversial politician's contribution on the cover of its August 9 1997 issue with the words, "Alan Clark names the famous person whom the press would most like to drive to suicide." Inside, under the heading PRESSED TO DEATH, Clark wrote: "The suicide of Gordon McMaster MP brings the press corps body-counts up to three… congratulations, boys! The big one still eludes you, but I expect you'll get her in the end."

Clark then attacked the paparazzi photographers, saying, "All moral impediments are discarded in the thrill of the chase." His essay ended, "And still elusive, though one must assume in the telescopic sight of every editor, is the ultimate trophy – the most brightly plumaged of all: *"to accelerate, and then be the first to capture, the sudden death of Diana, Princess of Wales, in unexplained circumstances."* [My italics.]

Clark's use of the words *"accelerate"* and *"thrill of the chase"* seemed unconsciously to forecast what would actually happen in the infamous Paris tunnel on August 31. The security guard driving the Mercedes 600 with Diana and Dodi al Fayed in the back accelerated to shake off seven photographers pursuing on motorbikes. The Mercedes smashed into a concrete post. Controversy over the crash's true cause has continued ever since.

Also predictive were the words *"capture the sudden death of Diana."* A particularly ghoulish paparazzo began taking pictures of her in the wrecked Mercedes. Infuriated onlookers attacked him.

• • •

Alan Clark heard the news of Diana's death when he arrived back from a fishing trip in Scotland. He told *The Times* (September 12 1997): "I was horrified... it was very, very creepy to happen within three weeks of my writing about it. But I don't see why I should feel terrible. It's a fairly medieval precept to believe that people who predict things actually cause them to happen."

No scientist has yet produced a satisfactory explanation of precognition: the ability (usually inadvertent) to foretell future occurrences. But some adventurously minded physicists might be coming close, in their belief that the phenomenon possibly involves quantum mechanics, a discipline which has demonstrated a mysterious connection between distant particles. That link, discovered relatively recently, shows that the particles seem to transcend the boundaries of time and space.

Most precognitive visions are brief, exploding in a flash during dreams or daylight reveries. But harder to comprehend are cases like that of author Tim Heald, who spent months – and hundreds of pages – unconsciously constructing a sprawling, detailed landscape of future time.

But what of the professional clairvoyants? After news of the tunnel tragedy broke, armies of "psychics" around the globe came forward to say they had foreseen it all – and had described their visions either in obscure radio broadcasts or to witnesses. But to my knowledge none [with the honorable exception of Lebanese clairvoyant Michel Hayek, below] seemed to have written or published any circumstantial prediction before the event. Provided she had read it, a detailed letter of warning to the already fearful Diana might have saved her life.

On national TV, psychic Michel Hayek foretold Diana's "death in a car accident" – eight months before it happened.

A Middle East Magician Muzzled

THE FUTURE SEEMS more accessible to Michel Hayek than to the rest of us. By his 27th birthday Hayek's accurate predictions had won him such celebrity in his native Lebanon that a national TV network engaged him to present annual forecasts for the 12 months ahead. In his December 1996 telecast, preserved on tape, he said: "England will experience sadness when their princess, Diana, is killed while traveling in a car."

Viewers had learned to take such forecasts seriously. Hayek had a nose for imminent death, having starkly, and publicly, predicted the destruction of US space station *Challenger* in the mid-1980s.

In his December 2004 program Hayek said, "A major incident in downtown Beirut will shake the area for a long time." In February 2005 a truck bomb killed 23 people including a former prime minister, Rafiq Hariri.

During the same alarming telecast Hayek tipped that the government would collapse. It did. He also said the media and cabinet would come under violent attack – naming publisher Gebran Tueni, his friend, president Emile Lahoud and defense minister Elias al Murr as particular targets. Two months later the men were blown up by a bomb. Tueni and one of his journalists died.

As his other forecasts of assassination attempts kept reliably proving correct, Hayek grew increasingly defensive. "It's not my fault that these things happen – I just see them," he said. "I wish my predictions did not come true and all those people did not die."

But a proportion of the Lebanese population had become convinced that Hayek was not only predicting the troubles, but causing them. Several Beirut businesses threatened to sue him for ruining their trade.

In December 2005 Hayek announced via media release that he would make no further prophecies for the time being: "After all the clamor surrounding my predictions for this year I have decided to stop. I don't want to be the reason people are afraid to go to the grocer or send their children to school."

Dream Screams Warned of Heart Attack

THE MOST CONVINCING EVIDENCE of precognition can be found in print, on film, or in dated and stamped letters and reports. An example of the latter type of documentation involved the British actor Roy Kinnear. A Hertford woman wrote to ASSAP – Association for the Scientific Study of Anomalous Phenomena – to describe a vivid nightmare in which she had seen him fall to his death from a boat.

The woman's letter, comprising several closely written pages, was unnervingly circumstantial. The dream-glimpsed accident had occurred on a warm day during a film-shoot in a sunny location. The crew, who had been laughing at some joke, suddenly screamed, horrified as the actor stumbled and plunged headfirst into the water.

An ASSAP investigator, Ken Phillips, was sufficiently impressed by the letter to send a photocopy to Roy Kinnear at London Weekend Television, suggesting he try to avoid the described situation. Following standard procedure Phillips then date-stamped and lodged the original letter in ASSAP's files. He received no reply from Roy Kinnear.

The letter's contents became public months later, when most of the dream's details came true. Kinnear died while filming *Return of the*

Musketeers in Spain. The one "mistake" in the nightmare was that no boat was involved. The actor, in reality, suffered a heart attack while riding a horse over a drawbridge.

The Man Who Painted the Future

IN 1976, AFTER RETIRING from his art-lecturing job at a Scottish university, David Mandell took up painting as a 50-hour-a-week hobby. The activity proved a boon to him psychologically. It enabled him to give artistic expression to the nightmares which had for unknown reasons begun to plague his sleep.

Before long Mandell was startled to find that some of his dream canvases had foretold future events, small and large, ranging from train accidents to massacres. He wanted to share this information with people who might be able to explain what was happening – but he realized that he'd probably be dismissed as a delusional old pensioner.

Determined to prove that he was regularly painting visions of disasters yet-unfolded, Mandell persuaded the local bank manager to have him photographed beneath the branch's calendar clock (showing date and time) whenever he had a new picture to display. The results were dramatic enough to have him invited onto TV programs in England and USA.

- Mandell's most famous artwork – painted, annotated and photographed precisely five years before events overtook it – shows the destruction of the Twin Towers on September 11 2001. The painting depicts a silhouetted airliner approaching the towers which collapse into each other, gushing black billowing smoke. In the air floats the head of the Statue of Liberty. [David Mandell was not alone in producing a graphic "prediction" of this kind. The Inner City Hustlers' rock album *Time to Explode* was released in July 2001. After September 11 2001 it was hastily removed from stores. It bore a prophetic picture of the Twin Towers ablaze.]

- Another work, which Mandell completed four months before the terrible event, shows Scotland's Dunblane elementary school massacre of March 13 1996, in which 16 children and a teacher were murdered.

- He also painted an image of a Concorde crashing while flying a Tricolor flag [a sinister preview of the Concorde disaster at Paris airport]... and a picture of Tokyo commuters dying in the sarin gas attack. In an accompanying note he identified the city as "Tokio."

In March 2003 Britain's Channel 5 subjected David Mandell to stringent scientific testing – checking the photographic negatives, which showed no evidence of tampering, and putting the artist through a polygraph test, which he passed. A skeptical panel admitted that it had found no evidence that the artist was a hoaxer or fantasist.

David Mandell had never sought money – only an acknowledgment that his gifts were genuine. He announced that he was delighted by the investigation's result.

The Child Who Foreglimpsed JFK's Murder

AS A 10-YEAR-OLD schoolboy Cuban-born Tony Cordero experienced a distressing vision in which he saw President John F. Kennedy fatally shot.

The FBI placed the youngster's statement on file, but took no action. The president was assassinated several days later.

The federal agency's records of the interview, released under the Freedom of Information statute, reveal that the boy had accurately described many major details of the killing.

In adult life Cordero's precognitive abilities made him a celebrity. Journalists Bernard Gittelson and Laura Torbet told his life story in the book *Intangible Evidence* (Simon and Schuster).

Cordero recalls that he was at school when the knowledge of the president's fate "washed over" him:

> All the Cuban kids had gathered around a little TV set to watch President Kennedy at the Orange Bowl in Miami. The picture was in black-and-white – but I could see blood coming out of the president's head, and it was in color. I was really shook up. I started hyperventilating.

Tony was taken to a children's hospital, where he was so insistent the president was in danger that a young doctor rang the FBI. "Three agents came to talk to me, but they just took notes. Two days later President Kennedy died, in the way I'd seen it."

To his parents' relief, Tony Cordero's warning attracted no publicity at the time. But the situation had changed by October 28 1971 when, as an already nationally known 18-year-old, he appeared on the radio program *Speak Out, Washington* – predicting that a scandal would force President Nixon to resign.

The Watergate Hotel break-in did not occur until June 17 1972. When the scandal broke, the tape of Cordero's interview was replayed across America.

Moon-Visions Mystery

IN JUNE 2004 the space probe Cassini took the first-ever close-ups of Mimas, one of Saturn's 31 moons.

The Saturnian moon Mimas, photographed by NASA
space probe Cassini.

Bemused NASA scientists noted that the tiny satellite, with its distinctive circular crater, was almost identical to the Death Star, which had awed *Star Wars* audiences years earlier.

The crater on Mimas is of colossal size and has a central mountain taller than Mount Everest. The uncannily similar crater-like feature on the spherical Death Star was used in the *Star Wars* scenarios to launch gigantic superweapons.

Death Star's Hollywood designers could not possibly have copied from nature. While they were building the model, no earthly telescope would have shown Mimas as more than a pinprick of light.

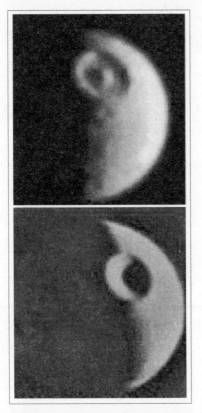

The Death Star (lower) was created by *Star Wars* set designers, years before NASA photographed the stunningly similar moon Mimas.

The Novelist Whose Dreams Came True

IN 1975 GERARD DE VILLIERS, a moderately popular author of political thrillers, published a novel with the unwieldy title *Irresistible Ascent of Mahommed Rizza.* The book, a thinly disguised speculation on the possible fate of Mahommad Reza, then Shah of Iran, received little publicity.

But its fortunes changed in 1979, when the Shah was overthrown – and newspapers pointed out that the novel had quite precisely foretold the time and manner of the leader's political demise.

Questioned by journalists, de Villiers seemed confused. He could not understand how he had been able to foresee the Shah's downfall in such detail. The novel, he lamely supposed, was a pattern of coincidences.

But the following year – 1980 – he did it again. In his novel *Terror at San Salvador* he described the city's archbishop being killed by a bullet

A controversial novel precisely foretold the time and
nature of the Shah of Iran's death.

to the head while celebrating mass. Two months after the book appeared,
San Salvador's Archbishop Romero was felled by a single shot. This time,
however, the media reacted harshly – blaming the novelist for inspiring a
copycat murder.

In a future-probing novel, writer Gerald de Villiers circumstantially
predicted the murder of Egypt's president Anwar Sadat.

Gerard de Villiers, now a bestselling writer, defended himself by saying
his plots were partly based on disturbing dreams or intuitive flashes. "But

my novels are also built around known facts – and information I receive from political sources," he said. "I don't in any way consider myself to be a psychic author." His editor, Ganari Ali of Pion Publishing, Paris, disagreed. "This author's track record for accurately writing about the future defies all odds and explanations," he said.

In 1981 de Villiers published another novel, *The Egyptian Plot,* which described the imaginary assassination of Egypt's President Sadat. The "fictional" narrative came true within months.

Possibly the most astonishing of de Villiers's books was *Red Grenada,* published in 1982. It forecast in detail the communist-inspired execution of Grenada's Prime Minister Maurice Bishop, followed by the subsequent US marine invasion.

A Prescient Parade of Popes

IN 1139 AN IRISH CATHOLIC bishop, known today as St Malachy, reportedly fell into a trance while visiting Rome – and experienced a strange vision of monumental proportions. When he woke (according to his contemporary biographer Bernard of Clairvaux) Malachy wrote down everything he could remember from the dream. It was a list of popes, each of whom he identified by a prophetic description. His roll-call stretched into an unimaginably distant future.

Malachy gave his manuscript to Pope Innocent II, who incuriously deposited it in the Vatican archives, where it lay forgotten for several centuries. Then, in 1590, it was rediscovered and the full list published.

Doubters argued at the time that the descriptions up to 1590 might have been doctored and "improved" before going to print. And possibly they had. But because Malachy's list has been on the public record ever *since* publication, people interested in precognition can study the post-1590 entries with greater interest.

- Malachy describes Leo XI, for example, as *Undosus vir* – "The man who will pass like a wave." Leo did just that: surviving for only 27 days in 1605.

- Similarly intriguing is the motto "Lily and rose", which Malachy attaches to Pope Urban (1623-1644). It was Urban who gave permission for the marriage of England's Charles I to Henrietta of France. The lily dominated Henrietta's coat-of-arms. Charles's symbol was the rose.

- The pope whom Malachy dubs "guardian of the hills" is Alexander VII, enthroned in 1655. Alexander's coat-of-arms depicts a star glittering above six hills.

- He describes Clement XII as *Columna excelsa* – "The lofty column." History records that Clement, a frustrated architect, ordered – and interfered with – the building of many churches. When he built the chapel at Mantua he used two immense columns salvaged from the ruins of the Pantheon.

Malachy's descriptions of popes become, if anything, more direct as he enters the 20th and 21st centuries.

- His motto for Pius X, whose reign ended in 1914 is *Ignis ardens* – "Burning fire", conceivably a reference to the devastation of World War I which erupted that year.

- Benedict XV (1914-1922) is linked to the words *Religio depopulata* – "Death of the religious." This has been interpreted to refer not only to the unprecedented millions of Christians killed during the Great War, but to the Russian Revolution in which countless churchgoers were murdered and their places of worship destroyed.

- John XXIII (1958-1963) is accorded the motto *Pastor et nauta* – "Shepherd and sailor." Before his election he was patriarch of the maritime city of Venice.

- Paul VI (1963-1978) is described in the prophecies as *Flos florum* – "Flower of flowers." His personal arms bore three fleurs-de-lis.

- John Paul I is identified as *De medietate Lunae* – "The average age of the moon." Albino Luciani became pope on August 26 1978, the day after the moon reached its last quarter – and reigned for 33 days, approximately five days longer than a lunar cycle. Scholars have noted that he was born in the diocese of Belluno, a placename with echoes of *Bella luna* – "Beautiful moon." This short-lived Pope's name is also interesting: *Albino,* related to *albus* (white) – and Luciani, derived from *Lucius,* reducing to *lucis* (light)… arguably suggesting the moon's "White light."

- John Paul II: *De labore Solis* – "Travails of the sun." During World War II Karol Wojtyla worked in a quarry, from which optimistic analysts have derived "labouring in sunlight." A more persuasive interpretation might be that *labore solis* is a metaphor for solar eclipse. The future pope was born on May 18 1920 during a partial solar eclipse – and was buried during a rare "hybrid" eclipse over South America on April 8 2005.

- Benedict XVI: *Gloria olivae* – "Glory of the olive." Cardinals participating in the papal conclave speculated that the next pontiff might come from the Order of St Benedict, whose symbols include the olive branch. Joseph Cardinal Ratzinger, elected in April 2005, is not a Benedictine, but chose Benedict as his regnal name: a case, perhaps, of a prophecy fulfilled by its own subject.

This is the last of Malachy's prophecies that scholars overwhelmingly agree to be genuine. His predictions have been in print for more than eight centuries. As they have unfolded, pope by pope, into the 20th and 21st centuries skeptics have had increasing difficulty in dismissing them. At the very least, Malachy, lying in a trance-dream in the old Rome of 1139 AD, seems to have glimpsed vast landscapes of future time, in a manner which defies explanation.

The Film that Foresaw 9/11

IN 1984 – 17 YEARS BEFORE suicide bombers flew hijacked jets into New York's Twin Towers – journalist Bob (Watergate) Woodward completed a screen-play, *Under Siege*.

His 240-minute television movie, starring Peter Strauss and Hal Holbrook, was screened by the NBC network in February 1986.

Following the dark date of September 11 2001, DVD and tape sales of the film spiked sharply. Journalists, and the public, realized that the movie had foretold, in multiple detail, many of the murderous events of 9/11.

When the film was first screened in 1986, numerous critics and international friendship groups slammed it as being discriminatory. The plot, disparaged at the time as "unlikely" and "far-fetched", features an onslaught on "the heart of America" by terrorists, thought by the FBI to be Arab fundamentalists. Fanatical suicide squads attack a mall and crowded restaurants. Using truckloads of explosives (as were later central to the World Trade Center bombing of 1993) they also destroy a Washington DC military base in scenes reminiscent of the 9/11 assault.

Suicidal hijackers explode passenger jets in mid-air – and security analysts speak presciently of danger to the World Trade Center. Many Americans call for an immediate war on Iran, believed to be the culprit behind the holocaust. In a pre-echo of the controversy surrounding the invasion of Iraq, moderates call for Iran's guilt to be proved first.

- *Under Siege* was not the only teleplay to pre-mirror the terror assault on America. The first episode of a series, *The Lone Gunman,* was televised on March 4 2001, only six months before the 9/11 massacre. The hero, created by writers Chris Carter and Vince Gilligan, is tipped off about an impending terrorist action: the bombing of a domestic airliner. He and colleagues board the plane expecting to find a bomb – only to learn that *the plane IS the bomb.* The hijackers take him prisoner – and as he listens to their sneering hints, he realizes what they are planning to do: *"...World Trade Center. They're going to crash it into the World Trade Center."*

A Presidential Premonition?

J.W. DUNNE, author of *An Experiment with Time,* postulated that world-shaking events can sometimes resonate "backward from the future" into our dreams. Perhaps he should have added: "and drawings."

In 2006 Basic Books USA released a volume *Presidential Doodles:* a collection of random squigglings perpetrated by presidents from Abraham Lincoln onward. The section devoted to John F. Kennedy (assassinated 1963) contains a curious entry. In a circle JFK writes the numbers *9/11.* Beneath, underlined, he scrawls *Conspiracy.*

Strange Case of the Psychic Stock-tipper

IN AUGUST 2001 – one month before the Twin Towers tragedy – Arch Crawford, a successful Wall Street stock adviser – delivered a strange recommendation to his popular newsletter's subscribers. He advised them to go 100 per cent short – and sell every share they owned, along with just as many they didn't, with the intention of buying them back later at drastically lower prices.

The respected market analyst's tip created great consternation among clients, especially as he reminded them of his *Crawford Perspectives'* warning in May 2000 of a "bloody bear market in six to 18 months" – a prediction into which, in hindsight, the date September 11 2001 snugly fits.

In his September newsletter, released 10 days before the WTC attack, Crawford published the headline CRASH BY OCTOBER 5th? He added, "According to a Chinese tradition, the *I Ching, or Book of Changes,* we are faced with the Darkening of the Light."

Unashamedly basing his analysis, in part, on ancient Chinese wisdom and astrological charts, he proceeded to predict that planetary movements on September 8 would be "leading as to war"… that September 9 would be another turning point for markets and that financial dealings could be "occulted" (hidden) on September 10, 11, and 12. In the Melbourne *Age* (September 24 2001), financial commentator Brian Hale wrote, "Arch Crawford's reasoning for his market predictions was based partly on technical analysis – and largely on looking at the positions of the stars and planets. That's not what the major investment banks do, of course. But it's always worth reading what Arch has to say because experience has shown that he can be more right than the rest; which is why he is always among, and often leads, the Top 10 ranks of market-timers, even for five- and 10-year periods.

"He did predict the 1987 crash. He did get the 1994 bonds crisis. He did warn of the approaching Tech Wreck in 2000 – and he also got a lot of the upswings too."